T0305719

Managing Information Technology Outsourcing

For decades, outsourcing has been a major international phenomenon in business. The areas of Technology, Information Technology and Management represent a unique case for outsourcing both in terms of benefits and potential interorganisational problems.

This fully updated text has been brought up to date with this new landscape, including discussion of Robotic Process Automation, Internet of Things, cloud computing, low code and DevOps and agile. With a range of new global case studies in manufacturing, logistics, chemical industry and cloud services, this textbook offers a strong grounding in real-world industrial experience that effectively combines theory with practice. Uniquely, this book focuses on both sides of the outsourcing relationship, providing a balanced exploration of the ways in which these partnerships can be managed successfully.

Accessible and cutting-edge, the third edition of *Managing Information Technology Outsourcing* provides an in-depth, practical perspective on this important and far-reaching challenge in information technology management. It is an ideal text for students, academics and practitioners alike.

Erik Beulen is Professor of Information Management at Tilburg University, the Netherlands, and Academic Director of the Executive MSc in Information Management at TIAS Business School, the Netherlands.

Pieter M. Ribbers is Emeritus Professor at Tilburg University, the Netherlands, and was Chair of Information Management at their School of Economics and Management.

Managing Information Technology Outsourcing

Third edition

Erik Beulen and Pieter M. Ribbers

Routledge
Taylor & Francis Group

LONDON AND NEW YORK

Third edition published 2022
by Routledge
2 Park Square, Milton Park, Abingdon, Oxon, OX14 4RN

and by Routledge
605 Third Avenue, New York, NY 10158

Routledge is an imprint of the Taylor & Francis Group, an informa business

First edition published by Routledge 2006
Second edition published by Routledge 2010

British Library Cataloguing-in-Publication Data
A catalogue record for this book is available from the British Library

Library of Congress Cataloging-in-Publication Data
Names: Beulen, Erik, author. | Ribbers, Pieter, author.
Title: Managing information technology outsourcing /
Erik Beulen and Pieter M. Ribbers.
Other titles: Managing IT outsourcing
Description: Third edition. | Abingdon, Oxon;
New York, NY: Routledge, 2022. | Includes bibliographical
references and index.
Identifiers: LCCN 2021021754 (print) | LCCN 2021021755 (ebook)
Subjects: LCSH: Information technology—Management. |
Contracting out. | Electronic data processing
departments—Contracting out.
Classification: LCC HD30.2 .B475 2022 (print) |
LCC HD30.2 (ebook) | DDC 004.068/4—dc23
LC record available at https://lccn.loc.gov/2021021754
LC ebook record available at https://lccn.loc.gov/2021021755

ISBN: 978-1-032-12253-3 (hbk)
ISBN: 978-1-032-12254-0 (pbk)
ISBN: 978-1-003-22378-8 (ebk)

DOI: 10.4324/9781003223788

Typeset in Bembo
by codeMantra

Access the Support Material: www.routledge.com/9781032122540

Contents

Preface

The business landscape is in a state of constant change. Digital transformations are here today, and outsourcing has played an important role in these changes for decades. Much attention has therefore been paid to both practice and theory. It is the aim of the authors, who have extensive experience in both fields, to combine them in this book. We, the authors, hope that the combination of theoretical developments in the management and economic disciplines with the emerging practice of how to manage interorganisational relations will provide guidance for those who manage outsourcing relations.

For this third edition, we have updated the reference lists and added the newest insights on outsourcing, including agile software development and DevOps. In this edition, we also emphasise innovation largely in the context of stronger managing outsourcing and have added a chapter on compliance. Regulators across the globe are interfering in technology and outsourcing. In this third edition, we explain how organisations can deal with this interference.

The first two editions of this book were co-authored by our colleague Prof. Jan Roos. Unfortunately he passed away recently. With his extensive experience as director of the Rijkscomputer Centrum (RCC) and as author of several books that have been on the reading list of various computer science courses, he had important input. As Jan Roos has been retired for some time, his name no longer appears on the cover; however, his influence on the content has remained. We look back with respect and appreciation on a long, fruitful collaboration. We are dedicating this third edition of our book to him.

Erik Beulen
Pieter Ribbers
August 2021

1 Market trends in Information Technology outsourcing

The Information Technology (IT) outsourcing timeline, starting in the 1960s, provides the foundation for this chapter. To shed some light on market trends, historic landmark deals are detailed, such as Eastman Kodak (1989) and British Petroleum (1993), as well as market collaborations, including General Motors and EDS (1984–1996) and Philips and Atos (1989–2005), at that time BSO followed by Origin in 2000. The market trends in IT outsourcing are dictated by digital transformations requirements – basically, an unprecedented need for innovation and speed. What can be learned from these great case studies?

1.1 Introduction

In essence, there are three components in Information Technology (IT): services, hardware and software. The boundaries between these components have never been very clear, and they have and will change over time. What will not change is the shortage of skilled professionals and constant innovation. This sets up the context for IT outsourcing. The below timeline is far from complete but paints a picture over the decades of this still young industry.

1960–1970s. IT outsourcing started in the 1960s by time-sharing of processing power, predominantly consumed by large corporates. Also, universities were early adopters as processing power increased the efficiency of their research, besides IT being a research object. Electronic Data Systems (EDS), founded in 1962, was one of the leading suppliers together with IBM, which was also the dominant hardware and software provider. The IT outsourcing market continued to grow steadily, predominantly regionally and nationally.

1980s. Due to their international presence and scale, IBM and to a lesser degree EDS started to expand in the 1980s in providing mainframe data centre services to clients across multiple countries. The international presence of EDS started in the Middle East in 1976 with King Abdulaziz University in Saudi Arabia and the government of Iran. In Europe, Hoskyns, founded in 1968 and acquired in 1990 by Capgemini, signed a large IT outsourcing agreement with the Greater London Council in 1986. In 1989, IBM and

DOI: 10.4324/9781003223788-1

Eastman Kodak signed an IT outsourcing contract including the building of a dedicated data centre.

1990s. Meanwhile, the reputation of outsourcing was crumbling, due to job insecurity and quality of service concerns. The dominant reason to outsource was the belief that IT is not part of the core competencies of organisations. All IT outsourcing contracts were first-generation contracts. The transfer of staff was an important topic in negotiating and closing deals. Most deals were contracted "as-is" – the supplier continued to provide the service. Contracting "as-is" fuelled the debate about the desirability of IT outsourcing.

2000s. In this decade, transformational IT outsourcing contract began to emerge. Improving the services by a pre-agreed transition plan and adjusting the contracted services over time became easier.

The rise of Indian suppliers was very apparent, e.g. Infosys, Tata Consultancy Services (TCS) and Wipro. Labour arbitrage was the name of the game. In parallel, the traditional suppliers are also ramping up delivery centres in low-cost locations, including the Philippines, Central America and Eastern Europe. Large organisations also began setting up their captive centres, which for the non-IT organisations was an intermediate step towards outsourcing, e.g. Bayer Business Services' captive IT service centre in Mumbai, India, with around 550 employees was transferred to 2012, and Cognizant acquired UBS India Service Centre, including 2,000 associates for $75m in 2009/2010. Most shared service centres lacked scale, except for the shared service centres from technology companies, and faced high attrition and recruiting challenges.

An increasing number of IT outsourcing contracts were second generation, and changing suppliers was perceived as risky. At the end of the initial IT outsourcing, contracts are renegotiated; this included adjusted services, including service levels and pricing. Also, the terms and conditions were discussed as part of these renegotiations.

2010s. Traditional suppliers continue to grow, some predominantly by autonomous growth, e.g. Accenture from 204,000 employees in 2010 to 492,000 employees in 2019, and others by acquisitions, e.g. Atos acquiring Siemens IT Solutions and Services (2011) followed by Siemens Convergence Creators (2018) and CGI acquiring Logica in 2012. The Indian services also continue to grow and in some cases merge, e.g. Satyam and Tech Mahindra, due to Satyam fraud followed by public auction of 46% of Satyam in 2009 and a merger in 2013. TCS grew from 160,000 employees in 2010 to 446,000 employees in 2019, whereas Wipro grew from 120,000 employees in 2010 to 170,000 employees in 2019.

The argument to provide services from nearshore or offshore locations has changed from cost-efficiency to access to capabilities. Furthermore, significant investments are made in certification (think ISO and CMMi for individuals) to ensure quality and bridge time zone, language and cultural barriers.[1]

Also, the deal size is reduced. Currently, there are fewer global 5+-year full outsourcing deals. Shorter tower deals by region came into fashion. However, suppliers lock-in reduces complexity and management effort required is increasing.

In addition, cloud services are an integral part of the offerings, including Infrastructure as a Service, Platform as a Service and Software as a Service. The services are pay-as-you-go, which is aligned with the increasing need for flexibility in digital transformations. Many organisations are in jeopardy. The threat from start-ups and platform companies triggers the need for digital transformations. The ecosystem, including technology partners, needs to be built and is based on an added value instead of straightforward client–supplier relationships.

1.1.1 Software

Cloud services are dominant in software. All software providers transform their transaction models to subscription models. Despite offering full flexibility, this also helps outsourcing organisations to avoid incompliance, e.g. using unlicenced software.

There is constant consolation of software providers, and start-ups and scale-ups are acquired to incorporate their functionality. Larger acquisitions result in increased market shares. Let us take a closer look at Oracle's acquisition of Peoplesoft (2005), Siebel (2006), BEA Systems (2008), Sun Microsystems (2010), Taleo (2012), MICROS Systems (2014), NetSuite (2016) and CrowdTwist (2019) and many more. It is an integral part of their strategy[2]:

> Through our acquisition activities, Oracle seeks to strengthen its product offerings, accelerate innovation, meet customer demand more rapidly, and expand partner opportunities. An integral part of Oracle's Mergers and Acquisitions philosophy is our consistent commitment to customer service and product support while achieving our financial return objectives and creating value for our shareholders.

1.1.2 Hardware

Manufacturing of hardware is capital-intensive and must deal with shortage of raw materials, such as silica sand, iron ore, gold and bauxite. Recycling hardware is therefore essential. The manufacturers include Apple, Cisco Systems, Dell, Fujitsu, HP, Hitachi, IBM and Toshiba and many more. The demand for "as a service" has significantly increased. Because of this increase, the hardware manufacturers' position in the value chain is downgraded. This increase for "as a service" demand has started with processing, storage, network and printing devices but is currently also entering into the area of office devices. Underneath, there are many component manufacturers – think CPUs, dynamic random-access memory, fans, hard disk drives, network cards and video cards. These entire ecosystems and the value chains are not visible for outsourcing organisations entering in or engaged in IT outsourcing contracts.

1.1.3 Market size

Many analyst companies estimate the market size and IT spending for decades. Definitions and data collection are not an exact science, and cost allocation by outsourcing organisations is not straightforward, as IT costs are not only in the central IT unit.

The current size of IT spending was in total $3.7 trillion in 2019 – 1% growth.[3] Due to COVID-19, Gartner expects an 8% decline in 2020; this includes increases in cloud-based telephony and messaging (+8.9%) and cloud-based conferencing (+24.3%).[4] Also, external spending is increasing. IT services market grew 7.2% in 2019.[5] Gartner's market analyses are in line with other analyst companies such as Everest, Forrester and ISG.

1.2 Historic landmark deals and collaborations

To understand the IT outsourcing market better, this section details first the Eastman Kodak 1989 contract and subsequent developments, second the British Petroleum (BP) 1993 contract and third the EDS–General Motors (GM) and BSO/Origin (Atos)–Philips collaboration. The objectives and deal constructs are then detailed.

1.2.1 Eastman Kodak

Eastman Kodak signed in 1989 a landmark outsourcing deal with IBM.[6] The deal was, as with any outsourcing deals at that time, infrastructure-centric. The deal included the building and maintenance of data centres and the transfer of Eastman Kodak staff to IBM's Integrated Systems Solution Corporation (ISSC). The Eastman Kodak requirements are detailed in the contract. IBM set up dedicated service delivery teams to provide the services to their client. The dominant motive of Eastman Kodak was cost reduction, as IT was perceived as non-core. The cost savings were backed in over the contract duration. IBM fully benefits from efficiencies. At that time, IT was not about service (quality) or about security,[7] or compliance. There was also no concern about job losses in the US.[8] All the transferred Eastman Kodak employees became IBM employees, with no transfer of service to low-cost countries.

This landmark deal initiated an IT outsourcing snowball effect; many companies followed the strategy of Eastman Kodak and outsourced their infrastructure services.[9] The dominant suppliers at that time were Anderson Consulting, CSC, DEC, EDS and IBM.[10] This deal was also for IBM an important win against EDS, the market leader at the time. It was also the continuation of a long-term relationship. In 2005, Eastman Kodak signed a five-year agreement to provide a broad range of business support services. IBM will operate a broad range of business support functions for Eastman Kodak, including payroll services and credit and collections management. The objectives are a combination of cost reduction and increased business flexibility and responsiveness.[11]

The industry has changed, and so has Kodak: "The Kodak name is recognized around the world for its long heritage of delivering imaging innovations. The company is now writing its next chapter as a technology company focused on imaging" (https://www.kodak.com/en/company/page/history). The current focus is on including a blockchain-based document management platform for business. Kodak's claim is to secure document management combined with cost savings. Furthermore, Kodak changed their business model and linked to platform economy. Kodak launched an image rights management platform – KodakOne project.[12] Photographers and agencies can share their work and sell their work via the platform. This project was combined with the KodakCoin, a photo-centric cryptocurrency.[13] This change obviously sets different requirements for the partnerships and contracting than back in the late 1980s.

1.2.2 British Petroleum contract

Prior to signing a multi-tower deal in 1993, BP was facing serious challenges.[14] The company was privatised in 1987 and had to make redundant around 22,000 of their staff in the period 1990–1992. BP was a fallen angel.[15] Reshaping the internal IT department was one of the actions taken by the Board of Directors. At that time, the IT department employed about 1,400 staff, which on the back of the outsourcing deal was reduced to as little as 150 staff. This was the retained organisation, not only managing the suppliers but also aligning with the business.[16]

BP considered all contracting options, ranging from single outsourcing to short-term contracts with a large number of suppliers. The supplier dependency was perceived to be too much of a risk, and single outsourcing was ruled out as an option. The management effort required to manage a bundle of short-term contracts made this an unfavourable option. BP decided to explore the market thoroughly. In an open process, about 100 potential suppliers were invited to engage in the bidding process. From these 100 suppliers, 65 suppliers submitted a response. BP used the submission of all 100 suppliers as input in their contracting process. This resulted in a longlist of 16 suppliers and finally in a multi-tower contract with three suppliers.[12] This approach simply will not work today. Client organisations are not able to process the large number of offers, but more importantly, suppliers will be more careful to engage as the cost related to participating in a bidding process needs to be in line with the anticipated chance to win business.

In 1993, BP awarded the contract to Sema Group, Science Application International Corporation and Syncordia, which is a BT subsidiary. The unique aspect of this deal was that the three suppliers have to act as one.[12] The collaboration between suppliers was a key deal construct, which has made this into a successful contract.[17] The reality is that managing multi-(tower) outsourcing contracts requires a lot of effort from the retained organisation. Also, Shell has structured their IT supplier landscape in a similar way. Initially, they had separate ecosystems for application services and infrastructure services. Since the early 2010s, Shell has combined these two services in a single pool of preferred suppliers that engage seamlessly. Important in these types of outsourcing deals is first, maturity of the selected suppliers and second, scale. Only large and mature outsourcing organisations can successfully contract and manage these types of deals.

1.2.3 EDS–General Motors and BSO/Origin (Atos)–Philips[18] collaboration

GM and Philips both understood the need to have access to capabilities and the value of IT business. Both have treated their business units as part of their portfolio. There are no current examples of this business strategy. In the context of innovation and digital transformation, a good example is Randstad which operates in the HR services industry (www.randstad.com). They have launched a Tech & Touch strategy. They are monitoring industry-related tech companies, their partners, and take a stake in or acquire industry-related tech companies. Recent Randstad acquisitions are RiseSmart (2014) and Monster (2016). Randstad has an investment fund – Randstad Innovation Fund (RIF). Over the years, this strategic corporate venture fund has tracked some 2,500 early stage to expansion-stage HR technology players and emerging technologies.[19]

1.2.3.1 General Motors–Electronic Data Systems

GM realised that IT capabilities were crucial. To elevate their IT capabilities, GM bought EDS in 1984. In 1986, GM bought the remaining shares from Ross Perot, ex-IBM and founder of EDS. As an aside, he founded in 1988 Perot Systems, which was bought by Dell in 2009 and rebranded as Dell Services. EDS[20] joined Hitachi in 1989 to sell Hitachi computer products, and at the last minute, EDS rejected a merger with Sprint in 1994.

In addition to providing IT services to GM, EDS also provided services to other external clients. This always creates tension in allocating resources (technical experts and consultants) and setting prices. Both GM and the external clients are battling for the best EDS resources. GM can escalate via both the IT outsourcing contract and the hierarchy, as they fully owned EDS, where clients only can escalate via the IT outsourcing contract. In terms of price-setting, GM can set pricing for its own contracts, which is cost-neutral but potentially impacts the EDS valuation. Pricing towards external clients is set by market competition, which is similar to price-setting for any other supplier.

In 1996, GM decided to float off EDS. EDS was Wall Street stock listed, with a second listing in London. This decision included a ten-year revenue commitment of $30.6b from GM to EDS. This was a decreasing revenue commitment – from $4b per annum to $2b in 2005. At the end of the revenue commitment term in 2006, Chief Information Officer Szygenda signed outsourcing contracts with multiple suppliers, including Capgemini, EDS, HP, IBM and Wipro. Following the spin-off by GM, EDS was bought by HP in 2008.

A more recent twist was the GM IT strategy to bring back jobs to America in response to large-scale offshore outsourcing, predominantly to India. A relevant context to this strategy was that there were upcoming presidential elections, and prior to this statement, GM received a $50b government bailout. Chief Information Officer Mott, ex-Walmart, Dell and HP, set clear objectives in terms of data centre reduction from 23 to two certified data centres and a 40% reduction of 4,000+ apps, in combination with the reduction of the 90% outsourcing to 10% in 2015. The cost savings funded the transformation. Over time, GM created four innovation centres located in Southeast Michigan on the Warren Campus, downtown Detroit, Austin, outside of Atlanta and just outside of Phoenix. As part of the transformation, GM hired more than 3,000 new college graduates to supplement the thousands of experienced IT professionals. The workforce is approximately 10,000 now, with more than 80% of them dedicated to innovation.[21]

1.2.3.2 BSO/Origin (Atos)–Philips

Different from the approach of GM, Philips decided setting up a joint venture to safeguard and optimise their IT. This joint venture included the internal "Philips Application and Software Services" and "Bureau voor Systeem Ontwikkeling" (BSO) – 50%/50%. To further strengthen the relationship, Philips also invested in the BSO's holding company – initially 15%.

A Dutch company founded by the maverick IT entrepreneur Eckart Wintzen, BSO had international ambitions, which appeared to be difficult without the help of a partner. Aggressive international growth targets were set, partly on the backbone of supporting international Philips branches, followed by acquiring additional business with non-Philips customers. From the start in 1976, BSO has had a growth strategy which is still remarkable: as soon as an organisational unit, including corporate units, reached a head count of 100 staff, it was split to ensure competitiveness, innovation and lean functioning.[22] Over time, BSO was transformed into Origin.

In addition to the application services, Philips was also focusing on their infrastructure services. In the late 1980s, there too were maybe islands of automation, across Philips product groups and corporate functions. Also, the focus in Philips was too technology-driven. The central IT department, Corporate Automation, implemented significant improvements and realised a single infrastructure backbone and e-mail, as well as a Philips-wide properly functioning EDI. Furthermore, security and corporate data policies were brought into place. This was all in the domain of their infrastructure organisation, Communication & Processing. With regard to IT outsourcing, decision-making power was with the Philips product groups, not with Corporate Automation.

Another important step in revamping IT services, starting in Europe, was implementing a clear demarcation between demand and supply. This demarcation included the opportunity to provide services to external client. This was granted to Philips Application Software Services in 1989 and to Communication & Processing in 1991, due to the sensitivities of providing these services to non-Philips clients. The focus was on ensuring cost control; therefore, there was an obligation for Philips organisations to procure their IT services internally.

In parallel, Philips president Timmer initiated in 1990 operation Centurion, which included large layoffs, 15–20%. These layoffs were not applied to their IT departments, as these were able to acquire contracts with non-Philips customers.

In 1996, Philips included both IT groups in Origin. In 2000, Origin was acquired by Atos, a French company, and was branded as Atos Origin. Philips remained a shareholder after this acquisition; the company also acquired KPN Data Centres in 2001, KPMG Consulting in 2002 and SchlumbergerSema in 2004. In 2005, Philips divested their stake in the company. Still, Philips is an important customer, but Philips also has large IT outsourcing contracts with other suppliers.

1.3 Digital transformation[23]

In this day and age, digital transformation is very much in fashion. Vial defined digital transformation as a process that aims to improve an entity by triggering significant changes to its properties through combinations of information, computing, communication and connectivity technologies.[24]

A lot of companies have embarked on digital transformations, with only 9% of organisations not yet started.[25] Digital transformations dominate the agenda of most executives. In reality, there is much scepticism, as most executives are risk-averse.[26] Not only are changes in business models[27] and technology required, but also collaboration and contracting require a complete overhaul. Digital transformations also dictate IT partnerships and IT outsourcing deals. As addressed in the previous section, Randstad is a perfect example of an organisation which is shaping their technology and innovations partnerships with their Randstad Investment Fund in a ground-breaking way.

Digital transformations can include enriching existing products and services, creating new services to improve the top line, making smart use of data, and using mobile devices, social media, analytics, the Internet of Things and the cloud.[28] In digital transformation it is important that organisations assess their cloud readiness.[29] Digital transformations are a combined business and IT effort and are performed by joint teams. Many organisations are very successful in initiating pilot projects but struggle to scale up. This is due to limited capabilities, a lack of governance and the absence of a foundational IT architecture. Becoming talent magnets and securing leaders with vision to lead the digital strategy and commit resources for execution are essential.[30] This is a challenge for many organisations.[31] Company culture, corporate image and brand are important. This challenge is a bigger challenge for traditional companies than for start-ups and tech giants.

Except for innovative technologies, digital transformations have been around for decades. Schein[32] defined four strategic IT visions, including "transform," which included "altering the products and markets." According to Andriole,[21] organisations must prepare for a "planned digital shock." However, one cannot wait for a strategy – experimentation must run concurrently to the traditionally structured approach. Also, fail fast! Nearly all organisations the authors have engaged with applied short-term cycles and agile implementations of digital transformations ranging from four to thirty weeks. However, integration across front, middle and back offices is important,[33] not only for efficiency and effectivity, but also for compliance.

Pivotal for digital transformation success is combining hard data and soft judgement.[34] Data analytics are the heart of any digital transformation. Organisations need to keep their models simple and straightforward and have proper Master Data Management in place.

It is important to acknowledge that innovations are rarely stand-alone. Organisations need to select their partners and decide about their role in an ecosystem.[35] In digital transformations, organisations need to take the lead to secure competitive advantage, select the right partners and focus on managing the ecosystem. In addition to the traditional client–supplier relationship providing commodity services at agreed charges and service levels, organisations need to select their start-ups and scale-ups. Selecting the right technology partners is difficult. Organisations can expect more exclusivity from start-ups. The start-ups also need to limit themselves to only a few (potential) clients, as they need to have a combined focus on further (co-) developing their services and products (with customers) and delivering contracted services and products. This is a balancing act. In assessing and selecting potential start-up companies, the anticipated ability of a start-up to scale up is important. Furthermore, organisations need to plan for an acquisition of these start-ups in case securing competitive advantage is required. Alternatively, contractual arrangements can be put in place. In partnering and contracting with scale-up, less exclusivity has to be expected; these partnerships typically are moving towards a traditional client–supplier relationship. An important point in the contract negotiations with scale-ups is the exclusion of named competitors. This is a good practice to protect competitive advantage. For both start-ups and scale-ups, it is important to make explicit contractual arrangement on their contribution to innovation and the associated confidentiality as well as the generated intellectual property (IP).

Finally, the funding of digital transformations attracts interest and debate, with organisations leveraging corporate investment, self-funding and hybrid models.[36] In most organisations, a hybrid of self-funding via IT cost-efficiencies and corporate investment is used to initiate digital transformations. The partnerships and IT outsourcing contracts need to deliver IT cost-efficiencies. Furthermore, the partnerships obviously also need to contribute to bring not only the IT innovation but also collaborate in bringing the technology business innovation. The hybrid funding combines the IT operations cost conscience and technology insight of the Chief Information Officer and the partners, as well as business sponsorship. Both are pivotal in the justification and success of digital transformations.

Notes

1 Beulen, E., Fenema, P. V., & Currie, W. (2005). From application outsourcing to infrastructure management. *European Management Journal, 23*(2), 133–144.
2 Oracle (2020). https://www.oracle.com/corporate/acquisitions/ - accessed 27 August 2020.
3 Gartner (2019). https://www.gartner.com/en/newsroom/press-releases/2019-10-23-gartner-says-global-it-spending-to-grow-3point7-percent-in-2020#:~:-text=Worldwide%20IT%20spending%20is%20projected,latest%20forecast%20by%20Gartner%2C%20Inc - accessed 27 August 2020.
4 Gartner (2020a). https://www.gartner.com/en/newsroom/press-releases/2020-05-13-gartner-says-global-it-spending-to-decline-8-percent-in-2020-due-to-impact-of-covid19 - accessed 27 August 2020.
5 Gartner (2020b). Market share: IT services, worldwide 2019, G00717813, 13 April.
6 Computerworld (1989). December 25, 1989/January 1, 1990, pp. 14–15.
7 Plant, R. (2011). https://hbr.org/2011/10/a-kodak-moment-to-reconsider-t - accessed 27 August 2020.
8 For further reading, see Anon. (2005). From Kodak to Intel: How global outsourcing means local problems: Investigating the corporate social responsibility of moving jobs abroad. *Human Resource Management International Digest, 13*(3), 6–8; Hemphill, T. (2004). Global outsourcing: Effective functional strategy or deficient corporate governance? *Corporate Governance: International Journal of Business in Society, 4*(4), 62–68.
9 Loh, L., & Venkatraman, N. (1992). Diffusion of information technology outsourcing: Influence sources and the Kodak effect. *Information Systems Research, 3*(4), 334–358.
10 Kirkpatrick, D. (1991). Why not farm out your computing? Hiring another company to do your data processing can save you big bucks. Some say it's the biggest trend since the PC burst on the scene a decade ago. *FORTUNE Magazine*, September 23. https://archive.fortune.com/magazines/fortune/fortune_archive/1991/09/23/75507/index.htm - accessed 27 August 2020.
11 IBM (2005). Press release. https://www.03.ibm.com/press/us/en/pressrelease/7933.wss#:~:text=ROCHESTER%2C%20NY%20%26%20ARMONK%2C%20NY,business%20support%20services%20to%20Kodak - accessed 27 August 2020.
12 Pollok, D. (2019). https://www.forbes.com/sites/darrynpollock/2019/06/06/kodak-unveils-blockchain-based-document-management-platform-for-business-claiming-40-cost-saving/#7ac9080c245a - accessed 27 August 2020.
13 Levine, M. (2020). https://www.bloomberg.com/opinion/articles/2020-07-30/kodak-is-relevant-again - accessed 27 August 2020.

14 Anon. (1998). BP in outsourcing bed with EDS. *Computer Weekly*, pp. 6–7.

15 Linder, J. C. (2004). Transformational outsourcing. *MIT Sloan Management Review*, *45*(2), 52.

16 Cross, J. (1995). IT outsourcing: British Petroleum's competitive approach. *Long Range Planning*, *28*(4), 128–128.

17 Aubert, B., Patry, M., Rivard, S., & Smith, H. (2001). IT outsourcing risk management at British Petroleum. In *Proceedings of the 34th Annual Hawaii International Conference on System Sciences Maui, Hawaii, 3 January 2001–6 January 2001* (pp. 8076–8076). IEEE.

18 The collaboration between BSO/Origin (Atos)–Philips is based on a case study described in Beulen, Ribbers, and Roos (1994, pp. 128–136 – in Dutch) supplemented with more recent publications. Beulen, E., Ribbers, P., & Roos, J. (1994). *Outsourcing van IT-dienstverlening: een make or buy beslissing*. Deventer: Kluwer Bedrijfswetenschappen.

19 Randstand (2017). https://www.randstad.com/s3fs-media/rscom/public/2020-02/randstad-annual-report-2017.pdf – accessed 27 August 2020.

20 At that time, EDS was fully owned by General Motors.

21 High, P. (2018). https://www.forbes.com/sites/peterhigh/2018/06/18/after-five-years-of-transformation-gm-cio-randy-mott-has-the-company-primed-for-innovation/#2898781543f1, 18 June - accessed 27 August 2020.

22 Bakel, van R. (1996). https://www.wired.com/1996/11/es-wintzen/, 11 January - accessed 27 Augustus 2020.

23 This section is based on Beulen (2018), actualised and supplemented with the IT outsourcing perspective. Beulen, E. (2018). *Information management leads top line information technology initiatives and contributes to bottom line targets: The chief information officer is a technical innovator and custodian of the it architecture*. Tilburg: Tilburg University.

24 Vial, G. (2019). Understanding digital transformation: A review and a research agenda. *The Journal of Strategic Information Systems*, *28*(2), 118–144.

25 Gartner (2020c). https://www.gartner.com/en/information-technology/insights/digitalization - accessed 23 March 2021.

26 Andriole, S. J. (2017). Five myths about digital transformation. *MIT Sloan Management Review*, *58*(3), 20–22.

27 Berman, S. J. (2012). Digital transformation: Opportunities to create new business models. *Strategy & Leadership*, *40*(2), 16–24.

28 See for further reading Westerman, G., & Bonnet, D. (2015). Revamping your business through digital transformation. *MIT Sloan Management Review*, *56*(3), 2–5; Adner, R. (2016). Navigating the leadership challenges of innovation ecosystems. *MIT Sloan Management Review*, *58*(1); Majchrzak, A., Markus, M. L., & Wareham, J. (2016). Designing for digital transformation: Lessons for information systems research from the study of ICT and societal challenges. *MIS Quarterly*, *40*(2), 267–277; Schoemaker, P., & Tetlock, P. (2016). Superforecasting: How to upgrade your company's judgement. *Harvard Business Review*, *94*, 72–78; Hirschheim, R. A., Heinzl, A., & Dibbern, J. (2020). *Information systems outsourcing: The era of digital transformation* (5th ed.). Cham: Springer; Stibe, A. (2020). Transforming technology for global business acceleration and change management. *Journal of Global Information Technology Management*, *23*(2), 83–88.

29 Beulen E. (2017). Cloud readiness as an enabler for application rationalization: A survey in the Netherlands. In: Oshri I., Kotlarsky J., Willcocks L. (eds) *Global sourcing of digital services: Micro and macro perspectives. Global sourcing 2017. Lecture notes in business information processing*, vol 306. Cham: Springer.

30 Majchrzak, A., Markus, M. L., & Wareham, J. (2016). Designing for digital transformation: Lessons for information systems research from the study of ICT and societal challenges. *MIS Quarterly*, *40*(2), 267–277.

31 Beulen E. (2020). Digital maturity: A survey in the Netherlands. In: Oshri I., Kotlarsky J., Willcocks L.P. (eds.) *Digital for global sourcing of services. Global sourcing 2019. Lecture notes in business information processing*, vol 410. Cham: Springer.

32 Schein, Edgar H. & Management in the 1990s (Program), (1975). "The role of the CEO in the management of change: The case of information technology." Working papers 89-075., Massachusetts Institute of Technology (MIT), Sloan School of Management.

33 Harvey Nash & KPMG (2017). Navigating uncertainty, research report. www.hnkpmgciosurvey.com/ – accessed 23 March 2021.

34 Schoemaker, P., & Tetlock, P. (2016). Superforecasting: How to upgrade your company's judgement. *Harvard Business Review, 94*, 72–78.

35 See for further reading Adner, R. (2016). Navigating the leadership challenges of innovation ecosystems. *MIT Sloan Management Review*, 58(1), 59–63; Hensmans, M. (2017). Competing through joint innovation. *MIT Sloan Management Review, 58*(2), 26.

36 Kane, G., Palmer, D. Nguyen Philips, A., Kiron, D., & Buckley, N. (2017). Achieving digital maturity, adapting your company to a changing world, research report, reprint number 59180 (MITSloan Management Review, in collaboration with Deloitte University Press).

2 Theoretical foundation

By providing a theoretical foundation, the concepts explained in this book can relate to the literature. Given the product or service strategy of a company, the subject of outsourcing has to do with the boundaries of the organisation. Which of the processes and activities are carried out by the company itself and which ones does it obtain from the market? This fundamental question has been considered on the basis of various theories. In this chapter, the contributions to this issue from economic, behavioural and management theories are discussed. These matters will be returned to in later chapters when discussing specific topics.

2.1 Introduction

It has been demonstrated how both business aspects and technological developments affect business models and outsourcing relationships. Naturally, much research has been done into the nature of this influence. Many approaches have been discussed in the economics and organisation literature and many organisation theories have been proposed on the subject.[1] The most important of these for this book's purpose are the theory of competitive strategy, the resource-based view, the theory of transaction costs, the agency theory and two social or organisational theories: the resource dependency theory and the institutional theory. These will be discussed in the following subsections.

2.2 The theory of competitive strategy

Strategy is a rather difficult concept to define. One relatively simple way of looking at it is as an attempt to make a fit between one's organisation and its environment. This attempt has been considered from many different points of view. Porter's theory on competitive strategy,[2] which is the subject here, focuses on the influence that external factors have on companies' strategic positions. It represents a school of thought that begins by analysing the company's position in its competitive environment and then considers how it may achieve a sustainable competitive advantage in the context of those external

DOI: 10.4324/9781003223788-2

forces. The structural attractiveness of a company is, according to this theory,[3] determined by five aspects:

1   customer bargaining position;
2   supplier bargaining position;
3   barriers new competitors face when entering the industry;
4   the threat of new, substitute products or services;
5   competition among current competitors.

Combined, these forces determine how the economic value generated from products, services, technologies and competitive methods is divided between the companies in an industry and their customers, suppliers, distributors and substitutes. Each of these competitive forces is, of course, itself determined by a number of factors. The bargaining power of one's customers, for instance, depends on the degree of product differentiation, on the size of demand and supply and on the parties involved, but also on how much it will cost customers to change to another supplier. The latter costs, called switching costs, effectively may cause a customer to be locked in. In the area of IT, this may be the result of proprietary standards. However, the improved personalisation of one's services, achieved by using modern databases, for example, or the implementation of customer-specific technologies and knowledge, may also make it costly or impractical for the customer to move to another supplier. In outsourcing matters, the customer's bargaining position is therefore an important issue to consider. The bargaining power of one's suppliers is a similar subject, but seen from the opposite position. Now it is one's own company that faces the lock-in risk, for example.

Newcomers in an industry face all kinds of barriers, generally of an economic or technological nature, but sometimes also caused by culture or language differences. Entering an industry requires capital and often scale, and one must have the expertise needed to be taken seriously. Likewise, new products or services face the barrier of switching costs. However, if they can add value without the customer having to make many such costs, they become a serious threat to the industry's current products. Consider the Internet, for example, which cost traditional mail services a significant amount of business by making e-mail accessible to everyone.

Competition is very different in different markets. It may be fierce but sometimes it is relatively relaxed. In addition, it is often influenced by developments outside the company's control. Here, too, the Internet is a good example. Companies and consumers are now directly linked, reducing search costs and increasing market transparency. Companies relying on information asymmetry see their profit positions seriously threatened.

Analysing these five aspects clarifies the fundamental attractiveness of an industry. It exposes the underlying drivers of average industry profitability and provides insight into how profitability evolves in the future. These factors determine the participants' profitability even if the industry's suppliers, channels, substitutes or competitors change.[7] According to this theory, achieving success is thus a matter of choosing the right competitive strategy, for which there are two major possibilities – either one concentrates on being a low-cost producer and customers buy because products are the least expensive; or one differentiates from competitors in terms of the quality offered, and customers buy because they believe that they are buying the best products. These strategies can be pursued either overall in the market or by concentrating on a particular niche.

Also, organisations should investigate the desirability of outsourcing core processes in order to achieve success. There are four circumstances where, if the right contracting processes are followed, outsourcing of core processes can be considered: the organisation is behind (catch up), one wants to change technology (technology shift), changing customer requirements (meeting changing customer needs) and entering new markets (new markets).[4]

2.3 The resource-based view

According to the theory of economic development, innovation is the source of value creation.[5] Several kinds of innovation have been identified: the introduction of new goods or new production methods, the creation of new markets, the discovery of new supply sources, the reorganisation of industries, etc. Effectively, innovation is in this theory considered a matter of using new combinations of resources to provide new products and production methods with which markets and industries are transformed. Economic development is then the result.

To achieve such innovation, one must, of course, have the necessary resources. The resource-based view therefore focuses on internal characteristics as factors for companies' competitive success. Enterprises are considered collections of competences and capabilities that must be maintained and developed,[6] and in the context of strategic sourcing.[7] Only their "core" and unique, difficult-to-imitate resources contribute significantly, as they are the foundation of the company's competitive position in their business environment.

Even these resources cannot do so on their own; one has to select the right ones and combine them in the right way for the company to be successful. The central idea of the resource-based view is, then, that combining a set of complementary and specialised resources in a unique way may enable a company to generate value from them – if these resources reduce costs and raise revenues in comparison to a situation without them.[11] The resources are of many kinds: capital, equipment, real estate, patents, brands, experience, skills, knowledge, organisational aspects, etc. Some resources are tangible; others are not. Some are easily bought and sold, but management skills, for example, are not. Consequently, not all resources are equally important. To be the basis of a sustainable competitive advantage, resources must be difficult to buy, difficult to imitate and difficult to substitute – or else a competitor will simply do the same and cannibalise the profit.[8] Besides, such resources must have been acquired against reasonable costs, or they will be a burden rather than an asset.

Generally, intangible assets such as knowledge and experience are more difficult to acquire, imitate or substitute than tangibles, like equipment, real estate and data centres. In addition, unprotected intangibles like organisational routines are in their turn more difficult to trade, replicate or replace than those whose property rights are well defined, such as patents or brand names. After all, trading involves disclosing, which at least partly destroys their value, for even licences and royalties only apply for a limited period. As far as information is concerned, unprotected information is therefore the best basis for a sustainable advantage. For other resources, different arguments may apply: using tankers to transport oil, for instance, may offer a perfectly sustainable competitive advantage if pipelines are impossible or unaffordable to build.

In the field of intangible assets, the concept of core competences has come to play an important role. Core competences are considered the root of the enterprise: its collective knowledge base, skill sets and activities, upon which its competitive position is built.[9] This concept plays an important role in analysing the viability of new business models. If one knows what the company's core competences are, then it is clear which resources cannot be outsourced, for example. Outsourcing all other activities may be a good strategic move, because one can then concentrate on the core competences and achieve a leaner, more flexible organisation that can respond quickly to the inevitable but unpredictable changes in its environment. Since the resource-based view offers insight into which resources are of critical importance, it helps determine which resources should be kept or acquired. In a similar vein, the resource dependency theory discussed in Section 2.6.1 looks at external resources, and considers ways to cope with the risks of one's dependence on outside suppliers for them. Resource theories help determine whether one should or should not outsource certain processes and capabilities.

In the case of IT outsourcing also, the demarcation of responsibilities and required resources is important and contributes to competitive success.[10,11]

2.4 Transaction cost economics

Implementing new business models has implications for companies' strategies. One important question already encountered is whether one should produce a certain good or service oneself or buy it from an external supplier. In part, the answer to this question depends on the efficiency of the transaction involved. According to transaction cost theory,[12,13] companies engaging in exchanges with external companies make several kinds of costs, collectively called coordination costs. These include many different kinds of expenditures: for finding and selecting the right trading partner (which includes the costs of information exchange and of determining the client's needs), for negotiations, drafting a contract that meets the needs of the parties involved, financing, distribution, monitoring, invoice settlement and the many after-sales aspects that arise from doing business.

Also included are operations risk costs, which arise from the possibility that one's partner may misrepresent the situation, withhold information or underperform, and opportunism risk costs,[14] referring to partners wanting to renegotiate after the other side has already made certain investments, or simply because there are few alternatives. For some products and services, these costs are higher than for others; some circumstances may cause them to rise and others to drop. However, companies will always weigh production costs against coordination costs, that is, the advantages of internal management (also called the hierarchy), against those of external procurement governed by a market mechanism.

The central issue addressed by transaction cost economics is why companies internalise transactions that might also be conducted in markets. Analytically, this boils down to two questions that companies facing outsourcing decisions should answer:

1   Which activities should they keep inside their organisation versus which activities should be outsourced?
2   How should they manage their relationships with their customers, suppliers and other business partners?

Put in another way, the focus is to devise the most efficient governance form for transactions, given their specific economic contexts, and the answer is found in the costs associated with these transactions. Essentially, companies will themselves produce the goods and services wanted if the costs of market coordination are greater than the benefits arising from the economies of scale and scope associated with outsourcing to specialists – and vice versa. Later scholars have extended the discussion to include quasi-hierarchical and quasi-market structures as alternative governance forms,[15] but the concept remains the same.

Many aspects of inter-business relationships play a role in this field[16]: uncertainty, exchange frequency, the specificity and complexity of the products and services delivered[17] and even human behaviour,[18] in particular bounded rationality and opportunism. These aspects will be discussed in the next two subsections.

2.4.1 Transaction aspects

There are three aspects to transactions that exert a powerful influence over the decision to insource or outsource: asset specificity, product complexity and transaction frequency. The asset specificity of a transaction refers to the degree to which it is supported by assets that are specific to this transaction alone and that cannot be used otherwise or elsewhere without incurring a significant reduction of their value. If one needs trained personnel for the transaction, this is called human capital specificity.[13] If a power station is

located close to the coal mines producing its fuel, one can speak of site specificity. Likewise, time specificity occurs when the product or service involved
must be delivered within a short period,[19] as is the case with some foods, for
instance. There are many different kinds of specificity, but they share one
characteristic: since the acquisition of the asset involved is generally a long
and possibly costly process, asset-specific transactions tend to be performed
by the user themselves because that reduces the risk to their continuity and
it increases the level of control and coordination. For rather more unspecific
transactions, markets usually work well.

Commodity products are simple and often standardised. Buyers choose on
the basis of their price, and markets offer a way to compare these. So that is
where most commodities are bought. Complex products, however, involve
a significant exchange of information. This exchange is less easily achieved
on markets because it increases the transaction costs. As product complexity rises, buyers therefore tend to prefer single-supplier relationships that are
more hierarchical.

Finally, even though some circumstances may point to insourcing a certain
transaction, setting up transactions hierarchically involves making significant
organisation costs. Such investments are only recouped if the volume or frequency of the transactions is high enough. If they are low, the goods or services
are still better procured from a market.[13] Companies facing outsourcing decisions must attempt to strike a balance between these conflicting arguments.

2.4.2 Behavioural assumptions

People all try to make decisions rationally, with a view to optimising the
outcome and turning it to one's advantage. The problem is that there are
often too many variables for us to take them all in. Quite a few questions are
simply too complex for human capacity to be able to give the answer, even if
one has all the information needed. A famous example is that of the game of
chess. The positions of the pieces on the board provide the players with all the
information needed, and yet not even the grand masters can think through
all possible moves.[13] This is called bounded rationality: the fact that human
beings intend to behave rationally but are simply incapable of doing so to
more than a limited degree. This challenge is all the more daunting in complex or uncertain situations. Chess players at least have all the information. A
government buying a new fighter plane (another well-known example) cannot be sure of the costs or even of whether all the intended technology will
really work. With so many specifications unknown, it will be very difficult
to reach a decision and lay it down in a contract. The coordination costs of
transactions may thus become very high in situations when bounded rationality and complexity or uncertainty reinforce each other.

Another human characteristic is that, regrettably, not all of us are equally
honest. Some people try to exploit situations to their own advantage by making what has rather euphemistically been called "self-disbelieved statements."[23]

Not everybody does, of course, and not all of the time. The problem is that some people do so some of the time, and when one does business, one cannot distinguish between honest and dishonest. In business literature, taking advantage of a partner's lack of knowledge and know-how is called opportunism: self-interest-seeking, with guile.[23] Since one can never entirely rule out the possibility that one's partner is less than fully honest, many transactions involve inspections, contracts and the like, even if the partner involved is considered perfectly trustworthy. The occurrence of opportunism may therefore increase transaction costs. This is especially important if there are few potential trading partners. Those partners will then care less about their reputations as there are few alternatives to which their clients might turn if they are not satisfied. Under such circumstances, of what is called small numbers exchange, the possibility of opportunism is very likely to make transaction costs rise.

The transaction theory can also be used to perform a risk assessment for IT outsourcing, to understand the implications of different scenarios better, such as lock-in, costly contractual amendments, unexpected transitions and management costs and disputes and litigations.[20]

However, applying the transaction cost theory to IT outsourcing is not straightforward and lots of questions are still open.[21,22] Less than half of the empirical ITO findings supported TCE logic.[23]

2.5 The agency theory

If one employs or hires another person or company to deliver certain products or services, there is always the problem of making sure that this supplier will really act in the client's interests. This issue is the subject of agency theory,[24] in which the two parties that in this book are often referred to as outsourcing organisation and supplier are called principal and agent, respectively. The principal may be a private person, a company acting as an employer or a group of shareholders; they are always the party who needs a certain product or service. Agents can be suppliers, employees or the management team of the company involved – the party delivering the products or services. Since the client's profits depend on the actions of the supplier, the principal must try to find ways of making an agent act in accordance with the principal's objectives. That said, this is difficult, for the principal usually does not have the expertise and information needed, often not even to properly assess the agent's work. Consequently, the outsourcing organisations face monitoring costs. There is always some degree of mistrust between the principal and the agent. Agency theory attempts to explain how such relationships are best organised.[25] Its analyses are based on four assumptions[26]:

1   both parties behave rationally and have rational expectations;
2   the agent's actions generate the principal's profit and success;
3   the parties' interests diverge;
4   the principal–agent relationship is characterised by information asymmetry.

Agents are always tempted to serve their own purposes rather than those of the principal. They can do so by hiding their real skills and abilities to do the job properly (hidden characteristics), by being unclear about their own goals (hidden intentions) and by maintaining a certain degree of freedom (hidden actions). The agent's degree of freedom decreases as the principal intensifies control over agent activities in order to decrease the principal's own uncertainty. However, doing so costs money. Agency costs essentially are a kind of transaction cost, and they include expenditures for selection, standard-setting, monitoring and possibly residual losses.

Already, albeit tacitly, the parallel has been introduced between the subject of the agency theory and the issue at hand in outsourcing decisions. Relationships between principals or outsourcing organisation on the one hand and agents or suppliers on the other generally fall into three stages.[31] In the first stage, the right supplier must be found; this stage ends when the contract is signed. Then, the contract must be executed. Finally, the relationship ends, or it is renewed. Each of these stages is characterised by its specific problems.

Outsourcing companies can never fully judge the quality of their potential suppliers, nor their real intentions. It is therefore important that they mitigate the risks of the selection stage by gathering as much independent information about them as possible. Sources for such information are market researchers and current or former clients, who know about the supplier's track record, and sometimes independent authorities or institutes, who may carry out benchmarks. This information need also explains the rise of certification procedures in the past decade or two. Once the contract has been signed and the products or services are delivered, the outsourcing organisation must make sure that these tasks are carried out in the outsourcing organisation's best interests. The agent, however, has a major information advantage, and this is not surprising, as this is probably one of the reasons for outsourcing in the first place – so, actions are difficult to assess. Agents may boost their own profits, for example, by spending less time or resources than agreed. Monitoring is one way of countering this risk, but it is costly since one must set performance standards and measure the actual work done or have it audited by independent authorities. Another method is to align the agent's interests with those of the principal, by introducing incentive schemes, for instance. Emotional pressure may also improve the agent's loyalty and prevent them from behaving opportunistically.

At the end of the contract period, both parties run certain risks. It was seen earlier in this section how a client may experience lock-in. However, suppliers also may have made investments that have not yet been recovered, a situation called hold-up. The switching costs either party faces in such circumstances may be avoided by minimising relationship-specific investments which are of little use in relationships with other clients or suppliers, and by limiting one's dependence on the other in terms of exclusive skills and knowledge.

To bridge the interest of the principal and the agent in IT outsourcing, the agency provides good insights, such as having incentives in the contracts.[27] Integrating risks assessments in IT outsourcing is critical, and in addition to the transaction cost theory, the agency theory can also underpin risk assessments.[28]

2.6 Social or organisational theories

Finally, one can distinguish a category of social or organisational theories that look at the dynamics of decision-making processes between multiple stakeholders. These describe interorganisational decision-making as a push-and-pull process based on negotiation and coalition-building, in which multiple ambiguous goals exist.[29] Proponents of this approach contend that the experiences and a shared (negotiated) understanding among key stakeholders are essential to effective decision-making processes.[30] According to the social exchange theorists, these interactions are based on trust, collaboration, co-operation and win-win relationships between the participants.[31] The notion is that the parties in a relationship share certain risks and rewards, which are reflected in the agreement. Specifically with regard to outsourcing relationships, several problems have been identified that may occur, such as hidden costs, the failure to implement new technology innovations, the failure to pass on savings to the client and differences in opinion regarding the interpretation of contract details and performance metrics.[32] However, the parties in an exchange are in mutual agreement that the resulting outcome of the exchange is greater than what could be obtained through other forms of exchange or from an exchange with a different partner. In this relational view, the focus shifts to the continuing strategic relationships between companies in generating value beyond what could be realised independently. This type of relationship is also called a partnership.[33] However, realising the benefits from such a partnership is contingent upon mutual trust and organisational complementarity in things such as decision-making processes, control systems and organisational culture.[35] For the purposes of this book, it will suffice to take a closer look at two such social or organisational theories: the resource dependency theory and the institutional theory.

2.6.1 The resource dependency theory

Section 2.3 discussed how the resource-based view focuses on companies' internal resources with which to achieve a sustainable competitive position. Now it is time to look at external resources – hence the "dependence" in the name of the theory discussed here, since that aspect must be managed. Resource dependence theories, first introduced in the 1960s by Thompson[34] and later elaborated by Pfeffer and Salancik,[35] work from the premise that companies strive for continuity: survival as the fundamental motivation for action. This means that one must attain control over critically important resources. Total autarky cannot be achieved, since no company can own all necessary resources, nor would it be efficient to do so. However, one can and therefore must adopt strategies to secure the acquisition of such resources from the environment. The consequent dependence on parties in that environment presents several difficulties. Dependences are multidimensional and the company's social, political and task environments influence them. They cause different degrees of interconnectedness and co-dependence, that is, the number and patterns of relationships and the type of interorganisational relationships, respectively. As concerns relationship type, the prime question is whether it is reciprocal (involving feedback) or unidirectional. Reciprocal relationships introduce the highest levels of interdependences and consequently require much management effort because they necessitate the involvement of others in one's strategic decision-making processes.

In such ways, dependencies interfere with companies' drive towards continuity: interconnectedness and co-dependence increase their environments' uncertainty and instability.[40] The resource dependency theory studies the arguments for and against procuring vital resources from external suppliers. The importance or power of a resource is a key issue here. The alternatives available in the market, which are an indication of the freedom left to change suppliers, as well as the discretion on the part of the supplier with regard to the resource's characteristics and availability, are also important factors to consider.[40] Likewise, if the outsourcing organisation can control their supplier to a certain degree, or if they can easily switch suppliers, they are more likely to outsource their needs[36]; otherwise, they will tend to produce the goods and services themselves. The theory also focuses on how to deal with the dependences that result when such resources are indeed outsourced. The risks involved can be mitigated by several strategies. Coalition-building will help reduce the uncertainty in the relationship. Cultivating alternative resources reduces the buyer's dependence on one supplier. Basically, the organisation will try to reduce its dependence on the environment by constantly balancing two contradictory forces: certainty and autonomy.[37]

2.6.2 The institutional theory

The institutional theory is based on the work done by Hughes,[38] Parsons[39] and Selznick,[40] who represent what is called the "old" institutionalism. The central aspects of their theory included influence, coalitions, competing values, power and informal structures. Their theory focused on finding explanations for the uniformity of many organisations, and it found that the environment played a major role. With respect to outsourcing, the "old" institutional theory can be applied to outsourcing organisations as well as suppliers. It explains why companies opt for outsourcing and why the phenomenon has therefore grown so much. It can also be used to explain the strategic motives of the suppliers, for example, with respect to offshore outsourcing or business process outsourcing. In the IT industry, for instance, mergers and takeovers have led to concentration, which is likely to continue for the next ten years or so. In reaction to the "old" institutionalism, a "new" institutionalism arose, which made a distinction between coercive, memetic and normative processes leading to conformity, a process also called isomorphic.[41] Later,[42] cognitive and cultural explanations were also added. Their central question concerned the impact of social choices on institutional arrangements. This includes shaping, mediating and channelling.

This issue applies to outsourcing as well – not just with respect to the "make or buy" question, but in the management of outsourcing relationships and the influence on them of institutional arrangements as well. On the basis of the developments of the past decades, it is certainly safe to conclude that outsourcing is institutionalised. It is an important phenomenon, well embedded in every industry.

Institutional theory distinguishes between two kinds of change: revolutionary and evolutionary change.[43] Outsourcing may in this context be considered an evolutionary change. It has grown inexorably but gradually. Institutional theory can explain this: the need to be able to cope with contextual forces that often change dramatically has become a key determinant of competitive advantage and organisational survival.[44] Bridgman and Willmott investigated a case of a major IT outsourcing contract and concluded that in bridging social and material facets of organisational change, the technology is treated as a material cause.[45]

Notes

1 See for further reading Dibbern, J., Hirschheim, R., & Jayatilaka, B. (2004). Information systems outsourcing: A survey and analysis of the literature. *Databases for Advances in Information Systems*, *35*(4), 6–102; Lacity, M., Khan, S., & Willcocks, L. (2009). A review of the it outsourcing literature: Insights for practice. *Journal of Strategic Information Systems*, *18*(3), 130–146; Lacity, M., Khan, S., Yan, A., & Willcocks, P. (2010). A review of the it outsourcing empirical literature and future research directions. *Journal of Information Technology*, *25*(4), 395–433; Hanafizadeh, P., & Zareravasan, A. (2020). A systematic literature review on it outsourcing decision and future research directions. *Journal of Global Information Management*, *28*(2), 160–201; Rajaeian, M., Cater-Steel, A., & Lane, M. (2017). A systematic literature review and critical assessment of model-driven decision support for it outsourcing. *Decision Support Systems*, *102*, 42–56; Liang, H., Wang, J., Xue, & Cui, X. (2016). IT outsourcing research from 1992 to 2013: A literature review based on main path analysis. *Information & Management*, *53*(2), 227–251.
2 Porter, M. (1980). *Competitive strategy*. New York: The Free Press.
3 Porter, M. (1997). Creating tomorrow's advantage. In Gibson, R. (Ed.), *Rethinking the future* (pp. 48–61). London: Nicholas Brealey.
4 Baden-Fuller, C., Targett, D., & Hunt, B. (2000). Outsourcing to outmanoeuvre: Outsourcing re-defines competitive strategy and structure. *European Management Journal*, *18*(3), 285–295.
5 Schumpeter, J. (1939). *Business cycles: A theoretical and statistical analysis of the capitalist process*. New York: McGraw-Hill.
6 Barney, J. (1997). *Gaining and sustaining competitive advantage*. Reading, MA: Addison-Wesley.

7   Watjatrakul, B. (2005). Determinants of IS sourcing decisions: A comparative study of transaction cost theory versus the resource-based view, *Journal of Strategic Information Systems, 14*(4/12), 389–415.

8   Douma, S., & Schreuder, H. (1998). *Economic approaches to organizations* (2nd ed.). Hertfordshire: Prentice Hall Europe.

9   Prahalad, C., & Hamel, G. (1991). The core competence of the corporation. In Montgomery, C., & Porter, M. (Eds.), *Strategy: Seeking and securing competitive advantage.* Boston, MA: Harvard Business School Press.

10 Gales, T. (2003). Schwerpunktaufsatz – vendor capabilities and outsourcing success: A resource-based view - causal modeling, outsourcing, partial least squares (Pls), resource-based theory, survey, vendor capabilities. *Wirtschaftsinformatik, 45*(2), 199–207.

11 Espino-Rodríguez, T., & Padrón-Robaina, V. (2006). A review of outsourcing from the resource-based view of the firm. *International Journal of Management Reviews, 8*(1), 49–70.

12 Coase, R. H. (1937). The nature of the firm. *Economica, 4*(16), 386–405.

13 Williamson, O. (1983). Organizational innovation: The transaction cost approach. In Ronen, J. (Ed.), *Entrepreneurship.* Lexington, MA: Lexington Books.

14 Clemons, E., Reddi, S., & Row, M. (1993). The impact of information technology on the organization of economic activity: The 'move to the middle' hypothesis'. *Journal of Management of Information Systems, 10*(2), 9–35.

15 Gulati, R. (1995). Does familiarity breed trust? The implications of repeated ties for contractual choice in alliances. *The Academy of Management Journal, 38*(1), 85–112.

16 Beulen, E. (2011, March). Maturing IT outsourcing relationships: A transaction costs perspective. In *International workshop on global sourcing of information technology and business processes* (pp. 66–79). Berlin, Heidelberg: Springer.

17 Klein, S. (1996). The configuration of inter-organizational relationships. *European Journal of Information Systems, 5*(2), 75–84.

18 Williamson, O. (1975). *Markets and hierarchies.* New York: Free Press.

19 Malone, T., Yates, J., & Benjamin, R. (1987). Electronic markets and electronic hierarchies. *Communications of the Association for Computing Machinery, 30*(6), 484–497.

20 Bahli, B., & Rivard, S. (2003). The information technology outsourcing risk a transaction cost and agency theory-based perspective. *Journal of Information Technology, 18*(3), 211–221.

21 Alaghehband, K. F., Rivard, S., Wu, S., & Goyette, S. (2011). An assessment of the use of transaction cost theory in information technology outsourcing. *Journal of Strategic Information Systems, 20*(2), 125–139.

22 Koo, Y., Lee, J.-M., & Son, I. (2016). Effect of relational structure with multiple vendors on it outsourcing performance: Transaction cost theory perspective. *Information Systems Review, 18*(1), 177–197.

23 Lacity, M., Willcocks, L., & Khan, S. (2011). Beyond transaction cost economics: Towards an endogenous theory of information technology outsourcing. *Journal of Strategic Information Systems, 20*(2), 139–57.

24 Jensen, M., & Meckling, R. (1976). The theory of the firm: Managerial behaviour, agency costs and ownership structure. *Journal of Financial Economics, 2*(October), 305–360.

25 Eisenhardt, K. (1985). Control: Organizational and economic approaches. *Management Science, 31*(2), 134–149.

26 Keil, P. (2005). Principal agent theory and its application to analyze outsourcing of software development. *ACM SIGSOFT Software Engineering Notes, 30*(4), 1–5.

27 Aubert, B. A., Patry, M., & Rivard, S. (2003). A tale of two outsourcing contracts – an agency-theoretical perspective outsourcing, incentive contracts, agency theory. *Wirtschafts Informatik, 45*, 181–198.

28 Bahli, B., & Rivard, S. (2003). The information technology outsourcing risk: A transaction cost and agency theory-based perspective. *Journal of Information Technology, 18*(3), 211–221.

29 Cyert, R., & March, J. (1963). *A behavioural theory of the firm*. Englewood Cliffs, NJ: Prentice Hall.

30 Dyer, J., & Singh, H. (1998). The relational view: Cooperative strategy and sources of interorganizational competitive advantage. *The Academy of Management Review, 23*(4), 660–679.

31 Kumar, K., & van Dissel, H. (1996). Sustainable collaboration: Managing conflict and cooperation in interorganizational systems. *Management Information Systems Quarterly, 20*(3), 279–300.

32 Earl, M. (1996). The risks of outsourcing IT. *Sloan Management Review, 37*(3), 26–32.

33 Rothery, B., & Robertson, I. (1995). *The truth about outsourcing*. Aldershot: Gower.

34 Thompson, J. (1967). *Organizations in action: Social sciences bases of administrative theory*. New York: McGraw-Hill.

35 Pfeffer, J., & Salancik, G. R. (1978). *The external control of organizations: A resource dependence perspective*. New York: Harper & Row.

36 Grover, V., & Teng, J. (1993). The decision to outsource information systems functions. *Journal of Systems Management, 44*(11), 34–37.

37 Davies, G., & Powell, W. (1992). Organization–environment relations. In Dunnette, M., & Hough, L. (Eds.), *Handbook of industrial and organizational psychology* (Vol. 3). Palo Alto, CA: Consulting Psychologists Press.

38 Hughes, E. (1936). The ecological aspects of institutions. *American Sociological Review, 1*, 180–189.

39 Parsons, T. (1951). *The social system*. New York: Free Press.

40 Selznick, P. (1957). *Leadership in administration*. New York: Harper and Row.

41 DiMaggio, P., & Powell, W. (1983). The iron cage revisited: Institutional isomorphism and collective rationality in organizational field. *American Sociological Review, 48*, 147–160.

42 Powell, W., & DiMaggio, P. (Eds.) (1991). *The new institutionalism in organizational analysis*. Chicago, IL: University of Chicago Press.

43 Greenwood, R., & Hinnings, C. (1996). Understanding radical organizational change: Bringing together the old and the new institutionalism. *The Academy of Management Review, 21*(4), 1022–1054.

44 D'Aveni, R. (1994). *Hyper-competition: Managing the dynamics of strategic manoeuvring*. New York: The Free Press.

45 Brigdman, T., & Willmott, H. (2006). Institutions and technology: Frameworks for understanding organizational change-the case of a major ICT outsourcing contract. *Journal of Applied Behavioral Science, 42*(1), 10–126.

3 Changing business models

Changing business models has an impact on IT outsourcing, as the business requirements are changing. New business models, such as platform-based, have arisen. Important are not only quality and speed of the IT services, but also the ability to work together as outsourcing organisation and supplier. How can IT outsourcing transform efficiently and effectively and adapt to the ongoing changes in business models?

3.1 Introduction

This chapter opens with a discussion in Sections 3.2 and 3.3 of economic and technical factors that put pressure on existing ways of doing business. The consequence of these developments is that traditional value chains unbundle, and new business models emerge. Determinative for the choice of a business model are internal and external factors and the use of information assets. These developments are discussed in Section 3.4. The traditional set-up of a company could be described as, "we do everything ourselves unless." With new business models, this principle is reversed: "we do nothing ourselves unless." This puts outsourcing on the map as a central and strategic choice and lays the foundation for the network organisation, which is the subject of Section 3.5. Network organisations lay the foundation for what are known as business ecosystems.[1] In ecosystems, organisations and suppliers are collaborating to achieve mutual success. The ecosystem perspective on business networks is discussed in Section 3.6. This changing business landscape impacts the sourcing of information services; these implications are discussed in Section 3.7. The matter of business models is concluded with a discussion of the impact of digital platforms in Section 3.8, with a presentation in greater detail of the example of a successful B2B platform that is having a major impact on chemical industries.

3.2 Core business

Concentrating on core business has become a trend in many industries. This means that those activities that are not core to the business are outsourced to

DOI: 10.4324/9781003223788-3

specialised suppliers. For companies doing this, decisions on how to acquire the basic products and services required to meet their customers' needs have come to be of strategic importance. They define the company's position in its competitive environment. The long-term relationships with suppliers that are the result of such sourcing practices are therefore included in the company's strategic planning processes.

Traditional sourcing was a matter of "make or buy" decisions, typically based on cost analysis and focused on limited numbers of specific goods and services, delivered for a limited number of times or over a limited period (rarely more than a year). Companies engaging in such transactions experienced little interdependence and their main motive was cost-efficiency. Many such sourcing decisions are still taken, of course, on a day-to-day basis and all over the world. Strategic sourcing, however, is completely different. The dependence between the participants, their motives, the contract periods and many other characteristics are unlike those of traditional sourcing.[2,3] Strategic sourcing concentrates on long-term motives such as making one's organisation more agile or gaining access to important resources that are better supplied by external parties than developed internally. Strategic sourcing therefore focuses on long-term relationships: the participants collaboratively plan their moves in what thus becomes a common competitive environment. Participants are therefore much more dependent on one another. In addition, since the contract periods involved are consequently much longer, the decisions to be made concern the company's strategic planning horizons. Strategic sourcing may then be defined as the way in which organisations obtain products and services in exchange for returns while considering the long-term impact on the context, intensity and scope of their internal and external relationships.[4]

3.3 The changing competitive agenda

Until recently, most companies usually decided for themselves which changes to make and when. If they decided to expand their market, they made small, carefully planned changes to their organisation and strategy. If they wanted to modify their organisation, they carefully considered the consequences for their customers and employees, trying to keep their company balanced. Today, they cannot afford such luxury. Companies constantly face unexpected developments that have a serious impact on their competitive environment and that occur with a startling and increasing frequency. It is no longer the companies themselves but their environment that dictates most of the changes to be made, even internally.[5,6]

This transformation is driven by both business factors and technological developments. The primary business factors are the shift in power balance from supply to demand and the significantly fiercer competition that many companies experience in their industries, which D'Aveni[7] described as "hyper competition." Business planning no longer begins with what one can deliver, but with what the customer wants – high-quality, customised goods and services. Demand-oriented markets set performance standards, and suppliers will either meet them or perish. Many authors have reported on the changes to business management that this transformation has caused.[5] In the early 1990s, a *Harvard Business Review* editorial observed that modern business involved thinking like a customer, not a producer,[8] hence the concepts of mass customisation and one-on-one marketing.[9,10] Mass customisation refers to the delivery of products and services meeting the specific needs of individual customers in mass markets. The idea is to compose one's products and services of standardised modules and to also modularise the assembly and distribution segments of one's supply chain, thus enabling the company to tailor its products and services to the needs of the individual. In one-on-one marketing, the collective marketing activities of a company are targeted towards individual customers who will thus receive individualised product offerings.

Technological developments – especially the application of IT – are as much a cause as an effect of the transformation to new ways of doing business. The convergence of IT and telecommunication, combined with the increasing availability of bandwidth, has generated a highly competitive market environment and made new organisational designs possible. The Internet makes markets more transparent and helps customers locate the suppliers best suited to meet their expectations. Also, the mobility of IT is rapidly increased by mobile online functionality, including new media such as Twitter and social networks like Facebook and LinkedIn. It effectively negates the former's lack of information symmetry. IT also reduces many transaction and coordination costs, enabling companies to restructure their value chains and focus on their core competences. However, the global nature of the Internet also makes competition much fiercer, as one's competitors cross former geographical boundaries. When looking at the impact of IT on the business domain, one may observe that its initial role in business organisations was reactive. Computer applications supported existing managerial and operational processes, and IT investments were viewed as replacement investments which enabled efficiency improvements by replacing manual information-processing activities. From the mid-1980s, however, it became clear that IT could have a fundamental effect on the way the company's business was conducted. This was called the strategic impact of IT. On the basis of several hundred case studies, four types of "strategic systems" were identified[11]:

1   systems linking the company with customers and suppliers, thus changing the nature of these relationships;
2   systems allowing a more effective integration of the organisation's internal processes;
3   systems enabling the organisation to market new or improved information-based products and services;
4   systems providing executives with high-quality information to support strategy development and implementation.

It is the first two strategic systems in particular that contribute to innovations in the ways companies collaborate.

3.4 Restructuring of value systems

Increased competition forces companies to fundamentally rethink their positions in their respective markets. Traditionally, companies carried out all necessary activities for the production and delivery of their products and services themselves, unless some were procured from external suppliers for specific reasons. However, companies think differently nowadays. They feel that there is no reason to do something themselves unless they really are uniquely good at it. In addition, they therefore ask themselves which of their competences are unique and of core importance, which of their resources and functional capabilities really add value and, consequently, which might more efficiently be procured externally. Because of this change in point of view, outsourcing and insourcing movements are expected to cause fundamental changes in the way companies are configured. Uniqueness and value-adding competences are the business drivers of the future.[12,13] In order to understand how companies develop their competitive positions, one may profitably use the concept of the value chain[14] by strategic out-tasking.[15] Value chains describe the series of activities connecting a company's supply side to its demand side, that is, its raw materials, inbound logistics and production processes to its outbound logistics, marketing and sales. This concept divides a company's activities into the technologically and economically distinct activities the company performs in order to do business. Here, these are called "value activities."[15] Value chains generally are used to describe major lines of business and then show which activities are of primary importance and which have a supporting role. Primary activities are those that have a direct relationship (potential or actual) with the organisation's customers. They contribute directly to the delivery of goods and services. Examples of such activities are inbound logistics, procurement, manufacturing, marketing and delivery. Support activities provide the necessary inputs and infrastructure to allow the company to perform those primary activities. This model is a tool to analyse and, if necessary, redesign the internal and external processes of companies in order to improve their efficiency and effectiveness.

As a result of the developments discussed in Section 3.3, traditional value chains are becoming unbundled. On the one hand, many support activities and some primary activities (logistics, operations) are being outsourced, including even some parts of the company's infrastructure (accounting, financial services and human resources). In companies made up of many business units, shared service centres for specific activities such as human resources or IT are often set up as a first step towards outsourcing. On the other hand, the outsourced activities have to be procured from one or more external suppliers, a process that rebundles them in another way. Clearly, this process causes the relationships between businesses to become increasingly complex.

The popular term used in business literature for these new ways of doing business is the "business model." Business models may be defined as descriptive representations of an enterprise's planned activities (also called business processes). They encompass three integral areas of attention[16]:

1   the internal aspects of the business venture: what it does and how, and how it intends to make money from it;
2   the external aspects of the enterprise: its relationships with its business environment, including its effective knowledge of these relationships;
3   the way in which the company uses its information assets (such as information systems and effective business processes, typically grouped in the domains of customer relations management, supply chain management and core business operations) to do so.

These three components will now be discussed in further detail.

3.4.1 The internal aspects of a business venture

The first major area to which a business plan pays attention is the company's internal aspects. Specifying the internal matters of a business venture means defining, among other aspects, the following elements:

- The products and services the company delivers to its customers. These customers may be consumers or businesses that use these products and services as a part of their activities.
- The sources of revenue that indicate how and to what extent a business venture is viable economically.
- The activities the company performs in order to deliver its products and services and to realise its strategic objectives. These encompass both primary and support activities and concern physical activities like manufacturing, as well as service activities like coordinating other parties' activities.
- The organisation the company has established in order to realise its objectives: company structure (task allocation, for example) and its processes (the combinations of tasks leading to a specific outcome, like order acquisition). This part of the analysis must include the processes that cross the company's boundaries, such as collaborative actions with external business partners for product development, for instance.

Since the shift in managerial focus from vertical, functional activities to the final customer during the 1990s, interest in business processes and their management has grown.[17] Business processes in this sense are taken to consist of one or more related activities that together constitute the response to a business requirement for action. Or, to put it another way, they are sets of interdependent activities designed and structured to produce a specific output for a customer or a market. A business process view therefore implies a horizontal look at the business organisation. The role played by IT may differ widely, between insurance companies and health care organisations, for example, but the process view applies to both. IT developments specifically oriented towards such a process view include workflow systems, workflow management systems and enterprise resource planning (ERP) systems.

3.4.2 The external aspects of the enterprise

As with internal aspects, the company's external relationships must also be defined. These involve several kinds of external actors, who are all in some way involved in the venture: customers, suppliers, shareholders, etc. As with internal focus, this external focus includes structure and processes, since these are needed to maintain external relationships as well. The external aspects discussed must also include the potential benefits for those actors, indicating under which conditions the company may expect to enjoy their support.

Another kind of aspect to be included in this category is that of the new collaboration patterns enabling trading partners to successfully respond to market demands. Traditional arrangements such as buying and selling, subcontracting and joint product design still apply, but outsourcing and specialisation are becoming increasingly important. Companies in the technology businesses, who work with very short product cycles, are taking the lead here. For example, Contract Manufacturing is especially prevalent in the electronics industry.[18] Market research reports signal that in general the expected growth of CM (until 2023) is around 6.5% per year.[19]

Adopting an outsourcing model means developing a strategic vision of one's role and position in the value chain. Companies must ask themselves how they will add value for their customers and for those providing the inputs.[12] They must also analyse their own and their partners' willingness to engage in long-term collaboration, as well as the strength of their collaborative links. Some external companies may want to be able to leave the partnership easily, in order to find new partners. Others are perhaps more willing to invest in close business relationships, integrating their business processes with those of their partners across their company boundaries. No company can afford to engage in outsourcing before it has analysed these aspects.

3.4.3 The use of information assets

Finally, the way in which the venture's information assets are to be used also must be included in the business model. Information Technology is becoming an integral part of all business processes and organisational designs – IT simply cannot be ignored on this level. An example may help to clarify this point: it makes a great deal of difference whether one sells books in a shop or through a website, and such differences must therefore be defined in one's business model. IT and the way it is used influence the company's internal processes as well as its external relationships, for even operational buying and selling activities may be pursued through e-markets. The extent to which IT is interwoven with the company's business processes also affects its outsourcing decisions. Not only is significantly interwoven IT more important than IT that exists only in a supportive role, but the role of its IT supplier increases if the company's IT is more highly integrated with its business. Thus, this business integration aspect influences one's "make or buy" decisions, even though a greater degree of integration does not necessarily lead to a "make" decision – after all, external parties may in fact be better able to guarantee services delivery than internal IT departments. In a similar way, the degree of integration affects the way in which outsourcing relationships are managed once they have been set up. Highly interwoven IT services will cause business managers to keep a close eye on their delivery. Such a situation therefore requires more IT knowledge on the part of the company's business managers and more business knowledge on the part of the supplier's IT professionals.

3.5 New forms of intercompany relations: the network organisation

A successful response to the new market situation described above demands not only new business models but also new trading patterns. The sell-and-buy relationships of old still exist, of course, but increasingly companies engage in all kinds of collaborative efforts, from joint product design to planning their market strategies together. Over the past 25 years or so, intercompany relationships have moved from the operational to the tactical level, then on to the strategic (Figure 3.1).

Traditionally, companies all operated independently from one another. They bought products, components, piece parts and services on the basis of their current needs, expecting that there would be suppliers able to deliver, from which they would simply select the one with the lowest prices. Likewise, product and service offerings were based on forecasts derived from the current demand. Such business patterns may be characterised as operational-level relationships. Buyers and sellers exchanged no information beyond that directly concerning the orders placed.

Independence has its advantages, such as flexibility and the possibility to change suppliers quickly if the current one does not perform satisfactorily.

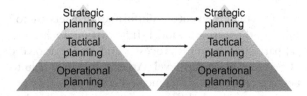

Figure 3.1 Levels of inter-business relationships.[18]

However, independence has also its price. It brings much uncertainty, which makes it impossible to plan far ahead, hence the long delivery times, high inventories and low utilisation levels per production unit (that is, production capacity standing idle). What also follows is the dominance of standardised products: customer-specific components can only be offered after the customer order has been received. When competition puts pressure on efficiency, delivery times and product customisation, suppliers must work together more closely. Their relationships then move to the tactical level. They include longer-term agreements on the product types and quantities to be bought or sold, and on the manufacturing of series and on production capacity, delivery moments, inventories and the like. As a result, both organisations benefit from a more stable supplier–buyer relationship. Reduced uncertainty leads to reduced inventory levels and improved delivery times. Tactical intercompany relationships induce participants to plan collaboratively.

The final step in this development is towards strategic-level relationships. The partners involved then decide to act collaboratively for a long period, and strategic planning becomes a combined activity. In such relations, suppliers (on the basis of their specific expertise and skills) develop, design and produce specific components and services for their customers. These collaborative relationships are also called value-added partnerships.[20] The stability they offer is even higher than on the tactical level. Collaboration is built around competence complementarities, and the partners share much information.

It is important to realise that companies engaging in higher-level collaboration still collaborate on the lower levels, too. Operational- and tactical-level relationships are always embedded in strategic-level collaboration. The result is that all three types of relationship can be found concurrently in almost every industry. In fact, almost every individual company nowadays engages in operational, tactical and strategic collaborations simultaneously.

- Companies buy and sell many goods and services on "spot markets." Here, relationships last only as long as the transaction and, although both parties are generally well informed about one another, they exchange little information. Spot market transactions are typically found in markets for basic raw materials and agricultural products.
- A regular need for specific products or services will usually be captured in a contract, specifying delivery conditions and volumes, and setting repeat provisions. Such longer-term relationships require the exchange of information for planning purposes.
- Finally, some relationships evolve into partnerships, in which the participants collaborate for a long period and even pursue a joint competitive strategy in their industry. Partnerships require an extensive exchange of information.

In this context of evolving business models, unbundling value chains and increasing collaboration, the concept of network organisations emerged. This development is considered a reaction to the narrow perspective of the original markets-and-hierarchies framework, which seems to suggest that the only choice is between market (or horizontal) coordination and hierarchical (or vertical) coordination. New organisational forms are emerging, where independent organisations engage in longer-term relationships. These relationships bear the characteristics of markets: the participants are independent; transactions are governed by contracts in which prices have been agreed; finally, the participants have the opportunity to put an end to the relationship. However, these relationships also bear the characteristics of hierarchies. Multiple coordination mechanisms are applied to improve the efficiency and effectiveness of the transactions. In addition, critical and even confidential information is shared, participants are engaged in collaborative processes and coordination occurs through mutual adjustment. Intercompany networks (or simply networks) are complex arrays of relationships between companies who themselves establish these relationships by interacting with each other.[21] The intercompany networks in which one is primarily interested exhibit the following characteristics:

- the links between the network's participants are based on various types of exchange (of economic goods, money, information, knowledge, etc.);
- networks have a distinct boundary with their environments;
- network participants pursue a common goal;
- all network participants nevertheless also have their own diverse, specific goals;
- networks consist of relationships characterised by mutual investments or interdependences (that is, not just simple transactional links).

The basis of these relationships is trust.[22] The companies' interactions imply making investments in order to build their mutual relationships, thus consolidating the network; caring for the company's relationships becomes a management priority. Lack of trust (a reaction to the possibility of opportunism) has been defined as the essential cause of transaction costs.[23] Thus, being able to generate trust is a fundamental entrepreneurial skill. Trust is needed to lower those costs and render the network economically feasible. Trust also contributes to efficient problem-solving: if the decision-makers feel no need to protect themselves from the others' opportunistic behaviour, information is exchanged freely and more solutions are explored. For such trust to develop, the emphasis on long-term relationships is essential because this shows that the relationships themselves are considered valuable. Competing is a matter of positioning one's company in the network rather than of attacking the environment.

The thrust of the previous discussion is that the activities necessary to produce a good or service can be carried out either by an integrated company or by a network of companies. If an arrangement is found in which companies keep to themselves those activities in which they have a comparative advantage while outsourcing other activities to the most efficient supplier, and if they manage to lower transaction costs, then a superior mode of organisation emerges: the strategic network. Partnerships are economically feasible because their participants' specialisation lowers the final total costs. Partnerships are sustainable because long-term relationships generate trust and thus lower transaction costs. Added-value-sharing fairness is achieved and problems are easily solved, because there is trust and because the relationships themselves are valued.

The potential variety of structures that may constitute network organisations is very large. Consequently, it is difficult to establish a single definition. Some authors even deny that intercompany networks represent a distinct way of organising transactions at all; they believe that they are simply another way to organise markets by new coordination mechanisms if their price mechanisms fail.[26]

3.6 Business ecosystems

A related development to the topic of network organisations in the business literature has been to study the relation between individual companies and the business networks around them as a business ecosystem.[24] James Moore introduced this concept into the field of business research with his Harvard Business Review publication,[1] in which he compared increasingly interconnected companies with a community of organisms adapting and evolving in order to survive. He suggested that a company should not be viewed as a single firm in an industry, but as a member of a business ecosystem, with participants spanning across multiple industries. This focus stresses the interconnectedness of the members of the network and the fact that they depend on each other for their success and survival.[29] The business literature suggests various definitions.[25] Summarising the different views, Adam Hayes suggests the following definition: a business ecosystem may be defined as a network of organisations, including suppliers, distributors, customers, competitors, government agencies and so on, which are involved in the delivery of a specific product or service through both competition and cooperation. The idea of the ecosystem perspective is that each entity in the ecosystem affects and is affected by the others, creating a constantly evolving relationship in which each entity must be flexible and adaptable in order to survive in a biological ecosystem. In case of a digital business ecosystem, the members of this community will be connected through an underlying, evolving technical system.[26]

A business ecosystem is a network, but not all networks are ecosystems. Ecosystems are networks with some special characteristics:

- The members of an ecosystem depend on each other for success and survival, to which they all actively contribute.
- Ecosystems are dynamic structures, flexible and adaptable to changing conditions.
- Ecosystems are loosely coupled systems.
- Ecosystems are modular, but the modules function as an integrated whole.

Considering the outsourcing of information services and approaching it as ecosystems is fairly obvious. However, this is only possible if the resulting network of suppliers and customers can meet the specific characteristics of an ecosystem. Concretely, for the outsourcing of information services, this means that the following conditions must be considered:

- Dynamic alignment of the supplier's services with the needs of each individual customer is crucial. This is a bilateral process: the supplier focuses on the customer, and the customer takes the supplier's capabilities into account.
- The services offered can be flexibly adapted to the changing information needs of the customers.
- To this end, it is important that information services can be offered through loosely coupled modules.
- Interoperability between systems is crucial and is realised by means of semantic, syntax, technical and process standards.

It goes without saying that these economic and technical considerations are necessary but not sufficient conditions for a business ecosystem to function. In addition, a culture of willingness to cooperate and mutual trust is essential.

3.7 Value system restructuring and IT outsourcing

To understand new business models and IT outsourcing better, this section will detail the outsourcing typology (Section 3.7.1) and the impact of IT on outsourcing (Section 3.7.2).

3.7.1 Outsourcing typology

Different types of relationships can be imagined between the outsourcing company and its IT suppliers. This relationship can be typified by the type of IT services being outsourced and the number of suppliers to whom they are outsourced. For example, a distinction is made between single sourcing and multiple sourcing on the one hand, and between selective and total outsourcing on the other.

Currie and Willcocks[27] distinguish between single outsourcing, in which the outsourcing organisation hires one supplier to supply it with the information services needed, and multiple outsourcing, in which a number of suppliers are involved. One may refine this distinction by subdividing single outsourcing into multiple integrated IT outsourcing partnerships and joint IT outsourcing partnerships. If one of the client's suppliers serves as systems integrator too, and the other suppliers subcontract to it rather than contracting directly to the client, the arrangement is called a multiple integrated IT outsourcing partnership. In joint IT outsourcing partnerships, the outsourcing organisation and its principal contractor set up a joint venture which provides the systems integration that the outsourcing organisation needs but also offers its services to other clients as well. A second distinction made by Currie and Willcocks is that between companies outsourcing all information services and those who outsource only a selection. The practice of total outsourcing is much criticised in business literature[28,29,30] because it renders the client dependent on the supplier. This difficulty may be removed, at least partially, by outsourcing to several suppliers and managing their services as a portfolio.[31]

As has been extensively reported in the literature, an increasing number of organisations have transformed their outsourcing operandi from single sourcing to multiple sourcing.[32] Single sourcing has the risk of supplier lock-in; in addition, one single supplier is probably not the best-in-class for all types of services. Multiple sourcing or best-of-breed sourcing offers several advantages in this respect. First, when subdividing the required IT services landscape into different tasks and sourcing them from different suppliers, organisations can compose a set of "best-of-breed" suppliers, i.e. contract with the perceived best supplier for a given service. Second, this practice increases the levels of supplier competition and consequently enables further improvement of the service quality, along with lower costs. Third, closing smaller contracts for clearly delineated IT services allows for improved agility and adaptability. If forced to do so by changing market circumstances or changed legal regulations, the company is more quickly able to add new suppliers to the existing ones or replace an existing one.

However, the advantages of multisourcing come at a price. Active coordination of the service delivery is required among the suppliers and between the outsourcing company and the suppliers. Consequently, for the company to enjoy the benefits of multisourcing, structures and processes for interorganisational coordination will need to be added to the existing governance.

3.7.2 Impact of IT on outsourcing

One important theory used to explain the outsourcing phenomenon is transaction cost theory. IT has a huge downward pressure on transaction costs, and this leads to the opportunity of sourcing services from those countries where production costs are low. The basic argument is that IT reduces the coordination cost between firms involved in supplier selection, price discovery, delivery scheduling and other activities associated with business transactions, enabling buyers to compare purchase alternatives at lower search costs and to transact with business partners more efficiently.[33] Low transaction costs combined with low production costs cannot help but lead to a shift in the sourcing landscape. The results are a reduced need for ownership and more outsourcing due to lower transaction costs (that is, a move away from ownership and vertical integration). However, reducing transaction costs will lead to more explicit coordination, which generates highly integrated interorganisational relationships involving significant investment in human relationships and organisational processes.[18] In this context, Clemons, Eddy and Row proposed an alternative view: the move-to-the-middle hypothesis,[34] which suggests the following:

1   There will be a greater degree of outsourcing as IT increases information availability, processing capacity and reduced transaction costs.
2   Companies will favour developing long-term value-adding partnerships with a small group of suppliers: companies will rely on fewer suppliers than before, with whom they will have long-term relationships and with whom they will cooperate and coordinate closely (that is, when outsourcing, they move away from the market in the direction of intermediate governance structures – a kind of "middle" position).

The second hypothesis consists of two elements: there will be fewer suppliers because of the use of IT, and relationships will be long-term and close.

Having fewer suppliers is attractive for three reasons[18]:

1   Outsourcing involves significant fixed investments in human relationships and business processes; these are more easily recovered by the economies of scale inherent in having only a small number of suppliers.
2   If a company buys specific commodities from a limited set of suppliers, the latter will recover their investments more quickly because they have a greater share of the business. This serves as an incentive for investing in services beyond the specifics of the contract, such as electronic data interchange systems, which are to the advantage of the buying company.
3   Suppliers are not evaluated on the basis of their prices only, but on lead times, flexibility, reliability, innovation and value-added services as well; since these service characteristics are more difficult to specify, having to compare the offers of a large number of suppliers is difficult and thus expensive.

The prediction that IT will lead to the development of long-term, close relationships between buyers and sellers is based on three arguments as well:

1   Long-term relationships allow outsourcing companies to recoup their investments in human relationships and organisational processes; they also incentive their suppliers with an incentive make the investments required.

2   The degree to which IT reduces coordination costs and facilitates monitoring depends on the duration of the relation (it takes time to coordinate
one's activities); long-term contracts allow both partners the benefits of a
learning curve.

3   Long-term partnerships will motivate suppliers to charge fair or even
relatively low prices, and to deliver better-quality, low-cost products and
services.

Based on the above argument, one may conclude that IT investments will
cause a shift towards more outsourcing and towards long-term relationships
between buyers and sellers.[42] Information Technology enables outsourcing
companies to achieve a level of coordination normally associated with in-
house production, without the offsetting increase in operations and opportunism risk costs that used to accompany it.

3.8 Digital platforms

In order to understand digital platforms better, a definition has been detailed
in Section 3.8.1 as well as the Elemica example (Section 3.8.2).

3.8.1 Platforms defined

The "move-to-the-middle" has led to the rise of digital platforms. As stated in
an earlier publication in the Economist, platforms are at the heart of the modern economy with a major impact on corporate strategy.[35] In a broad sense,
platforms can be defined as "foundational products, services or technologies
upon which additional complementary products, services or technologies can
be developed."[36,37] The term "platform ecosystem" in this respect refers to
the platform and all stakeholders interacting on the platform.[38] There are
two types of stakeholders: service providers (a.k.a. producers) and service
recipients (a.k.a. consumers). Both have to be attracted to the platform to
enable value creation.[39] This initiation of a platform is not straightforward –
platforms must create the network effect.[40] This initiation challenge is also
known as the "chicken-and-egg problem." B2B platforms are an important
channel for attracting new customers.[41]

In their literature research, Schreieck et al. identified more than 20 different definitions of the term "platform" which refer to the core of the platform
ecosystem.[46] In an attempt to cluster these definitions, the authors distinguish between technology-oriented and market-oriented definitions. These
are not mutually exclusive but rather complementary perspectives on platform ecosystems.[46] None of the platform-based businesses can be described
with only one of the perspectives.[42]

According to the technology-oriented perspective, a platform is defined as
"a set of stable components that supports variety and evolvability in a system
by constraining the linkages among the other components."[43] This definition

comprises software platforms, such as operating systems, and hardware platforms, such as IT infrastructure or computing hardware.[44]

Following the market-oriented perspective, platforms can be seen as "markets" where users' interactions with each other are subject to network effects and are facilitated by one or more intermediaries.[45] This definition comprises e-commerce marketplaces where goods and services are exchanged as well as communities where information is exchanged. The purpose of market platforms is to match supply and demand on a digital marketplace.

3.8.2 B2B platforms: the example of Elemica: outsourcing connectivity and interoperability

A successful B2B platform in the chemical industry is Elemica, founded in 2000 by a group of 22 chemical companies.[46] Elemica, according to the press bulletin issued at that time, would be an answer to supply chain inefficiencies by offering integrated solutions and services for buying and selling chemicals. In particular, Elemica aims at greatly reducing transaction costs and streamlining business processes on the purchasing and sales side.[47] CIO Bulletin recently announced Elemica as a winner of the Business Excellence Award 2020:

> "CIO Bulletin **Business Excellence Awards 2020** is a premier recognition programme which identifies companies that not only have the most innovative, diversified and reliable services, but also have a clear vision, self-evolving, and self-adaptable culture, and are working smarter than their competitors to create a business edge," said J.P Pande, Editor-in-Chief of the CIO Bulletin magazine. The publication has selected Elemica based on its vast customer base, openness to innovation, professional network and, moreover, its commitment to excellence.[48]

In 2000, an important business driver of the chemical industry was to increase efficiency in the supply chain. The industry was very fragmented. A complicating factor for the chemical supply chain was also that many companies both sold to and bought from each other. This did lead however to the fact that people knew and trusted each other well, which proved to be a good breeding ground for the creation of standards, the so-called "e-chem standards." These stimulated the development of EDI. The first ERP-to-ERP transaction took place in April 2001.[49]

The way EDI was implemented was to enable bilateral relations between companies. Needless to say, this resulting point-to-point architecture was very inefficient. Point-to-point integration is a model for unbounded growth of interfaces. To look at this mathematically, the number of possible integration points between systems (assuming two-way integration for each system connection) is given by $n \times (n-1)$, where n is the number of systems to be integrated. For example, for integrating two systems, the minimum number of connections is two; for ten systems, the minimum number of connections is 90; for 20, the number grows to 380![18] Point-to-point solutions are generally used to connect an organisation with a small number of key suppliers or customers, directly connecting a company's ERP solution with that of another, allowing the direct placing of orders and close inventory control. Point-to-point solutions tend to provide for high traffic dedicated requirements, supporting a small network and a very tightly coupled integration pattern.[18]

These new technology opportunities prompted the newly appointed CEO Kent Dolby to announce a change in strategy. Elemica was to become a connectivity solution provider, and to realise ERP-to-ERP communications between trading partners, but via a single connection to the Elemica network. This change in strategy introduced a middleware approach to connect incompatible software of all the members, enabling the various ERP systems to talk to one another.[50]

The Elemica platform has effectively standardised industry business transactions for all the network members regardless of the type of enterprise systems they have. This neutral platform now facilitates millions of transactions of all types, including order processing, billing and logistics management for industry suppliers, customers and third-party providers. It achieves this through two types of solutions:

1   Quick-link ERP connectivity enables companies to link their internal systems through a neutral platform so that information is moved into each company's database while maintaining confidentiality and security. This link is suitable for limited transactions between supply chains.
2   The smart link application developed a large amount of transactions. It provides specific support for customer management, logistics management, supplier management and sourcing management solutions.

Elemica as an IT supplier has had and still has a very big impact on the chemical industry by offering a platform which enables outsourcing intercompany connectivity and interoperability. On top of all this, Elemica offers a variety of services for suppliers and customers, to automate both their business processes and internal purchasing. A modular, cloud-based solution simplifies sales, procurement and financial processes; integrates supply chain partners to diminish communication barriers; and reduces overhead and errors.[51] To conclude with the words of Arun Samuga, CTO of Elemica,[52] today Elemica has developed into one of the most successful B2B platforms in the industry,[51] customers process over $600B in commerce annually on the network.[49]

Notes

1   Moore, J. F. (1993). Predators and prey: A new ecology of competition. *Harvard Business Review*, 71(3), 75–86.

 2 Sucky, E. (2007). A model for dynamic strategic vendor selection. *Computers & Operations Research, 34*(12), 3638–3651.
 3 Hvolby, H., Momme, J., & Trienekens, J. (2000). Planning and control in industrial networks. In *Proceedings of the 3rd Conference on Stimulating Manufacturing Excellence in SMEs* (pp. 222–231), April, Coventry, UK.
 4 Teich, J., Wallenius, H., Wallenius, J., & Zaitsev, A. (2006). A multi-attribute e-auction mechanism for procurement: Theoretical foundations. *European Journal of Operational Research, 175*(1/11), 90–100.
 5 Parker, M. (1996). *Strategic transformation and information technology: Performing while transforming.* Upper Saddle River, NJ: Prentice Hall.
 6 Parker, M. (1999). *Theory and practice of business/IT organizational interdependencies* (PhD thesis, Tilburg University).
 7 D'Aveni, R. (1994). *Hyper-competition: Managing the dynamics of strategic manoeuvring.* New York: The Free Press.
 8 Kanter, R. (1992). Think like the customer: The new global business logic. *Harvard Business Review, 70*(4), 9–10.
 9 Peppers, D., & Rogers, M. (1997). *Enterprise one to one: Tools for competing in the interactive age.* New York: Currency Double Day.
10 Pine, B. (1993). *Mass customization: The new Frontier in business competition.* Boston, MA: Harvard Business School Press.
11 Peppard, J., & Ward, J. (2016). *The strategic management of information systems – building a digital strategy* (4th ed.). New York: Wiley.
12 Gibson, R. (1997). *Rethinking the future.* London: Nicholas Brealy Publishing.
13 Croteau, A., & Raymond, L. (2004). Performance outcomes of strategic and IT competencies alignment. *Journal of Information Technology, 19*(3), 178–190.
14 Porter, M., & Millar, V. (1985). How information gives you competitive advantage. *Harvard Business Review, 63*(4), 149–160.
15 Krishnamurthy, K., Jegen, D., & Brownell, B. (2009). Strategic outtasking: Creating win-win outsourcing partnerships. *Information and Management, 46*(1), 42–51.
16 Papazoglou, M., & Ribbers, P. (2006). *E-business: Organizational and technical foundations.* Chichester: John Wiley and Sons.
17 Davenport, T. (1993). *Process innovation – reengineering work through information technology.* Boston, MA: Harvard Business School Press.
18 Contract manufacturer. Wikipedia, the free encyclopedia. https://en.wikipedia.org/wiki/Contract_manufacturer - accessed 10 March 2021.
19 BCC Research (2019). *Contract manufacturing: Global markets to 2023.* Downloaded from https://www.reportlinker.com/p05824780/Contract-Manufacturing-Global-Markets-to.html?utm_source=PRN - accessed on 10 March 2021.
20 Johnston, R., & Lawrence, P. (1988). Beyond vertical integration – the rise of the value adding partnership. *Harvard Business Review, 66*(4), 94–101.
21 Jarillo, J. C. (1988). On strategic networks. *Strategic Management Journal, 9*(1), 31–41.
22 Douma, S., & Schreuder, H. (1998). *Economic approaches to organizations.* Englewood Cliffs, NJ: Prentice Hall.
23 Williamson, O. E. (1981). The economics of organization: The transaction cost approach. *American Journal of Sociology, 87*(3), 548–577.
24 Anggraeni, E., Den Hartigh, E., & Zegveld, M. (2007, October). Business ecosystem as a perspective for studying the relations between firms and their business networks. In *ECCON 2007 annual meeting* (pp. 1–28).
25 See for a discussion Anggraeni, E., Den Hartigh, E., & Zegveld, M. (2007, October). Business ecosystem as a perspective for studying the relations between firms and their business networks. In *ECCON 2007 annual meeting* (pp. 1–28);

Graça, P., & Camarinha-Matos, L. M. (2017). Performance indicators for collaborative business ecosystems—Literature review and trends. *Technological Forecasting and Social Change, 116*, 237–255; Järvi, K., & Kortelainen, S. (2017). Taking stock of empirical research on business ecosystems: A literature review. *International Journal of Business and Systems Research, 11*(3), 215–228.

26 Graça, P., & Camarinha-Matos, L. M. (2017). Performance indicators for collaborative business ecosystems—Literature review and trends. *Technological Forecasting and Social Change, 116*, 237–255.

27 Currie, W., & Willcocks, L. (1998). Analysing four types of IT-outsourcing decisions in the context of scale, client/server, interdependency and risk mitigation. *Information Systems Journal, 8*(2), 119–143.

28 Lacity, M., & Hirschheim, R. (1993). *Information systems outsourcing.* Chichester: Wiley.

29 Willcocks, L., Fitzgerald, G., & Feeny, D. (1995). Outsourcing IT: The strategic implications. *Long Range Planning, 28*(5), 59–70.

30 Cullen, S., & Willcocks, L. (2003). *Intelligent IT outsourcing: Eight building blocks to success.* Oxford: Butterworth-Heinemann.

31 Peppard, J. (2003). Managing IT as a portfolio of services. *European Management Journal, 21*(4), 467–483.

32 Levina, N., & Su, N. (2008). Global multisourcing strategy: The emergence of a supplier portfolio in service off-shoring. *Decision Sciences, 39*, 541–570.

33 Malone, T. W., Yates, J., & Benjamin, R. I. (1987). Electronic markets and electronic hierarchies. *Communications of the ACM, 30*(6), 484–497.

34 Clemons, E. K., Reddi, S. P., & Row, M. C. (1993). The impact of information technology on the organization of economic activity: The "move to the middle" hypothesis. *Journal of Management Information Systems, 10*(2), 9–35.

35 The Economist (2014). Something to stand on, 18 January. https://www.economist.com/special-report/2014/01/16/something-to-stand-on – accessed 31 March 2021

36 Schreieck, M., Wiesche, M., & Krcmar, H. (2016). Design and governance of platform ecosystems – key concepts and issues for future research. In *Twenty-Fourth European Conference on Information Systems (ECIS)* (pp. 1–20), Istanbul, Turkey: DBLP.

37 Gawer, A. (2009). Platforms, markets and innovation: An introduction. In Gawer, A. (Ed.), *Platforms, markets and innovation* (pp. 1–18). Cheltenham: Edward Elgar Publishing Limited.

38 Gawer, A., & Cusumano, M. A. (2014). Industry platforms and ecosystem innovation. *Journal of Product Innovation Management, 31*(3), 417–433.

39 Parker, G., Van Alstyne, M. W., & Choudary, S. P. (2017). *Platform revolution: How networked markets are transforming the economy - and how to make them work for you.* New York: W.W. Norton.

40 Wallbach, S., Coleman, K., Elbert, R., & Benlian, A. (2019). Multi-sided platform diffusion in competitive B2B networks: Inhibiting factors and their impact on network effects. *Electronic Markets: The International Journal on Networked Business, 29*(4), 693–710.

41 Islam, A. N., Cenfetelli, R., & Benbasat, I. (2020). Organizational buyers' assimilation of B2B platforms: Effects of IT-enabled service functionality. *The Journal of Strategic Information Systems, 29*(1), 101597.

42 Basole, R. C. (2009). Structural analysis and visualization of ecosystems: A study of mobile device platforms. In *AMCIS 2009 Proceedings* (p. 292). San Francisco, CA: AIS.

43 Baldwin, C. Y., & Woodard, C. J. (2009). The architecture of platforms: A unified view. *Platforms, Markets and Innovation, 32*, 978.

44 Fichman, R. G. (2004). Real options and IT platform adoption: Implications for theory and practice. *Information Systems Research*, *15*(2), 132–154.
45 Eisenmann, T. R., Parker, G., & Van Alstyne, M. (2011). Platform envelopment. *Strategic Management Journal*, *32*(12), 1270–1285.
46 Laudon, K., & Guercio Traver, C. (2013). *E-commerce 2013 – business. Technology. Society* (9th ed.) Boston, MA: Pearson.
47 Anon. (2003). *Elemica (A) connect once connect all* (ESADE Business School case study series). Barcelona: ESADE Business School.
48 https://elemica.com/elemica-a-winner-of-business-excellence-award-2020/ - accessed 16 January 2021
49 www.elemica.com - accessed 18 January 2021
50 Rashad, W., & Gumzej, R. (2014). The information technology in supply chain integration: Case study of REDA chemicals with Elemica. *International Journal Supply Chain Management*, *3*(1), 62–69.
51 Laudon, K., & Laudon, J. P. (2013). *Management information systems, global edition*. London: Pearson Education UK.
52 Arun Samuga – CTO Elemica (2021). Elemica the best performing supply chain management company. www.Insightsuccess.com - accessed 18 January 2021

4 IT strategy and IT outsourcing

Business requirements and IT strategy are the starting point to develop and implement IT sourcing. IT sourcing provides guidance on the structuring and implementation of the supply. IT services can be provided by a combination of internal and external resources. IT sourcing therefore has a strong focus on the contracting and managing of IT services and IT outsourcing. How can IT sourcing contribute to business success?

4.1 Introduction

This chapter provides a strategic perspective on IT outsourcing (ITO). Section 4.2 begins by further defining the concepts of strategy and strategic. The strategic context of ITO is presented next. Then, two sections delve into a recent approach to strategy, namely the concept of capability. Also discussed is the consequence of a changing and uncertain environment, namely the need for dynamic capability. Also discussed is what the possible implications of dynamic capability are for the IT function. The conclusion consists of a discussion of the arguments for and against outsourcing. Writing here comes first from the point of view of general economic and social theory, then on the basis of the most frequently expressed arguments in the information science literature and practice.

4.2 Strategy: perspective and definition

In connection with the study of the management of organisations, it is common, following Ansoff[1,2] and Anthony,[3] to distinguish between three levels: the operational, the administrative (also called control) and the strategic. Planning levels form a hierarchy, with the strategic level at the top and the operational level at the bottom. The longer the effect of a plan, the more difficult to reverse, the more judgement is needed and the higher the importance of a decision, the more strategic the plan is. However, in practical situations, distinctions are not always that clear. Often, the distinction is more relative than absolute.

DOI: 10.4324/9781003223788-4

The operational level deals with day-to-day operations, in other words with maximising "profitability of current operations,"[4] and thus has a short planning horizon. This level is concerned with the shortest period considered by the organisation's management. The administrative/tactical level deals with regulating the operational level – or in Ansoff's terms, "with structuring the organisation's resources in a way which creates maximum performance potential."[4] The planning horizon here extends further and will span the period through the overall business plan, or at least a larger part of it. The strategic level deals with fundamental decisions, e.g. regarding the question: "What business are we in?"[5] It is primarily concerned with external rather than internal problems of the firm.[4] Strategic planning is long-range planning and has enduring effects that are difficult to reverse.[6] The organisation's strategy provides a set of rules for developing the firm's relationships with its external environment: *what* products-technology the firm will develop, *where* and *to whom* the products are to be sold and *how* the firm will gain advantage over competitors. This set of rules is called the product-market or business strategy.[4]

So, there is also a clear hierarchy between these management levels: the highest (the strategic level) determines the framework and context in which the management of the lower levels takes place. The operational level operates under the conditions determined by the administrative level, as the administrative level does with regard to the strategic level. At each of these levels, management takes place through planning and control. A good definition of planning is "anticipatory decision-making,"[8] i.e. within the planning horizon of that level. Control has to do with making sure that the plans made are realised and, if not, that corrective action is taken.

In many organisations, especially the larger ones, two levels of strategic planning can be recognised: the organisation-wide level and line of business level.[7] The first deals with the industries and markets in which the company operates, the second concerns how the company operates and competes in a specific industry. These are usually characterised by specific strategic questions and issues. This dichotomy does not exist in the so-called single business firms. In addition, there are the functional strategies, which are mainly about the elaboration and implementation of business strategies by individual functional departments, such as marketing, production and R&D.[8] Consistent with this, functional strategies are developed within the functional domain of Information Management. In this context, one can define information strategy as a set of implicit and explicit visions, goals, guidelines and plans regarding the supply and demand of formal information in an organisation, aimed at supporting the long-term goals of the organisation and its possible adaptation to changes in technology and environment.[9]

There are several important elements of this definition[10]: goals, vision and guidelines as components of information strategy; the distinction between supply and demand of information; the role of management as an essential source of support and sanction of information strategy; and the close relation to corporate strategy in both a supporting and enabling role.[11]

In this context, it is important to understand that the influence of information systems has changed dramatically over the decades. Well-known in this context is the "three-era model" of evolving IT application in organisations.[15] According to this model, the role of IT in organisations can be positioned as primarily supportive, aimed at improving operational efficiency or improving the effectiveness of management through better information provision, and finally strategic, where IT helps to determine the competitive position of the company. It is easy to understand that this three-era model shows a development over time of the influence of IT, from efficiency improving, to management effectiveness, to a factor of significance in the competitive strategy of the company. However, it also indicates that the influence of IT in today's organisations can differ per organisation. In other words, IT's impact is not always "strategic." It should also be clear that in any organisation, different systems may have a different impact; even if IT in general could be classified as strategic, not every application is strategic. This leads to a portfolio perspective where applications are classified into four categories, according to their contribution to ongoing operations and their importance to the future of the business[15]:

1 Strategic are those applications that are critical to the future success of the business.
2 Key operations are those applications that are critical to the current functioning of the organisation.
3 Support are those applications that provide some support, for example, through cost reduction or management support, but otherwise do not play a critical role, either in ongoing operations or in competitive position.
4 High potential are those applications that have the potential to make a significant contribution to the business in the future.

In addition to this development in the business contribution of IT, there is also a development regarding the integration of IT into the organisation's operational processes. Core processes such as production, order acquisition, procurement, invoicing and management of HR are increasingly run on IT platforms. Being able to rely on the guaranteed availability of these platforms and thus on the functionality they offer is an important competitive necessity for almost all organisations. IT is therefore part of the core business.[12]

4.3 A strategic perspective on (out)sourcing

As detailed in Chapter 1, outsourcing of IT is not a recent phenomenon. Computer applications were already being outsourced in the 1960s. These included financial packages, general ledger and payroll, but also support for various business processes such as inventory management and production planning. Outsourcing was primarily a back-office activity with a focus on efficiency and thus a contribution to profit through cost reduction. However, with the increasing importance of IT to enterprise, the importance of ITO is also becoming more prominent in guarding one's competitive position in rapidly changing environments, and by extension the economic position of the enterprise. The technology purpose evolves to aim at supporting both short-term goals of an organisation and long-term competitive advantage. In this sense, ITO is both tactical for satisfying current portfolio requirements and strategic for future value creation. Traditional back-office outsourcing evolved to a more cross-functional and interorganisational business process. This development can also be observed with respect to the position of procurement function in the business organisations.[13]

Also, in the literature, the increasing impact of IT on enterprise operations led to a broader view regarding outsourcing. In their 1995 MIT Sloan article,[14] Nolan and McFarlan argue that the options for outsourcing IT should be considered within the context of the strategic grid, discussed in the previous section. Companies that are in the support quadrant should definitely consider outsourcing; IT has little added value for them. The same applies to companies in the factory quadrant. IT does not contribute to competitive strategy, and outsourcing to a supplier for whom that is the core competency will often add good value to the business. A different recommendation applies to IT in the strategic quadrant: strategy should not be outsourced, and therefore this IT remains in-house; only a lack of the right IT competencies could be an argument to outsource. A similar recommendation applies to companies in the turnaround quadrant: transferring possible strategic developments is difficult to defend.

With the growth of the domain of information strategy in its contribution to corporate policy, strategic ITO also developed. Strategic ITO is to be defined as the identification, selection and management of IT suppliers for the establishment of a long-term partnership relationship, also aimed at making a commitment to the development of services that are mutually beneficial.[15]

A final note related to the term "strategy." "Strategy and strategic planning" means being in compliance with the prevailing literature, the highest level of control of an organisation, where the emphasis is on establishing the longer-term relationship with the environment. Hence, outsourcing strategy defines the longer-term relationship with the procurement environment. Mintzberg has given various descriptions of the concept of strategy in different publications.[16] Strategy can also mean to be a ploy or a trick to achieve something specific, or a deliberate plan to achieve a certain action or result. Examples include "bring your own device" (BYOD) with the goal of saving costs and Shadow IT to accommodate specific employee requirements. Employees who either bring their own hardware to the company or download an application from the Internet are obviously not engaging in strategic sourcing. However, the fact that this conforms to a formal policy of the organisation does make it a strategy. This may be a policy of the enterprise, but it is not strategic in the sense discussed here. For this reason, the term "policy" is used instead.

4.4 The IT capability[17]

A major contribution in the strategy literature is the viewing of an organisation as a set of resources and skills necessary to achieve its goals. Identifying, maintaining and applying critical resources and skills are critical for any organisation to be successful.

To achieve its goals, an organisation needs to have capabilities related to each of the functional areas (e.g. marketing and purchasing) and capabilities related to general management. An organisational capability is basically the firm's ability to achieve its goal, and that depends on specific skills of people, internal processes and culture. Capabilities are essentially collections of routines, the essential question of which is how well they are performed in comparison to the competition.[18] Examples are the ability to continuously delivering a "highly reliable service, a repeated process or product innovations, manufacturing flexibility, responsiveness to market trends and short product development cycles."[19] Which capabilities these are depends on what the organisation intends to be and do, activities, processes, external markets, legal regulations, etc. Identifying, developing and maintaining these capabilities is a crucial part of the management of any organisation, as well as aligning capabilities with the capabilities of suppliers and (business) ecosystem partners. This capability alignment is also important in ITO contracting and managing ITO relationships. The fulfilment of capabilities requires competences. The concept of organisational competences provides a way to focus attention on the integration and coordination of organisational knowledge for particular purposes: a competence represents an organisation's ability to utilise and mobilise resources to affect a desired outcome.[20]

Applied to the functional area of IT, the IT capability refers to the enterprise-wide ability to apply IT in the context of the enterprise objectives, dependent on knowledge and commitment of both the IT function and the various business functions. As with any capability, this includes competences at various levels. From a policy standpoint, the appropriate technology must be identified, acquired and deployed. The deployment includes the possible reciprocal adaptation to each other of technology and organisation. The technology must be adequately maintained and, ultimately, effectively used in the work environment. Organisations use control frameworks, certification and audit to safeguard the usage of IT for their organisation. In the IT literature, the notion is widely accepted that competitive performance and differences in competitive performance are not so much a result of technology, e.g. hardware, middleware, software resources and cloud solutions, alone, but more of how well they are combined with non-IT resources, such as tacit knowledge

Table 4.1 The IT capability

The IT capability	The business contribution	IT's contribution
Strategic planning	Strategic innovation	Strategic innovation
	Business change	Business change
	Business outcome and programme selection	Business outcome and programme selection
Tactical and operational planning	Benefit realisation and project development	Benefit realisation and project development
	Information and process requirements	Software configuration and development
	Service requirements	Service design
Operational execution	Utilisation of Information services in business processes and management	Service delivery

capabilities in specific business processes that support a company's strategic intentions.[21] In order to be successful, organisations need to decide on the involvement and level of involvement of suppliers.

To understand the contribution of the IT function to the business, and consequently the competences that shape the IT capability, from the research conducted for this book, seven competencies can be distinguished[22,23]: operational service delivery, service design in accordance with functional and technical specifications, software configuration and development, project development and benefit realisation, business outcome and programme realisation, business change and strategic innovation. These are detailed below, explaining IT's contribution starting from the operational execution up to the level of strategic planning (Table 4.1).

4.4.1 Service delivery

At this level, the focus is on IT infrastructure and operations. The IT organisation must ensure that IT services are delivered according to specifications, including architecture and security guidelines and policies, and against agreed-upon service levels and at an acceptable cost. In addition, the right technologies and organisational capabilities must be in place or must be sourced, and appropriate standards, methods and procedures for the utilisation of IT resources must have been developed and applied, again here enterprise and IT architecture and security are important topics, as customer satisfaction. Available staff must possess the skills to answer the organisation's needs. At this level, the business views the contribution of the IT function as one that provides acceptable support for the technology infrastructure that has been deployed.

4.4.2 Service design

Functional, non-functional (such as security specifications) and technical specifications for the information services have been determined and agreed on. The contribution of the IT department is to design the services and their delivery according to the functional and technical specifications. The bases of this contribution are the enterprise and IT architecture.

4.4.3 Software configuration and development

The IT organisation must demonstrate the ability to develop, acquire and implement technology solutions, including the adoption of technology innovations that satisfy business processes and informational needs. The IT organisation has technical and organisational measures in place to ensure business continuity by a secure operation that guarantees confidentiality, integrity and availability. It is at this level that management typically recognises the critical nature of IT in providing and contributing to successful business operations and achieving competitive advantage.

4.4.4 Project development and benefit realisation

This area addresses the quality, predictability and timeliness associated with the deployment of projects. The IT function here expands its impact and contributes to the optimisation of business benefits from investments that have a high IT content; by making impact and risk analyse prior and during the project execution, the IT function also leads the project management board, which monitors and governs the project portfolio.

These first levels of service are foundational and represent performance levels that the IT organisation must master to create and grow trust. If these are not realised, the business cannot develop, or at least will be hampered in its development. Thus, being able to perform successfully within each of these competence areas is crucial for any organisation, even when the IT function is in a supporting (non-strategic) role.

4.4.5 Business outcome and programme selection

IT management actors are active participants and decision-makers in the planning and selection of business projects or programmes, as many business projects are technology-centric, especially in digital (business) transformations. The IT organisation must demonstrate its ability to work closely with the business organisation, with different functional areas and at different levels of management. Also, the IT organisation proactively proposes new innovative technologies. IT technology trends are not only actively monitored by the IT organisation but form an input for business strategic planning, including decisions concerning the strategic sourcing of IT which includes (business) ecosystem partnering.

4.4.6 Business change

This level refers to the ability to implement business strategies by investing in programmes with high levels of IT content, also known as digital business transformations. These transformations potentially change the processes or even the business model. These business investments invariably require significant change plans because of their effects on markets, products, structures, processes and procedures and IT. Plans are thoroughly integrated with business and IT change plans. This competence includes the ability to prioritise technology-enabled investments, including pilot projects to experiment with new technologies, across the organisation according to business objectives.

4.4.7 Strategic innovation

This competence relates to developing unique uses of IT that form the basis for a radical and sustainable change in the business model. IT is a driver of innovation and contributes to innovation. Business strategy development is the result of co-creation with external partners, including IT suppliers and (business) ecosystem partners. The business vision affects the IT solutions to be applied, and new IT solutions affect the business' vision. On this level, the digital business strategy – in short, the digital strategy – is created.

The latter three levels of service (particularly regarding business outcome and programme selection, business change and strategic innovation), concerning the so-called growth needs, need not be addressed to the same extent by every organisation. The role of the IT supplier depends on the role that IT plays in the industry and within the particular outsourcing organisation. If that role is already a strategic one, then indeed these growth needs are present and need to be fulfilled. If that role is limited to back-office, factory-type function, it is unlikely that growth needs will be actively pursued. Consequently, it is not necessary for every organisation to develop the responsibility areas in the same way.

The relationship between the supplier and the outsourcing organisation differs with delivering the so-called foundational services or growth services. For growth-type services, the IT function moves from a support function to a business partner, critical to the organisation's future. This partnership will also be reflected in the outsourcing contract. In addition to service levels also provisions related to the collaboration and co-creation are detailed in the contract. It has to mirror business change competences for IT-induced business change.

Of course, successful delivery and implementation of IT services does not depend on the supplier (internal or external) alone. The business organisation should have specific IT competences in this respect. The support role interactions between business and IT are operational/tactical and are concerned with service delivery to users. Business functions are assumed to have the appropriate competencies to adequately use the information systems, including the underlying technology. The business functions also have the responsibility for defining their information needs and the desired support for the business processes. These have to be met by the IT function's service delivery apparatus. The information and process requirements are the input for software configuration and development and the selection and parameterising of Commercial of the Shelf (COTS) solutions and Software as a Service (SaaS) offerings. For the level of project development and benefit realisation, a closer collaboration between business and IT is critical, where the focus for the business is on benefit realisation. On this level, ensuring adequate conditions for optimal implementation and utilisation of installed systems (like sufficient user/organisational acceptance and training) is a primary business responsibility.

Being successful with IT on the higher growth levels of IT use (business outcomes and programme selection, business change and eventually strategic innovation) depends as much on the business as on the supplier. The competences to identify, select, deploy and implement new IT-based solutions, including technology refreshment and innovation, which are in line with the business strategy, need to exist in the business functions themselves. These levels are characterised by intense business–IT collaboration.

4.5 A dynamic view on organisational capabilities[23]

The design and functioning of an organisation are highly dependent on the environmental conditions in which it operates. A stable predictable environment is associated with a different type of organisation than a dynamic and difficult to predict environment. The latter necessitates quick reactions and sudden changes. This means that being able to see these developments coming in good time and respond to them quickly and adequately become critical skills for the entire organisation. This also applies to organisational capabilities. Dynamic environmental conditions require another type of capability than static and predictable conditions: the dynamic capability. In today's reality, most organisations are operating in a dynamic environment.

4.5.1 The impact of change and uncertainty

Uncertainty and change impact IT at each of the levels of service. As for the three foundational levels, uncertainty directly affects the volumes, required quality and types of services. Changes in business volume impact the volume of required services and thus the available capacity in terms of processing capacity, bandwidth, staff and response times. Sudden changes in service requirements (e.g. by changing laws or regulations) require timely adaptations in the functional layer (e.g. the software) and possibly in the infrastructure layer (e.g. middleware and hardware). Timely communication between the supplier (outsourced or in-house) enables the supplier to make the necessary adjustments is mandatory for a smooth continuity of service delivery and timely adoption of the IT. In this respect, the technology of cloud solutions (e.g. Infrastructure as a Service, Platform as a Service, Software as a Service) offers opportunities of increased agility. Agility is supposed to allow organisations to get their application up and running faster, and agility enables IT organisations to adjust resources more rapidly to meet fluctuating and unpredictable demands.[24] Agile software development approaches in combination with DevOps are used to speed up software delivery.

As for the so-called growth areas, the question is how a company should include developments in a timely manner that trigger a more fundamental change to strategic business and IT management. Companies need strategies and plans to run its current operations and reach its objectives, in combination with reacting to new, unexpected events. Concurrent exploitation of existing resources and capabilities, along with exploring and taking advantage of or reacting to initially unforeseen opportunities, requires combining two fundamentally different management styles. Exploitation goes together with routinisation, control and mechanistic structures; exploration is associated with flexibility, autonomy and organic structures. The combination of these two fundamentally different sets of skills, processes, management styles, etc., is known as ambidexterity.[25,26,27] IT ambidexterity is the joint consideration of IT exploration (related to new IT resources and practices) and IT exploitation (related to current resources and practices).[28] In this respect, Gartner introduced the term bi-modal IT: "the practice of managing two separate but coherent styles of work: one focused on predictability, the other on exploration."[29]

The relationship between dynamic business conditions and IT is problematic to say the least.[30] In many cases, the installed IT is a hindrance for flexibility and agility and requires a major redesign. Functional silo architectures (often from a variety of suppliers) and hard-coded business rules embedded in information systems can make even the smallest adaptation difficult. Enterprise resource planning (ERP) systems that are have been implemented in response to these bad industry practices are often overly complex and create process silos as a replacement for functional silos. Their implementation often requires complex organisational changes and as a result can take relatively long to implement – longer still to master. As a result, there is precious little IT resource left to support business flexibility and agility. Cloud solutions are partly addressing these issues.

4.5.2 Dynamic capabilities

To understand the nature of a firm's sustainable competitive position in a changing environment, Teece et al. developed the concept of "dynamic capabilities."[31] They define dynamic capabilities as "the ability to sense and then seize new opportunities, and to reconfigure and protect knowledge assets, competencies and complementary assets so as to achieve sustained competitive advantage."[38] Key concepts in the definition are "change" and the ability to function effectively – to survive if not thrive – under changing conditions.

Dynamic capabilities have to be distinguished from static or operational capabilities. The latter capability refers to the ability to run an organisation that functions effectively under specific conditions and context; in other words, dynamic capabilities correspond to the efficient exploitation of existing resources. These capabilities, however, have to change when conditions change. Under high levels of turbulence, there will be a discrepancy between the required and the present operational capabilities. Digital (business) transformations increase the need for dynamic capabilities. The presence of dynamic capabilities ensures the possibility of changing the operational capabilities. Without dynamic capabilities, the organisation would stick rigidly to its known pattern of behaviour and would, in the end, lose its relevance and die. So, in this view, dynamic capabilities do not come in place of operational capabilities; rather, they complement each other. Examples of dynamic capabilities include sensing and shaping opportunities and threats, seizing opportunities and maintaining competitiveness by adjusting or reconfiguring business resources.[38] In fast-changing environments, firms need to invest in scanning and surveying external developments and learn how to interpret them. The sensing capability may be defined as "the ability to spot, interpret and pursue opportunities in the environment."[32] Once the organisation has become aware of a new opportunity or risk, it must have the bias for action to take appropriate measures to develop new products, services or market approaches. Finally, when the enterprise is successful in its reaction to the identified market and other opportunities, it will have to remain alert to changes and be willing and able to adapt accordingly. The essence of an organisation's dynamic capabilities resides in its organisational processes and the leadership skills of its management. Organisations with strong dynamic capabilities have the ability to adjust.

Karimi-Alaghehband and Rivard applied these concepts to ITO.[33] They define ITO dynamic capabilities as "the ability of an organisation to sense ITO opportunities, seize opportunities and orchestrate new and existing IT services through outsourcing arrangements." In line with Teece's distinction into the dynamic capabilities of sensing and shaping opportunities and threats, seizing opportunities and maintaining competitiveness, Karimi and Rivard distinguish the following dynamic capabilities for ITO:

- ITO sensing capabilities, which refer "to the extent to which an outsourcing organisation is able to scan the environment to identify new outsourcing opportunities and become alert to ITO market conditions and offerings." Organisations that are able to scan their environment are aware of IT service suppliers, as well as the types of activities that are outsourced in their and similar industries. They are also informed in a timely manner about new opportunities to adjust their portfolio of IT services.
- ITO seizing capabilities that are defined as "the extent to which an outsourcing organisation is able to identify potential ITO suppliers and select among them." The perceived outsourcing opportunities must be

converted in modified outsourcing arrangements. Vendor selection, which includes negotiation, establishing selection criteria and appropriate pre-purchase and post-purchase evaluation processes a critical activity in every procurement process.[34]

- ITO orchestrating capabilities, which refer to "the extent to which an outsourcing organisation is able to coordinate the work of one or more suppliers and integrate their resources and activities with the current IT department's resources and activities." Orchestrating capabilities refers to the necessity to integrate the newly acquired IT resources with the existing IT resources.

Karimi and Rivard's study on the role of capabilities in the success of ITO confirmed their supporting role in explaining the success of ITO.[35]

4.5.3 Enterprise architecture and dynamic capability

An important role in this relationship between IT and business dynamics is reserved for enterprise architecture.[36] As defined by Ross, Weill and Robertson,[37] enterprise architecture represents the organising logic for business processes, IT applications and infrastructure. The enterprise architecture is composed of a number of layers, each with their own architecture, all of which are interdependent. A common classification distinguishes the business layer, the application layer, the data layer and the infrastructure layer. In the past decades, each layer underwent architectural changes[38]:

- The business layer evolved from a strictly vertical hierarchical functional structure, to a horizontal business process orientation, to a focus on supply chains and eventually to a focus on flexible global business networks.
- The application layer developed from a silo structure offering support to individual business functions, to enterprise-wide applications like ERP and CRM, to (more recently) a services orientation powered by cloud computing.[39]
- The information layer evolved from centralised data per function, to shared data, to distributed data today. The growth of the data volumes and the growth of the analytic capabilities are exponential. Not only structured data but also unstructured data, such as social media data (e.g. Twitter, Instagram and Facebook) is becoming an integral part of the data available for decision-making and managing for many organisations.
- The infrastructure layer developed from mainframe architecture, to client–server, to ubiquitous computing. Architectural choices on this level today are challenged by developments like mobile computing, BYOD and cloud computing.

The common misperception on architecture is that it is merely a(n) (IT-) technical construct that belongs to the domain of the IT function and its staff, and is rarely outsourced to an external supplier. Some organisations involve external consultants to fill (temporary) knowledge gaps. Under this assumption, the business functions remain at a distance when it comes to discussions about architectural choices. However, from the layered model it is clear that IT architectural choices are not and must not be independent from business-focused architectural choices. When, for example, a business changes its functional or regional orientation to a corporate (enterprise-wide) orientation, this will directly affect the IT architecture. A move to an enterprise-wide orientation makes possible the standardisation of business processes and common use of company data, like customer and supplier data. This is a choice that may be driven by the business objective to reduce cost and enable cross-selling. However, a change in the IT architecture to a single instance of one enterprise system (to reduce IT costs) may be very detrimental to the business results of a highly diversified company. This example also shows that if for some reason or another (strategic or regulatory) a company has to change its business model, this change can be heavily constrained by earlier architectural choices in their IT systems.

4.5.4 IT's contribution to dynamic capability

What is the contribution of the IT function to the dynamic capability of the firm? From current practice and literature, some principles emerge[40]:

- Use modular structures instead of monolithic silos for both business processes and systems. Modularity allows easy reconfiguring in multiple combinations and facilitates changes and scalability.
- Ensure that interfacing between modules is based on open standards to enable interoperability, cloud solution are typically strong in interfacing with any module.
- Accelerate the software development process by applying rapid and agile software application development methodologies in combination with no-code or low-code platforms such as Mendix, Outsystems or Appain.
- Embed options in software functionality based on plausible scenarios and supported by clear business cases.
- Promote shareability of data; for structured data, this requires a policy of semantic standardisations. Addressing data ownership is also important, where the business is the proper data owner and the IT function is facilitating the data infrastructure and tooling, including Identity and Access Management tooling.
- Recognise that the basic infrastructure is probably the least affected by turbulence, provided it is easily scalable and does not stand in the way of compatibility, cloud computing, e.g. Infrastructure as a Service and Platform as a Service enable compatibility.

As a conclusion to this section, it can be stated that creating an agile IT support for business necessitates that all IT activities are managed and synchronised from the perspective of making the business increasingly more flexible. This vision achieves several objectives: it drives the design of the enterprise architecture in all its layers; it directly affects the way business processes are organised and managed; it has implications for software architecture and the accessibility of data; finally, it forces a high level of connectivity and scalability at the infrastructure level. The realisation of this vision is a shared responsibility of business and IT management. They must have a clear, shared vision on which processes and business units should be most focused in order to enhance flexibility and agility. The role of IT in this partnership and thus the immediate consequence for the outsourcing partner is to select and implement those technologies that best support the required agility.

4.6 IT capability and outsourcing

To ensure fit for purpose, IT capabilities outsourcing is one of the options for organisations. The below subsections detail the arguments for outsourcing by the economic and social perspective as well as the perspective from the management literature.

4.6.1 Why outsource: economic and social perspectives

Establishing the boundaries of a firm encompasses strategic decisions. Whether resources, competences and capabilities should be kept and developed in-house or procured in the market has a major impact on how an organisation will thrive. As discussed in the Introduction, explanations of how and on what grounds these decisions are made have been developed in economics, management and behavioural theory.

The classical analysis comes from economics with transaction cost economics. The transaction cost of in-house production encompasses, e.g. internal planning and coordination costs; the transaction cost of procuring in the market comprises, e.g., search costs (e.g. for a reliable supplier) and contracting costs. The type and context of transactions determines transaction costs and thus influences whether a transaction will be carried out in the market or in a hierarchy.

Asset specificity, product complexity, uncertainty, difficulty to measure performance and frequency are the factors that have an impact on transaction cost and in particular the contracting cost. These factors result in more complex contracts, which demand more resources to develop. The combination of these factors makes contracting even more problematic[41] and consequently favours in-house production.

Closely related to transaction cost theory is agency theory.[42] This theory studies the costs a principal incurs in order to verify that the contractor (the agent) is acting in the principal's best interest. Agency costs include monitoring cost, the cost of controlling and supervising the activities of the agent and residual loss, costs resulting from incomplete control and costs from monitoring. In this context, it should also be mentioned that contracts by definition can never be complete, which can also lead to surprises. Needless to say, difficulty in monitoring supplier performance encourages in-house production.

A rival theory in economics is offered by the resource-based view (RBV).[43] According to this theory, an organisation has a collection of resources that generate rents. Some of these resources are critical for its competitive position and some are necessary but not critical. Critical resources are those that are VRIN – valuable, rare, imperfectly imitable and not substitutable. A related theory to the RBV is the resource dependency theory (RDT), a social theory, which theorises about resources, which are outsourced, as they are not VRIN but nevertheless are critical for the company's operations.[44] These resources create critical dependencies for which organisations need to develop strategies to mitigate the risks.

4.6.2 Why outsource: an overview from Information Management literature

The arguments in favour and against ITO are detailed in this subsection.

4.6.2.1 Arguments in favour of IT outsourcing

The ten most frequent arguments in favour of ITO are detailed below and in Table 4.2. Remarkably, these arguments have changed relatively little with time. Another important remark has to be made: the order of importance of the arguments in favour of ITO is different for outsourcing organisations. The business strategy and the IT strategy have an impact on the order of the arguments.

4.6.2.1.1 DECREASING THE TOTAL COST OF OWNERSHIP OF THE IT SERVICES

External suppliers must provide the same services as the company's IT department, but against lower costs. The external suppliers can do so because of economies of scale, both on the delivery side and by using their buying power to obtain better hardware and software prices. The condition for the external suppliers to be able to do so is that their clients allow them to standardise their information services, which they probably will, as long as their information needs are fulfilled.

4.6.2.1.2 SHORTENING TIME-TO-MARKET FOR NEW IT SERVICES

Many companies operate in markets whose already considerable dynamics have been increased by the globalisation process and digital transformations. IT departments must therefore be able to react quickly, which means having substantial resources available. This makes it difficult for internal IT

Table 4.2 Arguments in favour of IT outsourcing

Arguments	Rationale
1 Decreasing the total cost of ownership (TCO) of the IT services	IT departments regularly overspends. IT projects regularly overspend. IT services are insufficiently standardised. IT service levels are insufficiently standardised.
2 Shortening time-to-market for new IT services	IT departments are unable to deliver, on time, the IT services that the business units need. Maintenance of the current information systems takes up too much of the budget. Most of the IT department's staff are occupied with keeping the current information systems working. IT departments are too slow in realising the connections between new information systems and their environment, which causes delays.
3 Increasing IT services flexibility	IT departments are unable to improve the level of their services temporarily (for example, by keeping the help desk open longer when new applications are introduced). IT departments are unable to increase the volume of their services temporarily (when a new ERP system is introduced, for instance). IT departments are unable to maintain the many different technologies used by all departments. IT departments are unable to deliver IT services cost-effectively in new company locations.
4 Achieving IT services innovativity	The number of an IT department's staff is too small to assess the applicability of new technological developments. IT department staff is insufficiently qualified to assess the applicability of new technological developments. IT department objectives focus on operational excellence. IT department budgets do not include innovation. IT services are insufficiently standardised.
5 Facilitating the IT consequences of mergers and disentanglements	There are no scenarios for disentangling the information systems when parts of a company are sold. Consolidating information involves the use of a great number of interfaces, many of which are hand-operated. Much of the information stored by an organisation is redundant.
6 Achieving a "technology shift"	IT departments lack sufficient knowledge to implement new technologies. IT departments lack the capacity to implement new technologies while keeping current systems working. IT departments cannot implement new technologies within the time limits set by a company's business needs. The architecture of the current information systems hinders the implementation of new technologies.

Arguments	Rationale
7 Realising a strategic focus on central competences	A company's strategy includes focusing on central competences.
	IT services are not part of a company's central competences.
	A company collaborates with other enterprises in many fields already – in alliances, joint ventures and partnerships.
	A company's business units all have their own profit and loss responsibility.
8 Rendering the IT services costs variable	There are insufficient funds to invest in IT.
	IT investments to be made are out of proportion to their use and utility.
	The need for IT services will increase but is still limited.
	The need for IT services is great but will soon diminish.
9 Improving the company's financial ratios	The number of staff in relation to a company's turnover is high in comparison with that of other companies.
	The costs of the IT services in relation to a company's turnover are high in comparison with those of other companies.
	The investments in hardware and buildings needed for an IT department have a serious impact on a company's balance sheet.[a]
	A company's cash position must be improved.
10 Solving the problem of not being able to recruit qualified IT staff	Local collective labour agreements offer little scope for incentive schemes with which to attract scarce IT specialists.
	The company's salary structure offers little scope for incentive schemes (such as lease cars, bonuses) with which to attract scarce IT specialists.
	The company's image is not attractive to IT specialists.

a Although IFRS16 has reduced the impact of this rationale.

departments to be cost-efficient. External suppliers, who as a rule have many more clients, are in a better position to handle fluctuations cost-efficiently.[45] Also, development and implementation often leave internal IT departments little time and resources to document the changes properly, again making outsourcing attractive. Achieving a short time-to-market is essential, especially for software development and implementation.

4.6.2.1.3 INCREASING FLEXIBILITY OF IT SERVICES

IT departments must be able to react to changes in the services requested, with respect to both the quantity of these services and their nature. On the basis of their IT strategies, companies may decide to change from one information services platform to another. Such flexibility is needed to maintain their competitive positions.[49] Nevertheless, attention must be paid to the IT department's staff: can the internal staff be retrained?

Nowadays, flexibility is needed to keep up with the market's dynamics. Organisations are on the move and many companies join networks. Mergers and acquisitions are the order of the day. In addition, and paradoxically, it is mergers and acquisitions that require a certain amount of standardisation in order to achieve flexibility.

This is explained by the fact that connecting and disengaging whole departments is only possible if they all use the same standards.

4.6.2.1.4 ACHIEVING INNOVATIVITY IN IT SERVICES

Since information services technologies are increasingly rapidly developed, IT departments face a growing complexity, certainly in companies operating in international markets. Keeping their companies' business processes connected requires much of the IT function's attention and much innovativity. The ability to explore the opportunities of new innovative technologies and to rapidly deploy them is crucial. Due to scale and their 1:N business model, suppliers are better positioned to achieve innovativity in IT services.

4.6.2.1.5 FACILITATING THE IT CONSEQUENCES OF MERGERS AND DISENTANGLEMENTS

Survival and/or strategic motives often require selling parts of companies, which means that the IT functions of the separate parts must be disentangled. Such changes require much of the IT departments' attention. Likewise, integrating the IT functions of merging or acquired companies must be done very carefully to ensure good collaboration. The disentanglement as well as the integration requires additional temporary capacity of the IT departments. External suppliers are better positioned to provide this capacity, as they can use resources in the future for new clients.

4.6.2.1.6 ACHIEVING A "TECHNOLOGY SHIFT"

For years, IT departments have adapted their companies' information platforms – a sensible thing to do at first, but not always cost-effective in the long run. "Legacy" problems are often the consequence. When it finally comes to transforming such platforms, this involves drastic operations that require substantial effort. Change is made even more difficult by the fact that, during the transition, two separate platforms must be kept working. Consequently, the risks to the continuity of the information services delivery are significant.[46,47] External suppliers are better positioned to provide this capacity, as they can use resources in the future for new clients.

4.6.2.1.7 REALISING A STRATEGIC FOCUS ON CENTRAL COMPETENCES

The trend to focus on central competences has passed the point where the question was whether information services should be considered core competences or not. Instead, companies ask how collaboration may be achieved. Increasingly, global and partner-based alliances are established, evolving from the client-centred view of outsourcing.[48]

4.6.2.1.8 RENDERING THE IT SERVICES COSTS VARIABLE

If a company's IT department is made responsible for information services delivery, the company will have to invest in IT. That said, since the IT department has only that one company as its client, there is no way in which it can spread the investment costs over several clients when the information services demand fluctuates.[49] As a result, the IT costs are mostly fixed costs.

4.6.2.1.9 IMPROVING THE COMPANY'S FINANCIAL RATIOS

Many – especially listed – companies are assessed by investors and analysts on the basis of their financial ratios, such as revenue and/or profit per employee. Outsourcing IT services improve the financial ratios as the number of employees of the outsourcing organisation reduces, while the revenue remains stable. Improving financial ratios is an important motive for offshore outsourcing as well, lowering IT spending as a percentage of total spending.

4.6.2.1.10 SOLVING THE PROBLEM OF NOT BEING ABLE TO RECRUIT
        QUALIFIED IT STAFF

The labour market has been tight for decades. Recruiting and remaining qualified IT staff is therefore difficult, a trend that is reinforced by the rise of offshore outsourcing. In order to be attractive for potential staff, much attention must be paid to education and personnel management.

Another aspect to be considered, related to the argument of remaining qualified staff, is staff turnover, which presents a considerable risk to service delivery continuity. Employees who leave take their knowledge and know-how with them. This is a serious problem in rapidly changing organisation.[50,51,52,]

4.7 Arguments against outsourcing

Companies who consider outsourcing must realise that there are also negative consequences. Like the arguments in favour of outsourcing, the arguments against outsourcing also have changed little with time. The four most important arguments are discussed below and in Table 4.3. Just as with those in favour of ITO, there is also no particular order in the arguments against outsourcing.

Table 4.3 Arguments against IT outsourcing

Arguments	Rationale
1 Increased dependence on suppliers	Managing the IT service delivery of suppliers on the basis of contracts is more difficult and less flexible than managing an IT department by internal agreements.
	Price changes during a contract period may significantly affect the outsourcing organisation's total cost of ownership.
	Companies performing their own information services delivery can independently decide to invest in technological innovations specific to their industry or situation; if IT services are delivered by suppliers, these will have to be convinced of the need to make the investments.
2 A loss of knowledge and know-how	By transferring IT experts to the supplier, knowledge of the business is lost, as well as technical IT expertise.
	Experts working for internal IT departments usually are all-round technicians with much knowledge of the business. Supplier staff usually have a narrower technical expertise and much less knowledge of the business; they are also generally quickly rotated between clients.
	For an outsourcing organisation, it is difficult, costly and time-consuming to acquire IT knowledge and know-how after the expiration of an outsourcing contract.
3 Confidentiality risks	IT departments work for their own company only. Suppliers may also work for the company's direct competitors, which causes confidentiality risks.
	IT service delivery may be too directly connected to the company's primary processes.
	While it improves the supplier's competitive position, outsourcing may decrease the outsourcing organisation's competitive power.
4 Difficulty in selecting the right supplier	Future information needs are unforeseeable for outsourcing organisations.
	Future mergers and acquisitions in the supplier market are unforeseeable for outsourcing organisations.
	Future changes in the supplier's strategy is unforeseeable for outsourcing organisations.

4.7.1 *Increased dependence on suppliers*

When information services are contracted out, the responsibility for their delivery is transferred to the supplier. This is a big step for many companies, since it renders them dependent on their supplier. Instead of managing an internal IT department, the company will now have to discuss its needs with outsiders. In addition, the fulfilment of these needs is based on a contract which narrows the outsourcing organisation's ability to manoeuvre with flexibility.

4.7.2 A loss of knowledge and know-how

Outsourcing processes may transfer IT department staff to the company providing the services. Their knowledge and know-how then also leave the outsourcing organisation, requiring much effort to acquire them again. In relation to knowledge, a distinction can be made between explicit knowledge and tacit knowledge.[53] Knowledge of the former type is acquired through books, documentation, etc. Knowledge of the latter type is difficult to formalise. Consequently, the transfer of this kind of knowledge is highly dependent on personal communication with experienced peers. In the case of digital strategies, which involve integration of IT and business processes, tacit knowledge is also particularly important. This should be taken into account in the transfer of systems in case of outsourcing. This is all the more true if, in addition, there is poor or partially maintained documentation. This may well be an argument to keep one's information services in one's own hands.[58]

4.7.3 Confidentiality and privacy risks

Much essential company information, including strategic plans and customer data, is embedded in information systems. Under no circumstances should such information fall into the hands of competitors or become publicly known. The confidentiality risks involved in outsourcing are therefore frequently cited as a reason for not contracting out IT services.[54,55]

4.7.4 Difficulty in selecting the right supplier

Based on today's information needs, an outsourcing organisation is able to select the right supplier. This requires a thorough selection procedure, including predefined objectives of the outsourcing and requirements. For outsourcing organisations, it is very difficult to predict future information needs; future information needs might impact today's outcome of the selection procedure. Also, future supplier mergers and acquisitions might impact today's outcome of the selection procedure. Also, changes in the supplier strategy might have an impact. However, the market is maturing. Difficulties in finding the right supplier are decreasing.[56,57,58]

Notes

1 Ansoff, H. I. (1968). *Corporate strategy*. London: Pelican.
2 Ansoff, I. (1984). *Implanting strategic management Prentice*. Englewood cliffs, London: Hale International.
3 Anthony, R. N. (1965). *Planning and control systems: A framework for analysis*. Cambridge, MA: Division of Research, Graduate School of Business Administration, Harvard University.
4 Ansoff, H. I., MacDonnell, E. J., & Harvey-Jones, J. (1987). *Corporate strategy* (Rev., Ser. Penguin business). London: Penguin.

5   Abell, D. F. (1980). *Defining the business: The starting point of strategic planning*. Hoboken, NJ: Prentice Hall.
6   Ackoff, R. L. (1969). *A concept of corporate planning*. Hoboken, NJ: Wiley-Interscience.
7   Grant, R. M., & Grant, R. M. (2008). *Cases to accompany contemporary strategy analysis*. Malden, MA: Blackwell.
8   Johnson, G., Scholes, K., & Whittington, R. (2009). *Exploring corporate strategy: Text & cases*. London: Pearson Education.
9   Smits, M. T., van der Poel, K. G., & Ribbers, P. M. A. (2003). Information strategy. Assessment of information strategies in insurance companies. In Galliers, R. D., & Leidner, D. E. (Eds.), *Strategic information management: Challenges and strategies in managing information systems* (3rd ed., pp. 64–88). Oxford: Butterworth Heinemann.
10 van der Poel, K. G. (1995). *Theory and practice of information strategy: A study of contemporary practice in six large organisations and development of a typology of information strategies* (PhD Thesis, Tilburg University Press).
11 See for a discussion and analysis on this subject: Peppard, J., & Ward, J. (2016) *The strategic management of information systems – building a digital strategy* (4th ed.). New York: Wiley.
12 Magnusson, C. (1999). *Hedging shareholder value in an IT dependent business society: The framework BRITS* (Doctoral dissertation, Stockholm University).
13 Hong, P., & Kwon, H. B. (2012). Emerging issues of procurement management: A review and prospect. *International Journal of Procurement Management 4, 5*(4), 452–469.
14 McFarlan, F. W., & Nolan, R. L. (1995). How to manage an IT outsourcing alliance. *MIT Sloan Management Review, 36*(2), 9.
15 After: Talluri, S., & Narasimhan, R. (2004). A methodology for strategic sourcing. *European Journal of Operational Research, 154*(1), 236–250.
16 Mintzberg, H. (1978). Patterns in strategy formation. *Management Science, 24*(9), 934–948.
17 An earlier version of this Section has been published in Benson, R. J., Ribbers, P., & Blitstein, R. B. (2014). *Trust and partnership: Strategic IT management for turbulent times* (Ser. Wiley cio series). Chichester: Wiley.
18 Winter, S. G. (2003). Understanding dynamic capabilities. *Strategic Management Journal, 24*(10), 991–995.
19 Amit, R., & Schoemaker, P. J. (1993). Strategic assets and organizational rent. *Strategic Management Journal, 14*(1), 33–46.
20 Peppard, J., & Ward, J. (2016). *The strategic management of information systems – building a digital strategy* (4th ed.). Chichester: Wiley.
21 Tallon, P.P. (2007). Inside the adaptive enterprise: An information technology capabilities perspective on business process agility. Center for Research on Information Technology and Organizations, University of California, Irvine, www.crito.uci.edu - accessed 1 February 2021.
22 After the 'Total Value Performance model' in Benson, R. J., Ribbers, P., & Blitstein, R. B. (2014). *Trust and partnership: Strategic IT management for turbulent times* (Ser. Wiley cio series). Chichester: Wiley.
23 Benson, R.J., & Ribbers, P.M. (2020). Strategic Sourcing in turbulent times – the impact of trust and partnership. In Beulen, E., & Ribbers, P. M. (Eds.), *The Routledge companion to managing digital outsourcing*. London: Routledge.
24 Knorr, E. (2017). What is cloud computing? Everything you need to know now. *InfoWorld*, June, p. 10.
25 See for this analysis Koch, A., Ribbers, P. M., & Rutkowski, A. F. (2020). Ambidexterity at Axa concern. In Beulen, E., & Ribbers, P. M. (Eds.), *The Routledge companion to managing digital outsourcing* (pp. 130–146). London: Routledge.

26 Gibson, C. B., & Birkinshaw, J. (2004). The antecedents, consequences, and mediating role of organizational ambidexterity. *Academy of Management Journal*, 47(2), 209–226.

27 March, J. G. (1991). Exploration and exploitation in organizational learning. *Organization Science*, 2(1), 71–87.

28 Lee, O. K., Sambamurthy, V., Lim, K. H., & Wei, K. K. (2015). How does IT ambidexterity impact organizational agility? *Information Systems Research*, 26(2), 398–417.

29 Gartner (2017). *From the gartner IT glossary: What is bimodal?* https://research. gartner.com/definition-whatis-bimodal?resId=3216217&srcId=1-8163325102 – accessed 31 August 2017

30 Oosterhout, M. van (2010). *Business agility and information technology in service organizations* (No. EPS-2010-198-LIS).

31 Teece, D. J. (2009). *Dynamic capabilities and strategic management: Organizing for innovation and growth*. Oxford: Oxford University Press on Demand.

32 Pavlou, P. A., & El Sawy, O. A. (2011). Understanding the elusive black box of dynamic capabilities. *Decision Sciences*, 42(1), 239–273.

33 Karimi-Alaghehband, F., & Rivard, S. (2019). Information technology outsourcing and architecture dynamic capabilities as enablers of organizational agility. *Journal of Information Technology*, 34(2), 129–159.

34 Ribbers, P. (1980). *Planning and organization of the purchasing function in an industrial enterprise* (PhD Thesis, Tilburg University).

35 Their study that covered 152 valid responses from large US-based firms (number of employees greater than 500) across different industries.

36 Mikalef, P., Pateli, A., & van de Wetering, R. (2020). IT architecture flexibility and IT governance decentralisation as drivers of IT-enabled dynamic capabilities and competitive performance: The moderating effect of the external environment. *European Journal of Information Systems*, 1–29.

37 Ross, J. W., Weill, P., & Robertson, D. (2006). *Enterprise architecture as strategy: Creating a foundation for business execution*. Boston, MA: Harvard Business Press.

38 Aerts, A. T. M., Goossenaerts, J. B., Hammer, D. K., & Wortmann, J. C. (2004). Architectures in context: On the evolution of business, application software, and ICT platform architectures. *Information & Management*, 41(6), 781–794.

39 Beulen, E., & Ribbers, P. (2004). Value creation in application outsourcing relationships: an international case study on ERP outsourcing. In *Value creation from e-business models* (pp. 283–310). Butterworth-Heinemann.

40 Benson, R. J., Ribbers, P. M., & Blitstein, R. B. (2014). *Trust and partnership: Strategic IT management for turbulent times*. Chichester: John Wiley & Sons.

41 Poppo, L., & Zenger, T. (2002). Do formal contracts and relational governance function as substitutes or complements? *Strategic Management Journal*, 23(8), 707–725.

42 Jensen, M. C., & Meckling, W. H. (1976). Theory of the firm: Managerial behavior, agency costs and ownership structure. *Journal of Financial Economics*, 3(4), 305–360.

43 Barney, J. (1991). Firm resources and sustained competitive advantage. *Journal of Management*, 17(1), 99–120.

44 Pfeffer, J., and Salancik G. R. (1978). *The external control of organizations: A resource dependence perspective*. New York: Harper & Row.

45 Lander, M. C., Purvis, R. L., McCray, G. E., & Leigh, W. (2004). Trust-building mechanisms utilized in outsourced IS development projects: A case study. *Information & Management*, 41(4), 509–528.

46 Lacity, M. C., & Hirschheim, R. (1995). *Beyond the information systems outsourcing bandwagon: The insourcing response*. New York: John Wiley & Sons, Inc.

47 Cullen, S., & Willcocks, L. (2003). *Intelligent IT outsourcing: Eight building blocks to success*. London: Routledge.

48 See Lee, J. N., Huynh, M. Q., Kwok, R. C. W., & Pi, S. M. (2003). IT outsourcing evolution – past, present, and future. *Communications of the ACM, 46*(5), 84–89; Tiwana, A. (2008). Do bridging ties complement strong ties? An empirical examination of alliance ambidexterity. *Strategic Management Journal, 29*(3), 251–272.

49 Lacity, M. C., & Hirschheim, R. A. (1993). *Information systems outsourcing; myths, metaphors, and realities.* New York: John Wiley & Sons, Inc.

50 Beulen, E. (2008). The enabling role of information technology in the global war for talent: Accenture's industrialized approach. *Information Technology for Development, 14*(3), 213–224.

51 Beulen, E. (2009). The contribution of a global service provider's human resources information system (hris) to staff retention in emerging markets: comparing issues and implications in six developing countries. *Information Technology & People, 22*(3), 270–288.

52 Beulen, E. (2010). Long-held perceptions of the consequences of IT offshoring will become a reality: fewer IS jobs in developed countries. *Journal of Information Technology, 25*(4), 376–377.

53 Collins, H. (2010). *Tacit and explicit knowledge.* Chicago, IL: University of Chicago Press.

54 Willcocks, L., & Fitzgerald, G. (1993). *A business guide to outsourcing IT: A study of European best practice in the selection, management, and use of IT services.* London: Business Intelligence.

55 Miller, R. I., & Anderson, A. W. (2004). Legal and ethical considerations regarding outsourcing. *Journal of Accountancy, 197*(3), 31–35.

56 Ernst, R., Kamrad, B., & Ord, K. (2007). Delivery performance in vendor selection decisions. *European Journal of Operational Research, 176*(1), 534–541.

57 Wadhwa, V., & Ravindran, A. R. (2007). Vendor selection in outsourcing. *Computers & Operations Research, 34*(12), 3725–3737.

58 Kumar, M., & Vardhan, M. (2018). Data confidentiality and integrity preserving outsourcing algorithm for matrix chain multiplication over malicious cloud server. *Journal of Intelligent & Fuzzy Systems, 34*(3), 1251–1263.

5   IT services

Demand and supply

Ensuring fit-for-purpose IT services for the organisation is essential. Outsourcing of IT services is in most organisations an integral part of ensuring fit-for-purpose IT services. On the one hand, outsourcing organisations can tap into the resource pool of their suppliers, but on the other hand contractual commitment also constrains outsourcing organisation. How can one align demand and supply of IT services while being engaged in outsourcing relations?

5.1 Introduction

This chapter focuses on a core issue of sourcing: demand and supply. Section 5.2 discusses in more detail the IT planning responsibilities of IT and business functions on each of the three planning levels and how they are linked. Section 5.3 discusses demand and supply with regard to IT planning and how they are linked to an organisation-wide capability. Section 5.4 introduces the concept of micro IT outsourcing competence and relates it to the discussion in Chapter 2 of the IT capability and competences. Section 5.5 discusses demand and supply in relation to sourcing. Sourcing IT fundamentally relates to obtain services, IT services either by procuring them externally or by producing them internally. Characteristics of this service relationship are analysed in Section 5.6. Digital (out)sourcing relates to the ongoing fusion between supply and demand: IT is increasingly integrated in business functions. Section 5.7 discusses how this impacts outsourcing. Section 5.9 concludes this chapter with a consideration of the impact agility has on the supply demand relationship, including a discussion of the experiences of ING-Netherlands.

5.2 IT planning on three planning levels

Chapter 4 introduced the three levels of planning, strategic, tactical and operational, that can be used to characterise the governance of an organisation.

On the strategic level, designing the business-IT strategy is a matter of shared responsibility and co-creation. IT discusses proactively with business the future options for an IT-enabled strategy, business models and organisation

DOI: 10.4324/9781003223788-5

structures. The Chief Information Officer (CIO) should not wait until asked to do so; this person is a permanent and active participant and driver of the discussion. Nor can Chief Executive Officers and their management teams "throw" the business issues to IT and then lean back and wait. Success with IT is also their responsibility. Good teamwork is the key to success. Also, working on good relationships between business and IT throughout the company starts at the top. Supply management is involved in the discussions (e.g. represented by the IT director) when technology choices are on the agenda. Supply management bears a direct responsibility for designing the target IT architecture in alignment with the target business architecture. Supply management on this level also includes identifying and selection of supplier with whom strategic partnerships may be developed.

The tactical level proactively plans for the quantity and type of service delivery for the upcoming planning period; it also reactively intervenes when problems or changes occur that put the daily service delivery at risk. Activities on this level require a close interplay between business functions and IT supply management; in this interaction, demand management is closely facilitated by demand management roles. In some organisations, to ensure a greater independence of demand management in relation to supply, the former may report directly to a business manager.

The operational-level activities are the clear responsibility of supply management. Good working partnership relations are maintained with business functions for which the services are delivered. Whenever needed, they are consulted and informed about the status of current operations. Essential in this stage is the reporting about the service delivery to business and demand management (on a tactical level) in business terms.

5.2.1 Strategic-level IT responsibilities[1]

Obviously, information systems strategy and IT strategy belong to a strategic organisational level. Technology strategies are derived from the company's overall business strategy, and the two must be aligned with one another.[2,3,4] This is all the more essential because the importance of IT is steadily increasing, and strategic decisions about them in return influence the company's business strategy. Therefore, two-way strategic alignment is required.[5] The IT strategy includes a sourcing strategy, which defines which IT services will be delivered by the company's internal IT department or which will be outsourced to external suppliers.[6] For those services that are outsourced, a choice must be made between contracting a single supplier or several.[7] The IT strategy also includes choices about the architecture needed, which involves the layout of applications and infrastructure – aspects that both require attention and influence each other.[8] This architectural element is also derived from the IT strategy,[9,10] and it includes choices for development platforms, operating systems, databases and middleware solutions as well as for hardware suppliers[11] and cloud solutions.[12]

5.2.2 *Tactical-level IT responsibilities*

Planning the quantity and type of IT services to be delivered during the up-coming planning period and assuring the proper utilisation of these services (e.g. through training) is a matter for tactical organisation levels.[13] The way in which IT services are managed is derived from the IT strategies.[14] Whether some or all delivery has been outsourced is less relevant at this level, since agreements with internal departments and external suppliers must both always be laid down in contracts.[15] In the case of outsourcing, the need for watertight contracts is of course greater, since there is no hierarchic relationship but only a contractual one between the parties.[16] Nevertheless, in practice, it is often impossible to foresee every eventuality and decide ahead of time.[17]

5.2.3 *Operational-level IT responsibilities*

Finally, the responsibility for the actual delivery and proper use of IT services is an operational matter. Nevertheless, the dynamics of such obligations have always been a source of trouble.[18] The situation continues to grow even more complex, with the ever-increasing number of companies involved in mergers and acquisitions and the rise of technological developments. These techno-logical developments, such as e-business around 1995 and recently digital strategy, introduce new possibilities and challenges in the field of IT services that must somehow be made to fit into the contractual framework agreed upon. This is called "technology push." To be able to handle such changes, it is important that the processes involved are treated seriously.

Finally, the responsibility for the actual delivery and proper use of IT ser-vices is an operational matter; contractual obligations entered into the tactical level point the way here. Nevertheless, the dynamics of such obligations have always been a source of trouble[19] and still are.[18,20]

5.3 IT planning responsibilities: linking supply and demand

With regard to the effective development of IT-supported information ser-vices in the business, three key areas of management responsibility can be distinguished.[1,21] First, the appropriate alignment of IT and business requires the development of a vision of how IT should support the business, and also of how IT may enable new innovative strategies and organisational designs. These two effects have been labelled alignment and impact, respectively. The second area of responsibility concerns the design of the appropriate IT archi-tecture, the choices of the technical platform on the basis of which IT services will be delivered. These choices, though technical in nature, are closely re-lated to current and future business models. Networked business models and blurring organisational boundaries pose new challenges for choices regarding the right IT architectures and how to cope with new needs for interoperabil-ity and integration. Finally, there is the challenge of delivery of low-cost and high-quality IT services. The functioning of modern businesses is increasingly dependent on the availability of high-quality IT services. Choosing the right supplier, either internal or external, is a key decision.

These responsibilities can be separated into activities and roles, which, in turn, can be assigned to each of the organisational levels – strategic, tactical and operational (see Table 5.1). Such an analysis is the subject of this section, and is based on the work of Feeny and Willcocks[21] and Willcocks and Feeny[22] and this book's authors' own experience with large outsourcing deals. The results are presented in Table 5.2. The analysis must begin with the definition of the roles to be played, that is, people's functions with respect to IT. At the outsourcing organisation's side (also called the IT function), there are six roles: business manager, CIO, information manager (IM), service delivery supervisor, purchaser and business analyst. At the service supplier's side, seven roles may be distinguished: IT director, account manager, contract manager, service delivery manager (SDM), process

Table 5.1 Overview of roles and responsibilities in outsourcing relationships

Role		Description
Outsourcing organisation (IT function)	Business manager	Business managers carry final responsibility for the execution of business processes.
	Chief Information Officer (CIO)	CIOs carry final responsibility for the IT services and for the development and implementation of their company's IT strategies.
	Information manager (IM)	IMs are responsible for the IT services and the implementation of their company's IT strategies. They serve as contact persons for the company's divisions who must define their information needs. In large companies there may be several IMs, each with responsibility for part of the company. IMs report to the CIO.
	Service delivery supervisor	Service delivery supervisors manage external IT suppliers and, if applicable, the internal IT department. They report to their IM.
	Purchaser	Purchasers support their IM and the supplier's contract manager in selecting and managing external IT suppliers and, if applicable, managing the internal IT department. They represent both the IT function's interests and those of the company's divisions. They do not report to any official within the IT function.
	Business analyst	Business analysts implement the IT strategies. They serve as contact persons for the company's divisions who must define their information needs. In large companies there are several business analysts, each with responsibility for part of the company. They report to their respective IMs.

Role		Description
Supplier	IT director	IT directors carry final responsibility for the delivery of IT services as well as for the continuity of service delivery by external and, if applicable, internal IT suppliers. They are the IT function's strategic-level contact persons. If the IT services are outsourced, this role is played by the supplier's general manager.
	Account manager	Account managers maintain relations with the IT function (and the managers of the outsourcing organisation's divisions). Their contacts partly focus on widening the scope and increasing the scale of their contracts. They are held accountable for the scale of the services delivered and for customer satisfaction. Account managers serve as tactical-level contact persons for the IT function; together with the contract managers they are the supplier's front office.
	Contract manager	Contract managers are responsible for delivering the IT services contracted and for reporting and invoicing. For these aspects contract managers serve as contact persons for the IT function; together with the account managers they are the supplier's front office.
	Service delivery manager (SDM)	Service delivery managers manage the IT professionals who deliver the IT services. They report to the contract managers.
	Process manager	Process managers set up and maintain the processes and certification of the IT services delivered. This responsibility does not pertain to any specific contract but to the IT services delivered for all the supplier's contracts. Process managers report to their IT director.
	Competence manager	Competence managers investigate the potential of new technologies. This responsibility does not pertain to any specific contract but to the IT services delivered for all the supplier's contracts. The intention is to ascertain delivery continuity. Competence managers report to their IT director.
	IT professional	IT professionals deliver the IT services and investigate the potential of new technologies. They report to either the service delivery manager or to the competence manager.

Table 5.2 Overview of responsibilities, activities and role in demand and supply management

Level	Responsibility	Activities	Demand management						Supply management						
			Business manager	CIO	IM	Service delivery supervisor	Purchaser	Business analyst	IT-director	Account manager	Contract manager	Service delivery manager	Process manager	Competence manager	IT professional
Strategic	IT strategy	Business systems thinking	S	A	R										
		Leadership	S	A/R	S			C							
		Relation-building		A/R	R	I			I	I	I				
		Architecture-planning		A	A				I	I	C	C		C	
		Making technology work		A					S		C	C		C	
Tactical	Managing IT services	Formulating information needs			A	R	S			S	C	I			
		Informed buying			A	R	S	S			C	C			
		Contract facilitation			A	R	S	S		S	S	S		I	
		Contract monitoring				A/R	S		S	S					
		Vendor development				A/R									
		Setting up, maintaining and certifying IT delivery processes		I	C	C	C	S	A	R	S		A/R		S
		Investigating the potential of new technologies		I	S	S		S	S	A	(S)			A/R	S
		Maintaining relations with the tenderer		I	S	S									
Operational	Delivering IT services	Delivering the contracted IT services				S	C				A	R			S
		Creating a skills base									A	R		A/R	S

Note: R: Responsible; A: Approves; S: Support; C: Consulted; I: Informed.

manager, competence manager and IT professional. The content of these roles is described in Table 5.1. Naturally, while there is always only one CIO and usually only one IT director, there may be several business analysts, account managers, etc. Additionally, the supplier may be an internal IT department, an external partner or both. One can now move on to the activities that must be carried out, and assign them to the three organisational levels and to the functional roles just defined. This is the subject of the following three subsections. For the purpose of this analysis, four levels of responsibility for the activities will be used. Final responsibility means that the company's general manager will hold the person involved directly accountable for the accomplishment of the tasks. This highest level of responsibility is called A, which approves or accepts. Next is the level called Responsible I, which entails carrying out the activity and involves being held accountable by the person in the A role. Sometimes, A and R are combined (A/R), in which case the incumbent is again held directly accountable by the company's general manager. The letter S signifies delivering support to the persons in the R role. C stands for people who must be consulted by the persons in the R role before the activity is carried out, because their expertise is needed to decide how it must be done. Finally, I stands for people who will be informed afterwards; this is only one-way communication.

5.3.1 Strategic-level activities and roles

On a strategic level, one may distinguish five activities[23]:

1 business systems thinking
2 IT leadership
3 relationship-building
4 architecture-planning
5 making technology work

These will now be discussed and assigned to the roles just described. Activities on a strategic level are mostly the responsibility of the outsourcing organisation's managers.

5.3.1.1 Business systems thinking

Business systems thinking is about envisioning how modern business management can be supported and how business processes may be reshaped exploiting the functionality of modern IT. The CIO's most important task is making sure the company's business information requirements are met. They must therefore deploy IT so that it makes a maximum contribution to business management. This means that CIOs must know the developments in the field of IT as well as in their company's markets, and consequently they must also maintain good relations with the company's business manager. These tasks are carried out on the basis of perceptions laid down in the company's IT strategies.

The importance of having well-aligned business processes has become increasingly clear. Since digital strategies to an increasing extent lead to integration of IT and business processes, many CIOs must also contribute to their alignment. The question becomes how the value of the business can be increased by changing the operations.

Because of the importance of business systems thinking, it is the company's CIO who is ultimately accountable (A) for business systems thinking. Their IMs, next in line, carry out this activity in a "responsible" manner (R), supported (S) by the company's business manager. Business analysts play a consulting (C) role.

5.3.1.2 IT leadership

IT leadership is needed to integrate IT with the business and its activities. Leadership sets out the vision and the direction in which to go. IT leadership creates a shared understanding and a shared vision between business and IT. The first person in the organisation to address this responsibility is the CIO. That person holds both final and executive responsibilities (A/R) and is supported (S) by the company's IMs. Together, they develop and implement the company's IT strategies.[1] They also serve as ambassadors who must alert their business manager to the potential of IT service.

5.3.1.3 Relationship-building

IT groups and business functions are differentiated in terms of departmental structures and mindsets of employees. Mental models differ between the "techies" and the business people. Building collaborative relationships based on shared understanding of IT/business issues is a requisite for the effective development, deployment and utilisation of IT systems. CIOs must, together with their IMs and the company's business manager, make sure people collaborate.

As with leadership, the company's CIO combines final and executive responsibilities (A/R) for relationship-building. Both the IM and the company's business manager provide support (S), as do the supplier's IT director and account manager. The contract manager of the supplier should be informed (I).

5.3.1.4 Architecture-planning

Architecture-planning refers to bringing about the technical platform that supports current and future business models. The close interplay of the development of modern technologies and the demands posed by new business models require a close collaboration between IT groups and business management. Architecture-planning is a technical activity that belongs to both the IT strategies. It involves an analysis of the development of current into future business management practice in order to establish how the information architecture should be adapted to meet the demands expected.[24] This includes both hardware and software,[25] and it means that trend analyses of technological developments must be made. Since the current architecture plays a role in this planning activity, suppliers too must be included in these deliberations.

Here, again, the CIO carries final responsibility (A). Executive responsibility (R) rests with the IMs, who are supported (S) by the company's business analysts. The service delivery supervisor should be informed (I). The supplier's contract manager and SDM play a consulting role (C) and the competence manager should be informed (I).

5.3.1.5 *Making technology work*

This activity addresses how to pick up problems that arise with the technical platform quickly and how to serve business needs that cannot be addressed by the standard solution offered by the system. Compared with the other strategic-level activities, this activity has many operational aspects. The information office, which consists of the CIO and the company's corporate IMs, must therefore be involved closely, certainly in the case of major projects and when short-term decisions must be taken (as is often the case).

Information Technology knowledge is of essential importance for this task, as is the involvement of the company's supplier. Suppliers must contribute knowledge and know-how concerning IT possibilities and risks, while the outsourcing organisation's information office makes sure its business information requirements are met. It also takes the decisions, on the basis of the information provided by its supplier. Thus, the information office has final responsibility.

This activity is complicated by the dynamics of the interaction between business requirements and technology developments. These two must remain well tuned, which requires constant effort. According to one expert in the field:

> We intend to move away somewhat from aligning business and IT because it sounds so static, and because it is quite possible to be aligned but still go wrong. It is more important to have a good "conversation" between IT and business. In a dynamic conversation there is tension because the future is unsure and one does not know what one should do. However, while this tension shows that the outsourcing organisation and the supplier are not exactly aligned, being able to have an open and respectful conversation about future developments and needs is much more important than being in close agreement all the time.

Again, the CIO is ultimately responsible (A) for this activity, which is carried out under the executive responsibility (R) of the IMs. They, in turn, are supported (S) by the company's business analysts. The contract manager, SDM and competence manager contribute (C) to this activity.

5.3.2 *Tactical-level activities and roles*

The tactical organisational level involves another five activities[26,27]:

1   formulating information needs
2   informed buying
3   contract facilitation
4   contract monitoring
5   supplier development

These tasks are shared between outsourcing organisation and supplier. Typical activities on this level to be taken care of by the supplier are as follows:

6   setting up, maintaining and certifying delivery processes
7   investigating and developing the potential of new technologies

The importance of these processes may even have a strategic dimension for the supplier. The execution of the service processes takes place on an operational level.

5.3.2.1 *Formulating information needs*

Feeny and Willcocks consider this activity a part of what they call "informed buying."[27] There is a big difference between knowing what IT *services* are available in the market and knowing what information *needs* the business units experience. The first of these presupposes a technical profile, the second business management insight, and the two are rarely found in a single person. Therefore, the task of formulating information need is mentioned separately here. To carry out this activity, one needs both technology experts and subject experts. They can contribute knowledge of their business and define their business management's information needs.

Final accountability (A) for this activity resides with the company's IMs. It is tried out (R) by the service delivery supervisor, with the support (S) of the outsourcing organisation's purchaser and business analysts and the supplier's account manager. The outsourcing organisation's contract manager and competence manager play a consulting (C) role and the SDM will be informed (I).

5.3.2.2 *Informed buying*

Purchasing IT services requires market knowledge and insight. The buyer must also maintain good relations with their IT suppliers, setting up transparent tendering procedures and open communications.

Informed buying is part of the IM's final responsibility (A). It is carried out (R) by the service delivery supervisor, who is supported (S) by the purchaser and the outsourcing organisation's account manager.

5.3.2.3 Contract facilitation

The objective of contract facilitation is to warrant the success of existing contracts for IT services. Sourcing relationships and contracts are becoming increasingly complex. Service agreements are not perfect, and neither are suppliers nor outsourcing organisations. It is important that upcoming problems can be solved swiftly and fairly within the framework of agreements and relationships. To facilitate contacts, both the outsourcing organisation and the supplier must make the effort to "lubricate" their outsourcing relationship.

The outsourcing organisation's service delivery supervisor holds both final and executive responsibilities (A/R) for contract facilitation. The service delivery supervisor is supported (S) by the purchaser. The supplier's contract manager and SDM may be consulted (C) and the competence manager should be informed (I).

5.3.2.4 Contract monitoring

Through contract monitoring the outsourcing organisation's current and future contractual position is protected. It involves keeping suppliers on track by gearing their performance to the existing contracts and developments in the service market. Regular reporting on the supplier's performance, usually monthly and on the basis of key performance indicators, is needed. A balanced scorecard may be used to assess the supplier's performance.[28]

The outsourcing organisation's service delivery supervisor holds both final and executive responsibilities (A/R) for contract monitoring. This person is supported (S) by the purchaser and by the supplier's IT director account manager.

5.3.2.5 Vendor development

It is important for the outsourcing organisation to exploit the potential added value of its current service suppliers. Selection of a supplier, arriving at a contract and the subsequent implementation require substantial efforts and costs. Changing from one supplier to another may require the same level of effort. As a result, it is in the outsourcing organisation's interest to maximise the contribution to its business by its existing suppliers. This requires looking beyond existing delivery agreements at how the IT service needs will evolve and how the suppliers might contribute to these. However, apart from the company's relationships with its current suppliers, contacts with other suppliers must be maintained too. They may be able to supplement one's current IT services or make a proposition to improve them or their price. Also, in the situation that existing suppliers cannot satisfy a company's need, a logical alternative may be to try to create a supplier that can. Outsourcing organisations would therefore do well to manage their IT services as portfolios. This makes it easier to transfer the responsibility for them to another supplier.[29,30,31]

This activity is carried out (R) by the IM, under the final responsibility (A) of the company's CIO. The IM is supported (S) by business analysts. Of course, the outsourcing organisation's IT director and account manager also support (S) this activity.

5.3.2.6 Setting up, maintaining and certifying service delivery processes

To ensure service delivery continuity, attention must be paid to setting up, maintaining and certifying service delivery processes – quite apart from the tasks already assigned to contract and SDMs. Service provisioning must be organised as a process.[32] As one might expect, certification plays an important role in supplier selection. Certification is essential in outsourcing and offshore outsourcing relationships. For certification, the infrastructure management guidelines of the International Organisation for Standards (IOS) may be followed, or the application development guidelines of the Capability Maturity Model (CMM). Customers preselect their potential suppliers on the basis of their being certified.

The supplier's process managers hold final and executive responsibilities (A/R) for this activity. They are supported (S) by their IT professionals, and the outsourcing organisation's information and service delivery supervisor may be consulted (C).

5.3.2.7 Investigating and developing the potential of new technologies

This activity is linked with the outsourcing organisation's IT strategies. By assessing the potential of new technologies and sharing that knowledge with their clients, suppliers may contribute to their clients' competitive positions.

It is important to understand that the SDM has a natural resistance towards the implementation of new technologies. These new technologies will impact the stability of the services. To successfully investigate and develop new technologies, consultants have to be added in the team. A fresh pair of eyes and out of the box thinking is required for this activity.

Final and executive responsibilities (A/R) for this activity rest with the supplier's competence manager. Their IT professionals and the outsourcing organisation's IMs, service delivery supervisors and business analysts support (S) them. The CIO should be informed (I).

5.3.3 Operational-level activities and roles

Finally, on the operational level, there are three activities[5]:

1   maintaining relationships with the tenderer
2   creating a skills base
3   managing IT professionals

These activities are mostly the responsibility of the supplier.

5.3.3.1 *Maintaining relationships with the tenderer*

In order to maintain their relationships with their tenderer (important to ensure the proper delivery of the services contracted), suppliers must set up an unambiguous contact interface. This is usually a combination of the supplier's account manager and their contract manager.

Maintaining relationships with one's tenderer is the ultimate responsibility (A) of the supplier's IT director. It is carried out (R) by the outsourcing organisation's account manager and the supplier's contract manager. The contract manager supports (S) the account manager, as the SDM sometimes does too. The outsourcing organisation's IM and service delivery supervisor, in turn, support (S) all of them. Finally, the purchaser can play a consulting (C) role and the CIO should be informed (I).

5.3.3.2 *Creating a skills base*

The supplier must have the right resources available to deliver the contracted services. It is important that the right people are available to deliver the services. However, if e.g. staff are moved from one project to another regularly, discontinuities may be the result. In addition, the supplier should also be prepared to support new technologies. This requires training and planned career paths.

Final responsibility (A) for this activity rests with the supplier's contract manager. Their SDM is responsible (R) for carrying it out, while their IT professionals and the outsourcing organisation's service delivery supervisor support (S) it. The outsourcing organisation's purchaser may be consulted (C).

5.3.3.3 *Managing IT professionals*

Gottschalk[33] assigns the task of managing professionals who deliver IT services to systems development managers, systems operation managers and helpdesk managers. An important aspect of this management task is ensuring sufficient career and development perspectives for the professionals involved. To maintain the knowledge base needed for a proper service delivery, the personnel situation preferably should be stable.

Managing IT professionals is an activity for which the supplier's contract manager holds the final responsibility (A). The SDM executes this activity (R). The IM and the service delivery supervisor should be consulted (C) and the CIO should be informed (I).

5.4 IT capability, macro IT competences and micro IT outsourcing competences

In Chapter 4, the concept of organisational IT capability was discussed. This is described as "an organisation-wide capability that depends on the competences of both enterprise and IT functions."[1] Based on the research conducted for this book, six specific IT competences are defined.[1]

Following Peppard and Ward,[34] these competencies are referred to here as macro-level competences, each of which consists of several specific micro-competencies. The latter are at the level where activities can be deployed and their effectiveness assessed. In conjunction with this, the activities and roles related to outsourcing described in the previous section can be considered as micro-competences, as intended by Peppard et al.[34] These are also located at the level where activities are deployed and their effectiveness can be assessed.

Macro- and micro-competencies can be broadly classified according to the planning levels strategic, tactical and operational. Of course, the boundaries of these are not sharp and are approximate.

For the strategic level, the following macro-competences are important:

• strategic innovation
• business change

These are supported by the following IT outsourcing micro-competencies:

• business systems thinking
• IT leadership
• relationship-building
• architectural-planning
• making technology work
• investigating and developing the potential of new technology

For the tactical level, the following macro-competences are important:

• business outcome and programme realisation
• project development and benefit realisation
• software configuration and development

These are, in turn, supported by the following IT outsourcing micro-competencies:

• setting up, maintaining and certifying delivery processes
• supplier development
• information needs formulation
• informed buying
• contract facilitation
• contract monitoring

Finally, the competence that applies to the operational level:

• service delivery

This competence is linked to the following micro outsourcing competences:

- Maintaining relationships with the tenderer
- Creating a skills base
- Managing IT professionals

5.5 Demand and supply impact on outsourcing

Outsourcing has different implications on each of the organisational levels discussed. Generally speaking, strategy cannot be outsourced, so neither can IT strategy.[27,35] Outsourcing organisations must maintain control over their IT services, and have clear guidelines for managing their IT suppliers. The minimum attention that outsourcing organisations must spend on IT is called the "residual in-house IT function."[36] IT service delivery can, of course, be outsourced, since this involves rather more operational tasks.

5.5.1 Outsourcing strategy-level responsibilities

As said before, strategic-level responsibilities of the outsourcing organisation, in principle, cannot be outsourced. Strategising, innovation, IT leadership, enterprise architecting and relationship-building belongs to the core of the outsourcing organisation's responsibility. Designing IT architecture as part of the enterprise architecture is, however, an exception in this list; being a supply side responsibility, it is an activity that may be sourced externally. Another example is innovation, when a company can link up with a major IT supplier. Although strategy is the responsibility of the outsourcing organisation, suppliers can be involved in strategic planning. Steering committees that involve senior managers from both the outsourcing organisation and the supplier are instrumental in this respect. They also deal with escalated issues from the tactical level.

5.5.2 Outsourcing tactical-level responsibilities

Supplier-related tactical-level responsibilities, such as managing cost and performance and setting up reliable (and certified) delivery processes, are related to making sure that service delivery on the operational level will meet the client's expectations. The outsourcing organisation's required competence on a tactical level will be influenced by outsourcing also. Contracts must be managed and monitored; continuous collaboration with the supplier is needed to ensure alignment between what the supplier can offer and what the company needs. Formulating information needs is a tactical-level responsibility that requires close coordination between the outsourcing organisation's demand organisation and the supplier. Coordination between outsourcing organisation and supplier is needed for planning near-future service delivery and for reviewing the supplier's performance for the previous period. Also, on this level, steering organisations help to structure these discussions.

Suppliers increasingly include tactical-level activities in their offerings. This enables them not only to increase their turnover but also to strengthen their grip on their clients – and then hopefully to generate their own turnover growth, as it were. For this reason, outsourcing tactical-level activities is not always a good idea.[16] It can, however, be a good idea to hire external expertise for specific activities, such as the tendering process. Tendering is a project activity, which means that hiring external staff can be appropriate. Besides, the purchasing department and the outsourcing organisation's IMs often have too little time or even know-how to carry out a tendering process themselves. Nevertheless, it is important that the outsourcing organisation's own staff remain involved in the process.

Then there are situations in which hiring external consultants is actually preferred over using internal staff. This is especially so in the case of auditing and mediation – incidental activities for which the independence of the staff carrying them out is of crucial importance.

5.5.3 Outsourcing operational-level responsibilities

Provided that the strategic-level and tactical-level activities are carried out by the outsourcing organisations itself, operational activities are candidates to be outsourced to external suppliers. Service delivery, accountability and application and software development and maintenance are all areas that may be placed outside the company. Whether in a specific company situation these will be outsourced or not depends on a number of external and internal factors. Examples of these are the extent to which the activity belongs to the core of the organisation, the business criticality of the applications involved and consequently in the case of outsourcing the dependence on the external supplier, the existing market for the services to be procured, the increase of transaction costs in the case of outsourcing, etc.

Care must be taken with several of the new relation's aspects. Good collaborative relations with the outsourcing organisation's demand organisation and business functions are needed, especially for handling upcoming problems and coordination needs in the process of service delivery. While ensuring a reliable service delivery on a day-to-day basis is obviously the main responsibility of the supplier, also the outsourcing organisation has its share here, making plans about the required services in the near- or longer-term future is a responsibility of the outsourcing organisation that also needs input from and collaboration with the external supplier(s).

5.6 The service relationship and user experience

The relation between the business organisation – its functions, departments and business processes – and IT may be described as a demand and supply relation. The business needs support for all data processing and information provisioning that basically shapes the business organisation. This support is provided by several technologies and several organisational units responsible for managing, operating and administering these technologies. The latter involve a set of several organisational arrangements, such as local and central IT departments, external IT suppliers, Cloud, BYOD solutions and Shadow IT. The relation of IT (technology and organisational arrangements) to the business organisation is fundamentally a service relationship: IT delivers a set of services to the business.

From an economic point of view, a service involves a transaction in which no physical goods are transferred from the supplier to the outsourcing organisation. Services are by definition intangible. Services are created in the direct interaction between the outsourcing organisation and the supplier. Services are produced and consumed simultaneously. Tangible and intangible resources, like tools, physical infrastructure and skills and experience of the supplier, are needed to produce the service. The benefits of such a service are demonstrated by the eventual outsourcing organisation's willingness to accept the service and eventually willingness to pay.

IT services should not be treated as homogeneous. Different categories and classifications of services have been defined. For example, Benson et al.[1] provide a classification based on the delivery and supply of IT components to the business. They distinguish:

1   Application and Information Services. Consists of installing, operating, maintaining and providing break-fix services to the business for each business application. The cost of these services includes all staff and infrastructure required.
2   Direct Infrastructure Services. Consists of the direct-to-the-user services such as e-mail and Internet attachment. The cost of these services includes all staff and infrastructure required.
3   Project Services. Consists of the full life cycle (whether traditional, agile or other methodologies) of project development. The costs include all staff and infrastructure required.
4   Technical (User) Services. Consists of the direct-to-the-user services such as helpdesk, PC and workstation support, and training.
5   IT Management Services. Consists of the CIO and all related management services to the IT organisation, and to the services that may be directly provided to users such as IT procurement, IT human resources (HR).

Peppard and Ward[34] prefer a distinction based on how services meet business requirements and how they support business operations and strategy execution. They distinguish IT services into four different categories:

1   Application Services, which refer to services delivered via software applications, which directly impact business performance; they are related to the information-processing ability of technology and software. They include services around information-processing, information-sharing, information storage and information access.

2   Operational services, they are connected to assembling and operating the core IT environment. These services include, e.g., specification and installation of hardware and software, upgrading software, configuration management, activities involved in running the data centre.
3   Value-enabling services, which include, e.g., IT strategy development, systems and process design, enterprise architecture development, purchasing and supplier development.
4   Infrastructure services, which relate directly to the technology itself. They include processing capacity, connectivity and scalability. On their own, they provide little immediate value to the organisation, but without them the applications cannot function.

In each of the service categories mentioned above, IT supply has to deliver services. The question pops up: how can this service angle to the relationship impact its management? And, what is considered a good service?

Service quality has been a frequently studied topic in the service marketing literature.[37] The analysis of service quality centres on perceived quality, defined as "a consumer's judgement about an entity's overall excellence or superiority."[38] The first question concerns the outsourcing organisation's expectation.[39] Does the customer get value for money? Value is largely based on expectation. The second is the quality of the service interaction itself. Does the customer perceive the service as friendly? Helpful?

Assessing service quality is a central aspect of service management. Quality of service has different dimensions. A well-known instrument applied to assess the quality of a service is SERVCQUAL.[40] Valarie Zeithaml has with others evolved a set of service management standards and measures that have been operationalised across many industries.[41] The core idea is that service management is about focusing on five basic parameters[1]:

- The tangible deliverable. In the case of the fast-food restaurant, this is the hamburger, the seat and table, the condiments, the napkins. In effect, this is the value proposition of the restaurant.
- The reliability of the service. This primarily means that the service experience is the same each time; this forms the basis for the expectation. This is the consistency of the service.
- The responsiveness of the service. This is not a timeliness variable, but rather whether the customer believes the service as expected can be adapted to specific requirements. This encompasses willingness to help customers and provide prompt service.
- The empathy of the supplier to the outsourcing organisation. "Are we in this together?" Ultimately, this means care and individualised attention to customers.
- The assurance of the supplier. This is based on the ability to convey trust and confidence.

The first two dimensions relate to what the users exactly receive, the technical quality. The last three relate to the user experience, the emotional quality. They concern how the users want to be treated by the supplier. The emotional quality is directly related to the process of service delivery and the nature of user involvement in that process.[34]

The performance of the IT services supplier is traditionally monitored and managed through SLAs (service-level agreements). These however tend to focus on the technical delivery and cost. The insight that next to technical criteria also emotional criteria should be included in the assessment of service delivery has led to the development of an alternative to SLAs: XLAs or "eXperience Level Agreement," with metrics that reflect how the customers feel how they were treated. It puts the emphasis on the eventual customer experience. Several authors have proposed frameworks composed of dimensions and measures the structure of service quality,[42] and when assessed give an indication of the overall service quality.

5.7 Digital strategy and outsourcing[43]

Digital strategy reflects the organisation's strategic direction for acquiring and deploying IT. Certainly, over the past 20 years, this has become a pressing concern for many companies, particularly those engaged in an industry where IT is pervasive. As one set of researchers put it: "To succeed today, companies need a unique value proposition that incorporates digital technologies in a way that is difficult for competitors to replicate."[44] The key question here is how strategic IT sourcing plays a role in achieving this. As another set of researchers put it: "How can we use technology as a strategic asset to enable new competencies or maintain a competitive advantage?"[45] This is more than just a better mousetrap strategy.

At times, the issue of IT strategy confuses the supply side issues (the ways in which IT is delivered to the enterprise) with the demand side (the ways in which IT is used and applied in the enterprise).[46] Both are considered in the IT strategy – but most importantly, thus affect the strategic IT sourcing relationship and the contribution of IT suppliers to ecosystems. The supplier has to be capable of supporting both – excellence in IT supply and effectiveness in meeting IT demands. From the strategy perspective, this also means effectiveness in building the relationships of "alignment" and "transformation" between IT and business in collaboration with suppliers.

This carries forward on the ideas presented about, that is, the emergence of digital strategy as a fusion of demand (use of IT to transform the business) and Supply (the expansion of opportunities such as cloud computing), and so forth. The issue is that the lines are increasingly blurring between supply and demand. IT is no longer something to be "aligned" with the business – rather IT is a major force transforming the business in fundamental ways, as technology innovations drive the change of business model, e.g. platforms.

An MIT study on digital strategy opened with this statement:

> Maturing digital businesses are focused on integrating digital technologies, such as social, mobile, analytics and cloud, in the service of transforming how their businesses work. Less-mature digital businesses are focused on solving discrete business problems with individual digital technologies.[47]

Also, innovative technologies such as the Internet of Things and blockchain significantly contribute to not only solving business problems but also creating business opportunities.

Both cases described here illustrate the profound role strategic IT sourcing can play, by providing the business and technology resources to achieve this integration and achievement of digital strategy. However, the first case – integrating technologies and transforming how businesses work – is the primary effect of integrating IT sourcing. In effect, this is managing the complete set of technology and sources, for the transforming benefit to the enterprise.

Also, just like the traditional strategic sourcing in an organisation's supply chain, the relationship between outsourcing organisation and supplier, between enterprise and IT, has to be managed, consistent with the notions of strategic sourcing. That is, with the elements of permanence, stability, cost and partnership that one must find in any sourcing partnership. To accomplish this, of course, raises the issue of trust, which is the single most important characteristic of the overall strategic IT sourcing relationships.

Management includes accountability. The business units (including corporate) rely on the IT management activity to deliver according to their requirements (that is, IT demand). IT management then provides those IT services by relying on one or more suppliers, some internal to the corporation, some external. For example, the system development suppliers may be in the internal IT department, while the technical network management and provision can be external.

5.8 The impact of change and turbulence[48]

Traditional analyses of outsourcing, which focus on choices of either markets or hierarchies, give little guidance for sourcing decisions under different environmental contexts. According to transaction cost economics, uncertainty in business and/or technological conditions cause complex contracts and consequently lead to higher contracting costs.[49,50] As such, uncertainty favours internal integration of activities. It is however clear that frequent changes, e.g. in markets, regulations or technology make it impossible for any organisation to keep all potential resources, competencies and capabilities in house to sustain its market position.[51] Thus, outsourcing comes to the table as a viable alternative. However, the same argument applies to external suppliers: they are equally not able to react instantly to these changes. That is why solutions to handle problems and opportunities caused by environmental turbulence are sought in the so-called intermediate organisational forms like alliances and partnerships. Trusted, long-term alliances create a safe environment to share (strategic and otherwise critical) planning information and commit resources that enable the future service delivery.

Intermediate organisational forms should create conditions of stability of internal integration, combined with the flexibility of the market. This is supported by management and economic literature, e.g. Jay Galbraith, in his information-processing view on organisations, discusses how an organisation can change the environment, and manage its dependence on others[52] by developing a variety of cooperative strategies.[53] The observation that change and uncertainty lead to intermediate organisational forms is also supported by Folta.[54] In later publications, additional advantages of intermediate organisational forms have been recognised.[55,56] Examples are accessing resources faster than internal development,[57] creating a way to access complementary resources from other organisations,[58] exposing a firm to new ideas, and learning about the level of technology held by competitors.[59] In line with the foregoing, a recent study by Irge Sener based on 16 interviews with top managers concluded that managers perceiving environmental dynamism and complexity tend to form strategic alliances.[60]

To conclude, this analysis adds an argument to the traditional (IT-) outsourcing discussion. Transaction cost economics explains outsourcing from an efficiency perspective: the rational manager should seek to minimise the sum of production and coordination (transaction) costs[61] of the organisation. Production costs comprise the costs of all primary processes that are necessary to produce and distribute the goods and services eventually delivered to a client or customer. Coordination costs include the transaction costs necessary to coordinate the activities of staff and equipment that perform the primary processes.[62] The resource-based view explains the outsourcing phenomenon from a (business) strategic angle. Resources, competences and capabilities that are VRIN should be kept internally in order to fence them off from competition. VRIN as an acronym relates to the features for a resource to be strategically important[63]:

- Valuable – When resources are able to bring value to the firm they can be a source of competitive advantage.
- Rare – Resources have to deliver a unique strategy to provide a competitive advantage to the firm as compared to the competing firms.
- Inimitable – Resources can be sources of sustained competitive advantage if competing firms cannot obtain them.
- Non-substitutable – Resources should not be able to be replaced by any other strategically equivalent valuable resources.

The VRIN characteristics mentioned above are individually necessary for the resources to be strategically valuable.

Resources that are non-VRIN are potential candidates for outsourcing; however, from a resource dependency perspective, the manager should watch out not to become too dependent from a critical and thus powerful supplier. The "uncertainty" perspective, adding to the strategic perspective, looks at outsourcing from the point of view of creating a flexible, responsive organisation. By creating a network organisation with a selected number of alliances and partnerships, the managers establish a structure that allows to be responsive to changing information systems requirements caused by business and/or IT changes.

5.9 Towards agility in supply and demand

It has already been mentioned frequently, the number of changes and their speed, with which the business world confronted today is unprecedented. This situation has an immediate impact on the organisation and functioning of companies, and therefore also on the relationship between supply and demand of IT services. As discussed in this chapter, the IT capability of an organisation is determined by the input of the IT function and of the various business functions. Competencies present in both these parts of the organisation are important here. Based on the research conducted for this book and case studies, a set of competencies is distinguished that, in a certain hierarchy to each other, represents what the business organisation can expect from and with IT. These competencies are completed by the IT function and mirrored by competencies of the business functions. One can represent this as two ladders. For the IT function, this runs, seen from the basis, from service delivery to strategic innovation. For the business organisation, it runs mirrored from defining service requirements to strategic innovation. The bottom four rungs of the ladder, with regard to both the business competencies and the IT competencies, concern competencies at the operational and tactical levels. The top three steps represent competencies on a strategic level.

As with any process in an organisation, for the sake of effectiveness, its concrete design and functioning depend on a few factors. In particular, the complexity of the tasks to be performed and the uncertainty and dynamics under which they are carried out apply. The more stable and predictable the process is, the more it can be managed with formal procedures and periodic reconciliations; the more dynamic and unpredictable the more flexibility and adaptability are expected. Complexity is a "complicating" factor here, as it immediately determines how much information exchange and communication is required for effective execution. The corollary is that under conditions of stability and predictability, processes (simple as well as complex) can be implemented through planning and procedures. In contrast, under conditions of change and uncertainty, this is much less possible, and execution and coordination take place through mutual agreement at the personal level. Complexity is a "complicating" factor here, as it immediately determines how much information exchange and communication is required for effective coordination and execution. This is true under stable, predictable conditions, but all the more so in the case of dynamics and uncertainty.

The foregoing impacts how supply and demand in IT and their relation is organised. Where the aforementioned business and IT competency ladders, could operate at a distance from each other, in today's dynamic timeframe this is no longer possible. The two ladders more or less slide into each other. Business and IT stand side by side and need each other to ensure an optimal contribution of IT to the business result. This applies to every step of the ladder.

Many organisations are struggling with this; some forward-thinking organisations are experimenting with new solutions. Not only do these solutions often mean a drastic change from the known ways of working, they also require a good and smooth transition from the old ways of working to the new. "Agility" and "resilience" are the key words here. Agility is to be understood as "an organisation's capability to anticipate or respond to market changes by rapidly adapting itself, and if necessary, progressing in a different direction."[64]

Rigby et al.[65] describe the conditions that are favourable for agile working. These conditions concern successively:

- the market environment: customer expectations and possible solutions change frequently
- the customer involvement: close cooperation and fast customer feedback
- the type of innovation: complex problems, changing scope and product specifications; time-to-market is crucial
- the modularity rather than monolithic structures (characterised by the absence of subsystems). Modularity allows work to be broken down into small autonomous parts and iterative cycles
- the impact of errors: errors offer the opportunity to learn from them

ING[66] is an example of a large company that has experimented, predominantly in the Netherlands, with an agile way of working on a companywide scale. Faced with various business challenges in the first decade of this century, such as the rise of fintech, a merger with the Postbank, and a global financial crisis, ING was forced to make a drastic change in its strategy.[67] ING had to change from a multi-channel bank, with each individual channel having its own process for exactly the same product, to an omni-channel bank, with one process for all the channels. One process for all channels supports a uniform customer experience. To meet the requirements set by the European Union to qualify for a comprehensive support package, smaller and more manageable business units had to be formed. In addition, the IT had to be overhauled: from the traditional waterfall methods to "agile" methods.[68] The whole organisation, not only IT, had to adopt the agile philosophy.[69] ING's management took inspiration from the experiences of large tech companies such as Google, Spotify, Amazon, Facebook and Netflix.[70]

Transforming the bank to an agile way of working included the following key elements:

- Squads: The basis of ING's agile organisation. Squads consist of up to nine people with a total final responsibility for a specific, customer-facing project.[71] Each of the 350 squads consisted of individuals with different backgrounds and types of expertise to bring the project to a successful conclusion (including IT).[71] The squad, in the person of the product owner, is responsible for the "what" and has a total final end-to-end responsibility. At the end of the project, the team is dismantled.
- Tribes: Squads working on interconnected missions were grouped in a tribe, coordinated by a so-called tribe-lead. The tribe-lead is the interface with other tribes. Each of the 13 tribes had a target of maximum 150 people.[71]
- Chapters: Provide horizontal coordination across squads, within a specific domain of expertise; they are basically responsible for "how," with the chapter leading as finally responsible for the mastery of realising the tasks.
- Agile coach: Assists several specific squads in their functioning as an agile team.
- Centres of expertise focused on areas with scarce knowledge.

The agile method was first applied in the corporate IT department with the introduction of squads and scrum. Given its success, squads were then introduced into the business environment.

The board dealt with the overall strategy of ING, which was translated to the individual tribes. Each tribe produced a so-called Quarterly Business Review (QBR), indicating what it had or will not achieve and its expectations for the next quarter. In this way, the board maintains an overall oversight and helps the tribe-leads to ensure alignment with ING's strategic objectives.

It was clear from the start that this change would require a fundamental overhaul of the corporate culture. Code orange, a set of principles that reflect the company's purpose, was introduced and implemented. Enterprise-wide, all managers were interviewed to see if they could work under these new principles. Senior leaders expected that the agile way of working would not suit everyone. The implication of this process was that everyone lost their job and then had to reapply. Eventually, 70% of senior management was reassigned; 30% lost their job.[72]

The transformation process that the bank had gone through was evaluated positively. Several internal measures were tracked and showed a positive development.[71] In addition, there was a realisation that there is no end-situation for an agile transformation. It is a continuous process of learning and evolution of the organisation to closely follow market developments.[27]

Notes

1 Benson, R. J., Ribbers, P., & Blitstein, R. B. (2014). *Trust and partnership: Strategic IT management for turbulent times* (Ser. Wiley cio series). New York: Wiley.
2 Henderson, J. C., & Venkatraman, H. (1999). Strategic alignment: Leveraging information technology for transforming organizations. *IBM Systems Journal, 38*(2.3), 472–484.
3 Shpilberg, D., Berez, S., Puryear, R., & Shah, S. (2007). Avoiding the alignment trap in IT. *MIT Sloan Management Review, 49*(1), 51.
4 Obwegeser, N., Arenfeldt, K., Dam, A. C., Fenger, K. H., & Silkjaer, J. V. (2020). Aligning drivers, contractual governance, and relationship management of IT-outsourcing initiatives. *Journal of Information Technology Case and Application Research, 22*(1), 40–66.
5 Rockart. J., Earl, M., & Ross, J. (1996). Eight imperatives for the new IT organization. *Sloan Management Review, 38*, 43–55.
6 Quinn, J. B., & Hilmer, F. G. (1994). Strategic outsourcing. *MIT Sloan Management Review, 35*(4), 43.
7 Currie, W., & Willcocks, L. (1998). Analysing four types of IT-outsourcing decisions in the context of scale, client/server, interdependency and risk mitigation. *Information Systems Journal, 8*(2), 119–143.
8 Aerts, A. T. M., Goossenaerts, J. B., Hammer, D. K., & Wortmann, J. C. (2004). Architectures in context: On the evolution of business, application software, and ICT platform architectures. *Information & Management, 41*(6), 781–794.
9 Sankar, C., Apte, U., & Palvia, P. (1993). Global information architectures: Alternatives and tradeoffs. *International Journal of Information Management, 13*(2), 84–93.
10 Duncan, N. B. (1995). Capturing flexibility of information technology infrastructure: A study of resource characteristics and their measure. *Journal of Management Information Systems, 12*(2), 37–57.
11 Luftman, J. (2004). Assessing business-IT alignment maturity. In van Grembergen, W. (Ed.), *Strategies for information technology governance* (pp. 99–128). Hershey, PA: IGI Global.
12 Debski, A., Szczepanik, B., Malawski, M., Spahr, S., & Muthig, D. (2017). A scalable, reactive architecture for cloud applications. *IEEE Software, 35*(2), 62–71.
13 Morton, M. S. (Ed.). (1990). *Corporation of the 1990s: Information technology and organizational transformation.* Oxford: Oxford University Press, Inc.
14 Feeny, D. F. (1998). Re-designing the IS function around core capabilities. *Long Range Planning, 31*(3), 354–367.
15 Heckman, R. (1999). Organizing and managing supplier relationships in information technology procurement. *International Journal of Information Management, 19*(2), 141–155.
16 Lacity, M. C., & Hirschheim, R. A. (1993). *Information systems outsourcing; myths, metaphors, and realities.* New York: John Wiley & Sons, Inc.
17 Beulen, E., & Ribbers, P. (2003, January). IT outsourcing contracts: Practical implications of the incomplete contract theory. In *Proceedings of the 36th Annual Hawaii International Conference on System Sciences, 2003* (pp. 10–pp). New York: IEEE.
18 Cullen, S., & Willcocks, L. (2003). *Intelligent IT outsourcing: Eight building blocks to success.* Oxford: Butterworth-Heinemann.
19 Dickson, G. W., Leitheiser, R. L., Wetherbe, J. C., & Nechis, M. (1984). Key information systems issues for the 1980s. *MIS Quarterly, 8*, 135–159.
20 Guo, H., Wang, C., Su, Z., & Wang, D. (2020). Technology push or market pull? Strategic orientation in business model design and digital start-up performance. *Journal of Product Innovation Management, 37*(4), 352–372.

21 Feeny, D. F., & Willcocks, L. P. (1997). The IT function: Changing capabilities and skills. *Managing IT as a strategic resource* (pp. 455–474). New York: McGraw Hill.

22 Willcocks, L. P., & Feeny, D. (2006). IT outsourcing and core IS capabilities: Challenges and lessons at Dupont. *Information Systems Management, 23*(1), 49.

23 Feeny, D. F. (1998). Re-designing the IS function around core capabilities. *Long Range Planning, 31*(3), 354–367.

24 Ross, J. W., Weill, P., & Robertson, D. (2006). *Enterprise architecture as strategy: Creating a foundation for business execution.* Boston, MA: Harvard Business Press.

25 Keen, P. G. (1991). *Shaping the future: Business design through information technology.* Boston, MA: Harvard Business School Press.

26 Beulen, E. J. J. (2002). *Uitbesteding van IT-dienstverlening.* Den Haag: Ten Hagen & Stam (in Dutch).

27 Feeny, D. F., & Willcocks, L. P. (1998). Core IS capabilities for exploiting information technology. *Sloan Management Review, 39*(3), 9–21.

28 Lacity, M. C., & Willcocks, L. (2000). *Global information technology outsourcing: In search of business advantage.* New York: John Wiley & Sons, Inc.

29 Andersen, T. M., & Christensen, M. S. (2002). Contract renewal under uncertainty. *Journal of Economic Dynamics and Control, 26*(4), 637–652.

30 Beulen, E. (2011). Contract renewal decisions in IT outsourcing: "Should I stay or should I go". *Journal of Information Technology Management, 22*(4), 47-55.

31 Beulen E. (2016). Contract renewal decisions in IT-outsourcing: A survey in the Netherlands. In: Kotlarsky J., Oshri I., Willcocks L. (eds) *Shared services and outsourcing: A contemporary outlook. Global sourcing 2016.* Lecture notes in business information processing, vol 266. Cham: Springer.

32 Beulen, E. J. J. (2000). *Beheersing van it-outsourcingsrelaties: een beheersingsmodel voor uitbestedende bedrijven en de it-dienstenleveranciers* (Doctoral dissertation, Tilburg University (in Dutch)).

33 Gottschalk, P. (2004). Managing IT functions. In van Grembergen, W. (Ed.), *Strategies for information technology governance* (pp. 246–268). Hershey, PA: IGI Global.

34 Peppard, J., & Ward, J. (2016). *The strategic management of information systems – building a digital strategy* (4th ed.).Chichester: Wiley.

35 Lacity, M. C., & Hirschheim, R. A. (1993). *Information systems outsourcing; myths, metaphors, and realities.* Chichester: John Wiley & Sons, Inc.

36 Lacity, M. C., Willcocks, L. P., & Feeny, D. F. (1996). The value of selective IT sourcing. *Sloan Management Review, 37*, 13–25.

37 Kang, G. D., & James, J. (2004). Service quality dimensions: An examination of Grönroos's service quality model. *Managing Service Quality: An International Journal, 14*, 266–277.

38 Zeithalm, V. A. (1987). *Defining and relating prices, perceived quality and perceived value.* Cambridge, MA: Marketing Science Institute.

39 Wei, C. L. (2021). How relationship quality, service quality, and value affect the intention to purchase IT/IS outsourcing services. *Information Systems Management,* 1–18.

40 Parasuraman, A., Zeithaml, V. A., & Berry, L. (1988). SERVQUAL: A multiple-item scale for measuring consumer perceptions of service quality. *1988, 64*(1), 12–40.

41 See, for example, the foundational books: Wilson, A., Zeithaml, V. A., Bitner, M. J., & Gremler, D. D. (2012). *Services marketing: Integrating customer focus across the firm.* London: McGraw-Hill; Zeithaml, V. A., Parasuraman, A., Berry, L. L., & Berry, L. L. (1990). *Delivering quality service: Balancing customer perceptions and expectations.* New York: Simon and Schuster.

42 For example, Kang and James built their framework on four constructs: Functional Quality, Technical Quality, Image and Overall Customer Satisfaction. Specific measures for Functional Quality are Reliability, Assurance, Tangible, Empathy and Responsiveness. Functional Quality and Technical Quality have a direct impact on Image (in particular the overall company's image); Functional Quality, Technical Quality and Image determine overall Service Quality Perception, which in the end is the basis for the Customer Satisfaction. See for a discussion their paper: Service quality dimensions: an examination of Grönroos's service quality model. *Managing Service Quality: An International Journal.*

43 An earlier version of this Section has been published in Benson, R., & Ribbers, P. M. (2020). Strategic sourcing in turbulent times – the impact of trust and partnership. In Beulen, E., & Ribbers, P. (Eds.), *The Routledge companion to managing digital outsourcing* (pp. 4–40). London: Routledge.

44 Ross, J. W., Beath, C. M., & Sebastian, I. M. (2017). How to develop a great digital strategy. *MIT Sloan Management Review, 58*(2), 7.

45 Mithas, S., & Lucas, H. C. (2010). What is your digital business strategy?. *IT Professional, 12*(6), 4–6.

46 Peppard and Ward (2016).

47 Kane, G. C., Palmer, D., Phillips, A. N., Kiron, D., & Buckley, N. (2015). Strategy, not technology, drives digital transformation. *MIT Sloan Management Review and Deloitte University Press, 14*(1–25), 12.

48 An earlier version of this Section has been published in Benson, R. J., & Ribbers, P. M. (2020). *Strategic Sourcing in turbulent times – the impact of trust and partnership.* In Beulen, E., & Ribbers, P. M. (Eds.), *The Routledge companion to managing digital outsourcing* (pp. 4–40). London: Routledge.

49 Beulen, E., & Ribbers, P. (2002, January). Managing complex IT outsourcing-partnerships. In *Proceedings of the 35th Annual Hawaii International Conference on System Sciences* (pp. 10-pp). IEEE.

50 Beulen, E., & Ribbers, P. (2015). Governance of complex IT outsourcing partnerships. In *Information Technology Outsourcing* (pp. 236-256). Routledge.

51 Teece, D. J. (2000). *Managing intellectual capital: Organizational, strategic, and policy dimensions.* Oxford: OUP Oxford.

52 Galbraith, J. (1977). *Organization design.* Reading, MA: Addison-Wesley.

53 Rossignoli, C., & Ricciardi, F. (2015). Theories explaining inter-organizational relationships in terms of coordination and control needs. In Rossignoli, C., & Ricciardi, F. (Eds.), *Inter-organizational relationships* (pp. 7–36). Cham: Springer.

54 Folta, T. B. (1998). Governance and uncertainty: The trade-off between administrative control and commitment. *Strategic Management Journal, 19*(11), 1007–1028.

55 See for a discussion on this King, D. R. (2006). Implications of uncertainty on firm outsourcing decisions. *Human Systems Management, 25*(2), 115–125.

56 Bramanti, A., Rocha, H., & Redelico, F. (2020). Inter-organizational forms and impacts in commodity sectors: A review and integration. *Journal of Cleaner Production, 276,* 123025.

57 Kogut, B. (1991). Joint ventures and the option to expand and acquire. *Management Science, 37*(1), 19–33.

58 Dyer, J. H., Kale, P., & Singh, H. (2001). How to make strategic alliances work. *MIT Sloan Management Review, 42*(4), 37–37.

59 Willman, P. (1996). Wellsprings of knowledge: Building and sustaining the sources of innovation. *MIT Sloan Management Review, 37*(2), 112.

60 Şener, İ. (2012). Strategic responses of top managers to environmental uncertainty. *Procedia-Social and Behavioral Sciences, 58,* 169–177.

61 Malone, T. W., Yates, J., & Benjamin, R. I. (1987). Electronic markets and electronic hierarchies. *Communications of the ACM, 30*(6), 484–497.

62 Williamson, O. (1975). Markets and hierarchies. New York: Free Press.
63 Barney, J. (1991). Firm resources and sustained competitive advantage. *Journal of Management, 17*(1), 99–120.
64 Girod, S. J., Fernandes de Pina, E. P., Svedjedal, S., & Tanfour, M. (2018). *ING: An agile organization in a disruptive environment*. Lausanne: Institute for Management Development.
65 Rigby, D. K., Sutherland, J., & Noble, A. (2018). Agile at scale. *Harvard Business Review, 96*(3), 88–96.
66 See https://www.ing.com/About-us/Profile/ING-at-a-glance.htm – ING is a global bank with a strong European base. Our 57,000 employees serve around 39.3 million customers, corporate clients and financial institutions in over 40 countries. Our purpose is to empower people to stay a step ahead in life and in business.
67 Calnan, M., & Rozen, A. (2019). ING's Agile transformation—Teaching an elephant to race. *Journal of Creating Value, 5*(2), 190–209.
68 Kerr, W. R., Gabrieli, F., & Moloney, E. (2018). *Tranformation at ING (A): Agile.* Boston, MA: Harvard Business Review.
69 Birkinshaw, J., & Duncan, S. (2018). Building an agile organization at ING Bank Netherlands: From Tango to RIO. *London Business School.* https://caserighted.com/building-an-agile-organisation-at-ing-bank-netherlands-from-tango-to-rio/ - accessed 31 March 2021
70 Kerr, W. R., Gabrieli, F., & Moloney, E. (2018). *Tranformation at ING (B): Agile.* Boston, MA: Harvard Business Review.
71 Girod, S. J., Fernandes de Pina, E. P., Svedjedal, S., & Tanfour, M. (2018). *Ing: An agile organization in a disruptive environment.* Lausanne: Institute for Management Development.
72 Kerr, W., Brownell, A. (2018). *Transformation at ING (C): Culture.* Boston, MA: Harvard Business School.

6 Information Technology innovation and outsourcing

Information Technology (IT) has been evolving at an unprecedented speed for decades. Of equal importance to speed are increasing market dynamics. Disruption has become the norm. IT innovation is more necessary now than ever before. Outsourcing of innovation has been on the agenda for over two decades. The outsourcing of IT innovation, as well as the outsourcing of innovation in general, is still challenging, due to many aspects, including opportunism, a paucity of in-house capabilities, leadership or lack thereof and leakage. Because IT innovation is closer to the core business and the ability to achieve a competitive advantage, these challenges must be managed with more senior management dedication than the outsourcing of IT services, such as computing power, desktop management and application development. In this chapter, outsourcing IT innovation is addressed by detailing relation governance and contract governance. What needs to be done to ensure IT innovation in outsourcing contract and relationship?

6.1 Introduction

Innovation is defined as the generation, development and implementation of new ideas in organisations.[1] Innovations in IT deliver long-term improvements, efficiency and effectiveness.[2] In addition, IT innovation adapts and extends the usage of the product and services offered.[3] IT innovation enables disruption, while the innovation trend itself also avoids being disrupted,[4] and it is for this reason that any organisation needs to focus on IT innovation. IT innovation outsourcing intent can be a transactional intent focused on adjusting processes and/or a market-oriented innovation focusing on new/adjusted products and services.[3] Most organisations innovate both the processes and the products and services.

Can innovation be outsourced through collaboration with one or more external suppliers? Not easily.[5] In addition, nowadays outsourcing innovation is still not straightforward. This is also applicable for IT innovation. Implementing emerging technology, new best practices and transforming to achieve a competitive advantage are hard work.[6] IT innovation is related to product and process innovations.[7] For avoidance of the doubt, IT innovation

DOI: 10.4324/9781003223788-6

is different from technology refreshment, e.g. upgrading software or replacing hardware. Can IT innovation be achieved without the involvement of external partners? The simple answer is no, and even if the organisation has a significant scale, this will never be sufficient to create critical mass and enable efficient and effective delivery of IT innovation. Achieving IT innovation success involves collaboration with partner(s), as technology developments follow up on each other very rapidly, while expertise and resources are scarce.

Organisations need to allocate for IT innovation in their budgets. The split in IT spent by most organisations is 75% on IT operations and only 25% on capital.[8] The 25% capital is the project part, and while it includes IT innovation, it is not limited to innovation. Typically, IT innovation is less than 10% of what is spent on IT, and for most companies, the amount is less than 5%. The remaining capital budget is spent on technology refreshment, replacing existing technology. The upgrade of legacy systems or application rationalisation projects qualifies as technology refreshment, not IT innovation. Organisations that underinvest in technology refreshment are building up technical debt and will face future budget challenges for investments in IT innovations.

In this chapter, the focus is on IT innovation, which can be assessed by six constructs,[9] including new service delivery system, which is the technological component and the primary focus in this chapter. This component creates competitive advantage. Contracting IT innovation is associational and constitutional.[10]

To successfully manage IT outsourcing covering both technology refreshment and IT innovation, the organisation needs ambidexterity.[11] Technology refreshments focus on stability (traditional mode – Gartner Mode 1),[12] and innovation on speed and investigating (agile mode – Gartner Mode 2). This ambidexterity is not limited to the outsourcing organisation; the supplier organisation also needs ambidexterity.[13] The agile mode is also linked to the digital transformations.[14]

The agency theory can be applied to IT outsourcing and to both IT operations and capital, including technology refreshment and IT innovation.[15] The decision (in IT sourcing) regarding the governance mode then becomes the input of agency theory, which helps specify the appropriate incentives, roles and responsibilities of the contracting parties and the selection of appropriate contractual mechanisms.[16] This chapter only focuses on IT innovation. The uncertainty about the outcome and the difficulties in measuring the outcome of IT innovation drives opportunistic behaviour of both the principal (client company) and the agent (supplier company). Also, the threat of misproportioning intellectual property rights[3] and leakage[17] requires attention from both. With regard to intellectual property rights, it is fair to say that the business model of suppliers is to reuse non-client-specific knowledge, including knowledge gained in previous client engagements. In contracting, a good measure for proper contract design is credible commitments, which include the investment in supplier's proprietary technology by the client.[3(p. 937)] The allocation of intellectual property rights will be addressed by relational governance and contractual governance. Motives for outsourcing IT innovation have to be understood first.

6.2 Why outsource Information Technology innovation?

Initially, IT outsourcing was a strategy to save cost. Beginning in the late 1990s, leveraging labour arbitrage has enabled additional opportunities to save cost. Additionally, over time, the capability argument has become stronger. Outsourcing organisations need a growing number of specialised resources to fulfil their continuously growing demand. For over a decade, business value creation has also become a driver for IT outsourcing. Also, over time, IT outsourcing has transformed from having a cost focus into having a quality focus and now an innovation focus.[18] In collaboration, suppliers and partners can unlock and/or fast-track the potential of IT innovation.

Quinn listed five general arguments in favour of outsourcing innovation.[19] These arguments are rebadged for outsourcing IT innovation. First of all, the resource limitation enforces organisations to consider outsourcing of IT innovation. Organisations do not have sufficient professionals or the competencies to focus on IT innovation and explore potential opportunities in parallel with implementing these innovations and with delivering technology refreshment. Vendors and partners can quickly absorb differences in volume of the demand over time. Related to this argument is the second argument of specialist talents. Vendors and partners are able to build up resources with deep knowledge for each upcoming IT innovation. Not only is scale important, but also the diversity of client engagements, which significantly facilitates the speed of the learning curve for employees of suppliers and partners. The third argument is that companies run the risk of missing out on innovation, as outsourcing companies cannot invest in any upcoming IT innovation. Vendors and partners provide services to many clients. They can allocate resources to all emerging technology innovations and build up capabilities on the back of their (existing) client base. The fourth argument is that suppliers and partners are also better positioned to attract talent. They can offer a more attractive career perspective to professionals, as employees have a focus on the core business of the organisation, which is different from outsourcing companies. IT has a supporting role in outsourcing companies. Also, in some countries, such as India, it is more prestigious to work for a supplier. With regard to recruiting and attracting talent, outsourcing companies benefit from having a focus on innovation. This focus facilitates attracting and retaining talent. Finally, suppliers have the ability to ramp up resources much faster. Recruiting staff in most outsourcing organisations requires a lot of effort and is not as fast as can be accomplished by most suppliers. Vendors and partners have a highly industrialised recruiting engine (Table 6.1).

However, in outsourcing IT innovation, it is difficult to define requirements and assess delivered work.[20] Also, agreement on the ownership of delivered work is essential[3] and not straightforward. In managing the outsourcing

Table 6.1 Arguments for outsourcing innovation[19 (p. 25)] applied on outsourcing IT innovation

Arguments for outsourcing innovation[19 (p. 25)]	Applied for outsourcing IT innovation – internal IT departments
Resource limitation	have limited opportunities to quickly absorb difference in the volume of demand over time
Specialist talents	lack the required diversity of engagements with different internal clients to build up resources with deep knowledge
Specialised talent	lack IT resources with required capabilities in new technologies
Attracting talent	are not be able to offer job opportunities which are related to the core process of the organisation
Increased speed	are not able to quickly ramp up IT resources with required capabilities in new technologies

of IT innovation, there are two dominant strategies: partnering and ecosystems. In partnering, innovation is developed in isolation with one or more IT suppliers, whereas in ecosystems, other organisations in the value chain and their IT suppliers and partners are also involved. These two strategies will be discussed in the section below.

6.3 Partnering versus ecosystems

The strategies for outsourcing IT innovation have to be integrated into the IT sourcing strategy. An outsourcing company can select one of the existing suppliers and partners for contracting IT innovation. The innovation will be contracted in a separate Statement of Work under the existing framework agreement. This reduces the required pre-contract contract management effort, as well as the contract management effort over the lifetime of the contract. The prerequisite here is that there be sufficient market force to select a supplier or partner for the ongoing concern that is also capable of delivering the IT innovation. The reality is that for IT innovation, collaboration with (niche) alternative suppliers and partners is also a feasible option: simply apply the selective sourcing mindset.[21] Of course, outsourcing organisations can also choose to work with multiple suppliers and partners on IT innovations, including existing and alternative suppliers and partners. This is no different from contracting traditional services. Also, for contracting IT innovation, the Statement of Work needs to have a sufficient scope to ensure coherent IT innovations across partnerships and to ensure commercial attractiveness for (potential) suppliers and partners. Prior to the start of the selection process, deliberate decision-making is required to ensure that the supplier landscape is fit for purpose.

An extension of the scoping of IT innovation is related to involvement of value chain partners in IT innovation. This significantly increases the

complexity and required effort to manage the partnership with the IT sup-
plier(s), but it also provides opportunities for increasing competitive advantage, as IT innovation is fostered in the value chain instead of only in the
outsourcing company's organisation. This integral approach strengthens the
ties between value chain partners. To implement IT innovation outsourcing
across the value chain, participating organisations need to look for trusted
networks which in general also reduce the risk of information leakage.[22]
Such networks are trusted circles – a group of organisations committed to
a non-transactional collaboration. Nowadays, there is also to some degree a
geopolitical collaboration, consider Arab Leagues, the European Union or
the Regional Comprehensive Economic *Partnership* (RCEP), including South
Asian countries, as examples of geopolitically trusted circles.

Furthermore, external consulting firms can be partners in IT innovation,
to avoid any doubt, not sourcing consultancy but innovation consultancy. Examples of innovation consultancy firms are strategy firms such as McKinsey,
BCG and BAIN; technology firms such as Accenture, DXC, IBM, TCS and
Wipro; as well as the Big Four accounting firms Deloitte, EY, KPGM and
PCW. Innovation consultancy can facilitate knowledge creation, improve
the exchange of knowledge and support the implementation of knowledge
exchange and knowledge capturing processes and tooling. However, the
added value of including external advisers is unfortunately limited; there is
only partial support for the complementary effect on familiarity between
the outsourcing company and the supplier, and this support is conditional
to the support already established between the outsourcing company and
the supplier and the supplier's prior knowledge of the client.[23] Instead of involving an innovation consultancy firm, outsourcing organisations, suppliers
and partners need to implement a proper relationship governance, which is
detailed in Section 6.4.

6.3.1 Specific collaborations – joint ventures and crowdsourcing

There are two specific collaborations which organisations can consider for
both partnering and ecosystems. First of all, setting up a joint venture for IT
innovation can be investigated.[24] In a joint legal entity, the outsourcing company and one or more suppliers and partners shape and co-develop innovation by collective knowledge creation. Joint ventures create opportunities to
work more closely and reduce operational coordination costs. Unfortunately,
joint ventures do not reduce the contracting coordination costs – quite the
opposite. Setting up a joint venture requires significant senior management
and (external) legal expert involvement which exceeds the involvement required for contracting IT outsourcing innovation. As a consequence, joint
ventures are only suitable for long-term engagement. A three-year timeline
is already perceived as short in the context of contracting and negotiation
costs for IT innovation joint ventures. More realistic minimal timelines for
setting up an IT outsourcing innovation joint venture range from five to ten

years. Furthermore, a joint venture reduces the risk of opportunistic behaviour of both the outsourcing company and the suppliers and partners. On the contrary, setting up a joint venture also limits the participating suppliers in two ways.

First, a supplier and/or partner needs to create a ring fence for joint venture resources. This is a more restricted way of allocation than the resource allocation restrictions related to Chinese walls in traditional contracting. Not only the flexibility in terms of size of the supplier and/or partner team over time, but also adjustment of capabilities is more difficult, as when it comes to joint ventures (full-time), named resources are typically involved. In creating joint ventures, both the outsourcing company and the supplier(s) and partner(s) need to be mindful of organisational slack[25]; this slack also includes assessment of capabilities of joint venture resources. Second, suppliers and partners can at best partly leverage knowledge gained in the joint venture with other clients. Leveraging gained knowledge across an existing client base and with new clients is an essential characteristic of the business model of suppliers as well as partners. Vendors and partners will take this impact into account while assessing the attractiveness of setting up and participating in joint ventures. Finally, to successfully set up a joint venture also requires participating organisations of comparable size and market impact as well as minimal size to avoid dependencies, as dependencies might trigger opportunistic behaviour.

The second specific collaboration is crowdsourcing. Crowdsourcing is related to open innovation and can also be applied to IT innovation[26] and can be defined as transferring tasks previously performed internally to a large, usually undefined group of external resources[27]; typically, platforms facilitate matching demand and supply. Crowdsourcing has developed over time; currently, there are four types of platforms, each with a different combination of buying trust for supplier or platform and project governance for buyer or platform.[28] As IT innovation requires longer-term collaborations, the platform needs to have a strong role, and intellectual property needs to be controlled between the outsourcing company and the platform. The preferred platform type is the Governor platform; examples of such a platform are TopCoder and uTest, as platforms of this platform type put the project governance in place for their buyers.[28] However, even with a strong platform, the continuity and confidentiality risks are significant. Also, outsourcing companies need to be mindful of potential ethical issues, including fair wages, transparency, social feedback and autonomy,[29] although these risks are mostly related to individual professionals who offer their services via platforms such as Upwork and Freelancer.

6.4 Relational governance

In contracting IT innovation governance, the risks are high, as there is a low level of certainty about the outcomes. Also, IT innovation is difficult to codify. If there is trust between involved parties, the outsourcing company and the suppliers and partners, relational contracting and the associated governance can be considered.[30] Relational governance is based on trust as well as cooperative norms, and information-sharing routines figure prominently in explaining the success and stability of interorganisational exchanges.[31] Relational governance complements contractual governance,[32] which will be detailed in the next section.

Trust in IT outsourcing, more precisely in application development projects, has been classified by Sabherwal: calculus-based trust, knowledge-based trust, identification-based trust and performance-based trust.[33] In relational governance in IT innovation, outsourcing is more reputation-centric, which is a combination of Sabherwal's classification based on the beliefs and experiences of decision-makers of both the outsourcing company and the suppliers. Reputation also includes the professional reputation of individuals as defined in social capital theory.[34] Outsourcing companies as well as suppliers and partners are aware of close professional as well as personal relationships of their management and staff. This awareness positively contributes to relational governance. Negative experience and feedback in engaging in innovation might jeopardise future involvement for outsourcing companies with the same partner and other partners, as well as for the suppliers and partners, with their existing client and other new and existing future clients. Job rotation in innovation strengthens this positive contribution to relational governance.

IT innovation strategy and management control system(s)[35] and monitoring are also essential in IT innovation outsourcing and are the basis for relational governance. Monitoring innovation is preferable to online/real-time monitoring, implementing an interactive use of management control systems. Online monitoring of innovation strengthens the innovation process and innovation capabilities, as well as the monetisation of innovation.[36] Relational governance (and contractual governance) also requires in-house capabilities and strong business leadership to manage outsourcing innovation.[37] The strength of in-house capabilities and business leadership also impacts relational governance. In addition, introducing the role of an innovation integrator, similar to the role of service integrator in IT outsourcing, might strengthen the relational governance in IT innovation outsourcing. This integrator role is different from an external adviser, which was discussed in the previous section. The innovation integrator coordinates innovation on behalf of the outsourcing company and manages innovation partners, as well as the innovation resources of their own company. In addition to being the innovation integrator, the service integrator participates in conducting innovation themselves. The implication of the introduction of this role is that the innovation integrator will onboard skills for managing innovation and will be able to detect, present and resolve concerns, issues and shortcomings earlier, more clearly and better than internal outsourcing company staff managing the innovation. Potentially, suppliers and partners will also be more sensitive to guidance from an innovation integrator, as this guidance potentially impacts their reputation and jeopardises collaboration with the innovation integrator for other clients.

Finally, it is important to add the observation that for IT innovation outsourcing, as with IT outsourcing, most conflicts between parties and/or contractual breaches are resolved by relational governance. Proving right or proving wrong is even more difficult in IT innovation outsourcing. Nevertheless, proper contracts and contractual governance avoid conflicts and encourage parties to take appropriate measures to avoid contractual breaches, including under- or non-performance.

6.5 Contractual governance

In any organisation, objectives are a moving target.[38] This characteristic creates challenges for the codification of, preparation for an agreement on contracts, including detailing contractual provisions. Flexibility is required, which, however, will reduce contractual protection and enforceability.[39] The uncertainty in IT innovation outsourcing is significantly greater than for traditional IT outsourcing contracting. Therefore, a lot of contractual governance effort is required to ensure an outcome of the collaboration, which is balanced and acceptable for both the outsourcing organisation and the supplier. There might even be obfuscations included in the contract by the supplier[40] or the outsourcing organisation, or both. These loopholes enable undesirable opportunistic behaviour. Casas-Arce et al. suggest explicit ex-post exploitation of contractual clauses, including performance incentives and control systems, in addition to information-sharing.[41] Doing so will reduce the likelihood of leakage itself, but at the same time, strict contract management is killing innovation behaviour. Aubert et al. suggested for IT innovation – loosely coupled contracts, low control on supplier's work, limited or untargeted innovation and difficulty/impossibility to assess work delivered to facilitate innovation.[42] The spirit of the contract is also important,[41] as it will provide guidance to all parties over the term of the contract.

A final consideration in contractual governance is the impact of a time lag on the contracting of IT innovation outsourcing. The competitive advantage associated with successful adoption of IT innovations is limited in terms of time. Commoditising in the IT sector is happening at an increased speed. Cloud computing is the most important enabler of commoditisation. As a consequence, IT outsourcing organisations should not spend too much time on contracting IT innovation. Rather, they should have the basic contractual provisions right and rely on relational governance instead of striving for the perfect contract and being caught up by competition. The elements in the contracts that require full attention are the pricing mechanisms, which are detailed in the section below.

6.6 Funding and reward in IT outsourcing innovation

Innovation and IT innovation are closely related to the business processes of any organisation. Therefore, decentralised innovations initiatives are more effective. For IT innovations, organisations have a larger need to understand the bigger picture and to identify potential synergies of the innovations. The enterprise and IT architecture provide good insights into these potential synergies. In most organisations, business processes and associated exchange of information and data are well-integrated. For these types of organisations, a central funding of IT outsourcing innovations works best. The central funding also ensures positive innovation effects from the perspective of economies of scale. Also, decentralised funding sets governance challenges, as the size of the IT innovation budget is relatively small and the coherence of all decentral initiatives has to be assessed. This is an explicit additional governance obligation, whereas in central IT innovation funding, this is an implicit integral part of the governance.

Finally, outsourcing organisations also need to explore whether their innovation qualifies for public funding schemes. That said, there is also a balance between the effort required for granting the public funding and reporting on spending (accountability) of the funding and the amount of public funding received. However, most suppliers and partners are attracted to work with outsourcing organisations which have received public funding, as these organisations are perceived as prestigious and can be used in strengthening the profile of their organisation.

The reward for the suppliers and partners can be based on agreed-upon pricing, such as time * material or lump sum or on risk and reward or a combination of the two, which is no different from traditional IT outsourcing. Casas-Arce et al. suggest lump sum contracts, where the outsourcing company can decide on the final project or service.[41] In lump sum contracts, the innovation management remains the responsibility of the outsourcing organisation. The assessment of the proposed supplier and/or partner team prior to contract signing is key in lump sum contracts.

Furthermore, these contracts avoid too much intermediate decision-making by the outsourcing company. Successful IT innovation requires a mid- to long-term strategy. By using the time * material pricing mechanism, the outsourcing company introduces internal as well as external uncertainties by the ability to scale up and down the volumes and short(er) notice periods. Both will potentially jeopardise the IT outsourcing benefits. However, lump sum contracts introduce opportunistic behaviour. Shared revenue contracts might be considered.[43] In IT innovation contracts, setting parameters for shared revenue is also not straightforward. A capped bonus for the supplier or partner is the feasible incentive to structure a shared revenue contract for IT innovation.

The rewards in joint venture are no different, but unfortunately rewards are even more complex, especially in relation to the alignment on transfer pricing of services and resources from both the outsourcing company and the suppliers and partners and the monetisation of innovation. This additional complexity further increases the need for proper relational and contractual governance to circumvent undesirable opportunistic behaviour. Typically,

IT innovation joint ventures are project-driven, which ensures sufficient strategic interdependence for the parent companies. This independence is pivotal for successfully managing joint ventures.[44] The management of the joint venture approves budgets and allocates resources. The approved projects are managed by portfolio management, and, if required, resources can be reallocated, as priorities might change over time.

6.7 Conclusion

Although IT innovation is only a small part of IT spending, IT innovation is crucial to ensure business continuity as well as to growing a business. IT innovation enables disruption and also avoids being disrupted. A deliberate IT innovation strategy and management control system are a prerequisite. Pro-active management of the IT innovation outsourcing enabled by online/real-time monitoring is a necessity. Of utmost importance is selecting the right suppliers and/or partners and continuously assessing the health of the relationship(s), regardless of whether it is a partnership or an ecosystem or whether it includes a joint venture or crowdsourcing. The relationship needs to be long-term rewarding for all participants, as IT innovation requires long-term collaboration to be beneficial. A fit-for-purpose relational governance combined with a contractual governance is a prerequisite for achieving IT innovation outsourcing success.

Notes

1 Damanpour, F. (1991). Organizational innovation: A meta-analysis of effects of determinants and moderators. *The Academy of Management Journal, 34*(3), 555–590.
2 Lacity, M. C., & Willcocks, L. P. (2013). Outsourcing business processes for innovation. *MIT Sloan Management Review, 54*(3), 63–69.
3 Susarla, A., & Mukhopadhyay, T. (2019). Can outsourcing of information technology foster innovations in client organizations? An empirical analysis. *MIS Quarterly: Management Information Systems, 43*(3):929–949.
4 See also Denning, S. (2016). Can new disruption research suggest defenses against threats and opportunities for innovators? *Strategy & Leadership, 44*(3), 3–8; Wagner, M. (2016). Managing disruptive innovation with technology acquisitions: The informing case of software-based high-technology industries. *Technology Analysis & Strategic Management, 28*(8), 979–991; Beulen, E. (2018). *Information management leads top line information technology initiatives and contributes to bottom line targets: The chief information officer is a technical innovator and custodian of the IT architecture.* Tilburg: Tilburg University; Chan, C. M. L., Teoh, S. Y., Yeow, A., & Pan, G. (2019). Agility in responding to disruptive digital innovation: Case study of an SME. *Information Systems Journal, 29*(2), 436–455.
5 See Quinn, J. B., & Baily, M. N. (1994). Information technology: Increasing productivity in services. *Academy of Management Perspectives, 8*(3), 28–48; Quinn, J. B. (1985). Innovation and corporate strategy: Managed chaos. *Technology in Society, 7*(2), 263–279; De Quinn, J. B. (2000). Outsourcing innovation: The new engine of growth. *Sloan Management, 41*(4), 13–28.

6 Peppard, J., & Ward, J. (2016). *The strategic management of information systems – building a digital strategy* (4th ed.). New York: Wiley.

7 OECD (2005). *The measurement of scientific and technological activities Oslo manual, guidelines for collecting and interpreting innovation data* (3rd ed.). Paris: Organisation for Economic Cooperation and Development, OECD EUROSTAT.

8 Gartner (2020). IT key metrics data 2021: Industry measures—executive summary, ID G00737583, 18 December.

9 Den Hertog, P. (2000). Knowledge intensive business services as co-producers of innovation. *International Journal Innovation Management, 4*(4), 491–504.

10 Grandori, A., & Furlotti, M. (2019). Contracting for the unknown and the logic of innovation. *European Management Review, 16*(2), 413–426.

11 Koch, A., Ribbers, P., & Rutkowski, A. (2020) Samurais and ninjas: Ambidexterity @ AXA Konzern AG. In Beulen, E., & Ribbers, P. (Eds.), *Routledge companion to managing digital outsourcing* (pp. 130–146, Ser. Routledge companions). London: Routledge/Taylor & Francis Group.

12 https://www.gartner.com/en/information-technology/glossary/bimodal. Note that Boston Consulting Group argues for all-agile, Mode 2 only – https://www.bcg.com/publications/2016/software-agile-digital-transformation-end-of-two-speed-it. Undoubtedly, the pace of market and technology changes has increased over time significantly, but the distinction between the two modes is still meaningful, as there is no business urgency to only engage in Mode 2 with more complex relational governance and contractual governance.

13 Du, W. D., Pan, S. L., & Wu, J. (2020). How do it outsourcing suppliers develop capabilities? an organisational ambidexterity perspective on a multi-case study. *Journal of Information Technology, 35*(1), 49–65.

14 See Carroll, N., & Helfert, M. (2015). Service capabilities within open innovation. *Journal of Enterprise Information Management, 28*(2), 275–303; Carcary, M., Doherty, E., & Thornley, C. (2015). Business innovation and differentiation: Maturing the IT capability. *IT Professional, 17*(2), 46–53; Beulen, E. (2018). *Information management leads top line information technology initiatives and contributes to bottom line targets: The chief information officer is a technical innovator and custodian of the IT architecture.* Tilburg: Tilburg University; Caputo, F., Cillo, V., Candelo, E., & Liu, Y. (2019). Innovating through digital revolution. *Management Decision, 57*(8), 2032–2051.

15 See Jensen, M. C., & Meckling, W. H. (1976). Theory of the firm: Managerial behavior, agency costs and ownership structure. *Journal of Financial Economics, 3*(4), 305–360; Fama, E. F., & Jensen, M. C. (1983). Agency problems and residual claims. *The journal of law and Economics, 26*(2), 327–349; Eisenhardt, K. M. (1989). Agency theory: An assessment and review. *Academy of Management Review, 14*(1), 57–74.

16 Aubert, B. A., Barki, H., Patry, M., & Roy, V. (2008). A multi-level, multi-theory perspective of information technology implementation. *Information Systems Journal, 18*(1), 45–72, 48.

17 Lai, E. L. C., Riezman, R., & Wang, P. (2009). Outsourcing of innovation. *Economic Theory, 38*(3), 485–515.

18 See Weeks, M. R., & Feeny, D. (2008). Outsourcing: From cost management to innovation and business value. *California Management Review, 50*(4), 127–146; Lacity, M. C., & Willcocks, L. P. (2013). Outsourcing business processes for innovation. *MIT Sloan Management Review, 54*(3), 63–69.

19 De Quinn, J. B. (2000). Outsourcing innovation: The new engine of growth. *Sloan Management, 41*(4), 13–28.

20 See Aubert, B. A., Kishore, R., & Iriyama, A. (2015). Exploring and managing the "innovation through outsourcing" paradox. *The Journal of Strategic Information*

Systems, *24*(4), 255–269; Oshri, I., Arkhipova, D., & Vaia, G. (2018). Exploring the effect of familiarity and advisory services on innovation outcomes in outsourcing settings. *Journal of Information Technology*, *33*(3), 203–15.

21 Weeks, M. R., & Feeny, D. (2008). Outsourcing: From cost management to innovation and business value. *California Management Review*, *50*(4), 127–146.

22 Hoecht, A., & Trott, P. (2006). Innovation risks of strategic outsourcing. *Technovation*, *26*(5–6), 672–681.

23 Oshri, I., Arkhipova, D., & Vaia, G. (2018). Exploring the effect of familiarity and advisory services on innovation outcomes in outsourcing settings. *Journal of Information Technology*, *33*(3), 203–215, 213.

24 See Lacity, M., & Willcocks, L. (2014). Business process outsourcing and dynamic innovation. *Strategic Outsourcing: An International Journal*, *7*(1), 66–92; Oshri, I., Kotlarsky, J., & Gerbasi, A. (2015). Strategic innovation through outsourcing: The role of relational and contractual governance. *Journal of Strategic Information Systems*, *24*(3), 203–216.

25 Lin, J.-Y. (2017). Knowledge creation through joint venture investments: The contingent role of organizational slack. *Journal of Engineering and Technology Management*, *46*, 1–25.

26 See Chesbrough, H. W. (2003). *Open innovation: The new imperative for creating and profiting from technology*. Boston, MA: Harvard Business School Press; Leimeister, J. M., Huber, M., Bretschneider, U., & Krcmar, H. (2009). Leveraging crowdsourcing: Activation-supporting components for it-based ideas competition. *Journal of Management Information Systems*, *26*(1), 197–224.

27 Howe, J. (2009). *Crowdsourcing: Why the power of the crowd is driving the future of business*. New York: Three Rivers Press.

28 Kaganer, E., Carmel, E., Hirschheim, R., & Olsen, T. (2013). Managing the human cloud. *MIT Sloan Management Review*, *54*(2), 23–32.

29 Schlagwein, D., Cecez-Kecmanovic, D., & Hanckel, B. (2019). Ethical norms and issues in crowdsourcing practices: A Habermasian analysis. *Information Systems Journal*, *29*(4), 811–837.

30 Ring, P. S., & Andrew, H. van de Ven. (1992). Structuring cooperative relationships between organizations. *Strategic Management Journal*, *13*(7), 483–498.

31 Poppo, L., Zhou, K. Z., & Zenger, T. R. (2008). Examining the conditional limits of relational governance: Specialized assets, performance ambiguity, and long-standing ties. *Journal of Management Studies*, *45*(7), 1195–1216.

32 Poppo, L., & Zenger, T. (2002). Do formal contracts and relational governance function as substitutes or complements?. *Strategic Management Journal*, *23*(8), 707–725.

33 Sabherwal, R. (1999). The role of trust in outsourced IS development projects. *Communications of the ACM*, *42*(2), 80–86.

34 Coleman, J. S. (1988). *Social capital in the creation of human capital*. Chicago, IL: University of Chicago Press.

35 Dunk, A. S. (2011). Product innovation, budgetary control, and the financial performance of firms. *The British Accounting Review*, *43*(2), 102–111.

36 Lopez-Valeiras, E., Gonzalez-Sanchez, M. B., & Gomez-Conde, J. (2016). The effects of the interactive use of management control systems on process and organizational innovation. *Review of Managerial Science*, *10*(3), 487–510.

37 See Willcocks, L., Feeny, D., & Olson, N. (2006). Implementing core is capabilities: Feeny-Willcocks IT governance and management framework revisited. *European Management Journal*, *24*(1):28–37; Kranz, J. (2021). Strategic innovation in IT outsourcing: Exploring the differential and interaction effects of contractual and relational governance mechanisms. *The Journal of Strategic Information Systems*, *30*(1), 101656.

38 See Lakatos, I. (1970). The methodology of scientific research programs. In Lakatos, I., & Musgrave, A. (Eds.), *Criticism and the growth of knowledge* (pp. 91–196). Cambridge: Cambridge University Press; Grandori, A. (1984). A prescriptive contingency view of organizational decision making. *Administrative Science Quarterly, 29*, 192–208.

39 Schreyögg, G., & Sydow, J. (2010). Organizing for fluidity? Dilemmas of new organizational forms. *Organization Science, 21*, 1251–1262.

40 Susarla A., & Krishnan, R. (2015). *Influence of observable but unverifiable information on contract form*. East Lansing, MI: Mimeo, Michigan State University.

41 Casas-Arce, P., Kittsteiner, T., & Martínez-Jerez, F. A. (2019). Contracting with opportunistic partners: Theory and application to technology development and innovation. *Management Science, 65*(2), 842–858.

42 Aubert, B. A., Kishore, R., & Iriyama, A. (2015). Exploring and managing the "innovation through outsourcing" paradox. *The Journal of Strategic Information Systems, 24*(4), 255–269.

43 See Grossman, S. J., & Hart, O. D. (1983). Implicit contracts under asymmetric information. *The Quarterly Journal of Economics, 98*, 123–156; Myerson, R. B. (1983). *Analysis of two bargaining problems with incomplete information* (No. 582). Discussion Paper.

44 Kumar, S., & Seth, A. (1998). The design of coordination and control mechanisms for managing joint venture–parent relationships. *Strategic Management Journal, 19*(6), 579–599.

7 Transitions and contracts

The transition of the service from the internal IT department or the incumbent supplier is the starting point for the contract. How can outsourcing organisations minimise the business continuity risk related to IT outsourcing? Contracts are not the only measure, but are an important measure, which is not limited to the transition. Contracts cover the relationship from the beginning to the end.

Several contract aspects require careful attention, obviously the responsibilities of both the outsourcing organisation and the suppliers. Furthermore, both the outsourcing organisation and the suppliers have benefit in contract flexibility to adapt quickly to changing circumstances and to ensure a fit-for-purpose service at competitive rates. Also, the structure of contracts matters. What does successful contracting look like?

7.1 Introduction

Contracts are very important to IT outsourcing partnerships because they enable participants to manage their relationships.[1] In parallel with contractual discussions, the transition of the contracted services to the new supplier has to be prepared and executed. The transition will be detailed in Sections 7.2 and 7.3. Knowledge transfer to a new supplier is costly, as the costs related to the knowledge transfer are associated with switching suppliers.[2]

When contracts are prepared and negotiated, it is important that their structure matches the partnership's context: the contract for a relationship with a limited scope and involving only one supplier will obviously be very different from that of a global partnership with many suppliers. Competitive pricing is important and can be enforced over the term of the contract by a benchmarking clause. Market dynamics, changing strategies and technology developments make it difficult to include provisions covering all these unknowns in the contract. Therefore, contracts must include change management clauses describing the contract adjustment process. In IT outsourcing partnerships, the responsibility of each supplier must also be clearly defined. The contract also needs to address the contract termination.

Cloud services have added an extra dimension to IT outsourcing. Contracting and managing cloud services are distinctly different from each other.

DOI: 10.4324/9781003223788-7

As cloud services are standard services, the contracting and management effort is significantly lower; however, the risks related to supplier lock-in have to be thoroughly assessed.

7.2 Transitions[3]

Transitions are defined by Cullen and Willcocks as "implementing the new way of operating."[4] A transition is immediately followed by contract signing and precedes the service delivery phase.[5] The transition sets the tone for the entire outsourcing relation and involves handing over the outsourced services from either the outsourcing organisation's internal IT department or their incumbent supplier. Transitions include critical steps, such as those of knowledge transfer, determining and implementing new governance structures and implementing the processes of the new supplier. On average, transitions take two to three months; when an outsourcing contract includes application maintenance services with a significant customised functionality, the duration of the transition can take as many as six months. In case of transferring knowledge to offshore locations of the supplier (e.g. India, China, Eastern European or Latin American countries), the risks related to knowledge transfer increase and potentially the timelines as well.[6]

Vendors propose knowledge transfer strategy with a focus on the transfer of specific knowledge, as generic knowledge is not supportive in taking over responsibility for the delivery of services.[7] Codification is important in transitions.[8] Knowledge transfer strategy includes location for the knowledge transfer and approach, such as a train-the-trainer approach or direct knowledge transfer from the knowledge-giver to the knowledge-taker.[9]

It is also important to distinguish between transfer and transformation. The transfer is related to the transfer of knowledge and the implementation of processes and tools to enable the new supplier to provide contracted IT services. IT outsourcing contracts can also include commitments to adjust services over time. These adjustments of services are typically initiated after the sign-off of the transition deliverables and not defined in detail at the start of the contract. The transformation is a separate programme with separate deliverables and timelines. Often, the transformation programme is planned for the first and second contract years. The main difference between a transition project and a transformation programme is that, in a transition project, the new supplier is dependent on the incumbent supplier and/or the internal IT department as knowledge-givers, whereas transformation programmes will be executed independently by the "new" supplier.

7.2.1 Transition phase

Prior to contract signing, negotiations are conducted that include responding to a request for information and a request for proposal, followed by a due diligence and a best and final offer (BAFO). The results of these contract negotiations are included in the contract, which includes a transition project to transfer the knowledge to the new supplier.

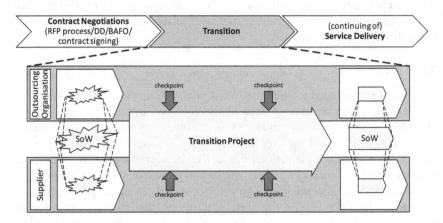

Figure 7.1 Transitioning a single Statement of Work (SoW).

The transition project is a prerequisite for the successful implementation of an outsourcing contract.[10] According to Lacity and Willcocks, the objective of the transition phase is to achieve operational performance.[11] It therefore includes activities such as validating the service scope, costs, levels and responsibilities for baseline services, as well as fostering realistic expectations of the supplier's performance. In addition, intermediate check points are important, for example, to ensure that the knowledge transferred has really been understood by knowledge-takers. A transition is a project, with a clear set of objectives, deliverables and milestones, along with a strict timeline (Figure 7.1).

In the past, costs of knowledge transfer in a transition were substantial – up to 50% of the service fees in the first year of the outsourcing deal. As the market has matured, these costs seem to be declining: currently, transition costs range from 15 to 25% of the service fees in the first year of the outsourcing deal. Transition costs depend on the kind of IT services to be transferred. The costs will be relatively low if the services are commodity services, such as desktop management, but they are much higher for the transfer of knowledge-intensive and highly customised IT services such as application management. Ensuring a sufficiently high budget for the transition is important for achieving transition success. Failed transitions jeopardise outsourcing success.

On the basis of the outsourcing, knowledge management and organisational learning literature, transitions may be conceptualised as combinations of three significant and interrelated organisational processes: transfer, learning and adaptation. Transitions contain key elements of each of these processes.[12] For instance, after an outsourcing contract is signed, client staff must transfer knowledge, experience and routines to new supplier personnel,[13] who must absorb them and learn to replicate the outsourced activities. That said, transitions do not only involve the transfer of broad organisational knowledge related to the outsourced activities, such as best practices.[14] More importantly, specific routines needed to perform these activities must be transferred as well. Doing so in the complex interorganisational setting of a transition is difficult mainly because these are highly contextualised routines characterised by emergent qualities such as accumulated experience, as well as aspects that are difficult to articulate, such as tacit knowledge.[15]

Learning during a transition takes place in two dimensions: learning to perform such outsourced tasks, as, for example, outsourcing organisation-specific application development activities[16]; and learning to adapt organisational settings, for example, by restructuring the outsourcing organisation's retained organisation[17] or by mirroring the outsourcing organisation's structure for the supplier.[18] Adaptation, which follows from learning and involves "modifying or combining practices," plays a significant role in integrating the knowledge transferred and the learning acquired during the transition.[19] For a successful transition, both these processes must be performed smoothly until the operational performance defined in the contract is achieved.[20]

These three aspects involve significant challenges. Learning, for example, may be difficult if the outsourcing company's staff in possession of the knowledge concerned lack motivation – because of job insecurity, for instance.[21] In addition, if the transfer has been limited and learning was insufficient, adaptation in the sense of modified structures and processes at the supplier and their outsourcing organisation is difficult to achieve. This increases the risks involved and may lead to costly mistakes.[19] From such considerations, a number of critical success factors for transitions may be derived. These are listed in Table 7.1.

Table 7.1 The critical success factors of transitions (in order of importance)[a]

1 Understanding the contractual agreements, including the service provisioning scope and the transition exit criteria
2 Implementing the transition's governance, monitoring and reporting
3 Approving the transition's planning, deliverables and budget
4 Ensuring the commitment of senior client and service provider managers
5 Ensuring clear and regular communication between the outsourcing organisation's and the supplier's teams during the transition, including proper collaboration between on-site and offsite teams, which includes offshore teams
6 Managing the expectations of the stakeholders
7 Conducting a comprehensive due diligence
8 Ensuring the capability and availability of the client's and the service provider's transition team resources
9 Preparing and executing knowledge transfer planning
10 Implementing change management initiatives at the client's organisation (including communication to the staff involved)

Note: client = outsourcing organisation and service provider = supplier.
[a]   These critical success factors and their ranking were established on the basis of the response to a questionnaire sent to 146 European-certified transition managers in Belgium, France, Germany, the Netherlands, the UK and Sweden in 2009. The authors thank Accenture for providing them with the mailing list used.

The critical success factors for transition in Table 7.1 are based on the insights of transition managers. Their insights were collected in 2009, but these critical success factors are not much different in 2021. The contract always remains the starting point for a transition. However, today in many cases, transition challenges are due to attrition of knowledge-givers in the outsourcing organisation or the incumbent supplier. Ensuring the availability of the knowledge-givers is a critical success factor in transitions. Furthermore, the sixth critical success factor has become more important, as IT has become a more integral part of doing business. Therefore, the expectations of senior business stakeholders need to be managed more closely.[22] Also, the ninth critical success factor has gained relevance. Preparation and execution of knowledge transfer planning has become more important, due to the increased speed required to implement new functionalities and increased dependencies in the IT landscape. Furthermore, most organisations are adapting to agile ways of working. Therefore, the tenth critical success factor is not as much of a challenge for most outsourcing organisations anymore.

7.3 Parallel transitions

Currently, second- and third-generation outsourcing engagements are the norm. There are hardly any first-generation outsourcing contracts anymore. Therefore, most transitions are from the incumbent supplier to the new supplier. Today's outsourcing engagements include offshore outsourcing and multisourcing as integral components. Multisourcing means outsourcing to several suppliers at once. In the analysis of Currie and Willcocks, "multiple sourcing" is therefore contrasted with "single sourcing," that is, outsourcing to only a single supplier.[23] Multiple sourcing is linked to portfolio management.[24] Levina and Su address the phenomenon of global multisourcing strategies.[25] By multisourcing, major cost savings and risk reductions can be achieved.[26] However, a transition is required first, and since multisourcing involves several suppliers, parallel transition processes are needed. The transition costs involved in multisourcing are therefore higher.[27] There are also other terms and conditions. Managing multisourcing engagements requires a mature, retained organisation,[28] because the management of intellectual property (IP) rights, compliance and security all require extra attention.[29]

Multisourcing also renovates the requirements for transitions. Instead of transferring the responsibility for service provisioning to a single supplier, it is transferred to two or more suppliers in parallel. Desktop management, for instance, is rewarded to supplier A, server management and network management to supplier B, ERP application management to supplier C and non-ERP application management services to supplier D. Consequently, the knowledge needed for these services must be transferred to these suppliers as well, which means that one has to run four transition projects simultaneously. A lot of coordination work is needed to manage the dependencies

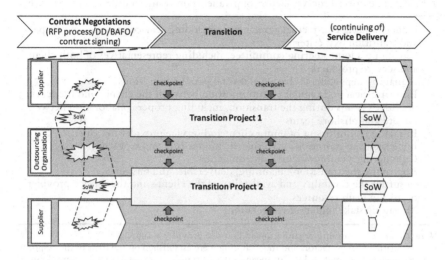

Figure 7.2 Transitioning multiple Statements of Work (SoWs) in parallel.

and to ensure proper service provisioning. This is conceptually detailed in Figure 7.2.

The dependencies involved relate to the availability and capabilities of the knowledge-givers, knowledge-takers and transition managers, and the retained organisation's information managers. Since the number of organisations involved in parallel transitions is greater than in single transitions, knowledge transfer will be more complex and thus lengthier and more difficult. Chua and Pan have identified five IS knowledge areas[30]: technology, application domain, IS application, organisation and IS development processes.[15] Predominantly, complexity has increased in terms of organisational knowledge. Blumenberg et al.[31] have reported that in IT outsourcing engagements, the sender-receiver dimension as described by Lin et al.[32] requires explicit, documented interaction structures between the parties. Additionally, this aspect becomes significantly more complex as the number of stakeholders increases.

In 2009, suppliers had not been very successful in addressing the challenges of offshoring and multisourcing. Worldwide, only 5% of them considered their competence sufficient to ensure well-developed and well-deployed multisourcing engagements.[29] In 2021, all mature suppliers have developed these capabilities and are able to transition and manage multisourcing engagements.

As with single transitions, ten critical success factors are distinguished for parallel transitions. They will be discussed in the following pages. This discussion includes a 2021 reflection on the in 2009 collected data, detailed in Table 7.2.

Table 7.2 The critical success factors of parallel transitions, in order of importance[a]

---

1   Understanding contractual agreements, including service provisioning scope and transition exit criteria
2   Setting up a joint steering committee, including representatives of both client and service providers
3   Managing dependencies between several parallel transitions
4   Ensuring clear and regular communication between the client's and the service provider's teams during the transition, including proper collaboration between on-site and offshore teams
5   Ensuring commitment of senior client and service provider managers
6   Implementing transition's governance, monitoring and reporting
7   Conducting a comprehensive due diligence
8   Approving the transition's planning, deliverables and budget
9   Ensuring the capability and availability of the client's and the service provider's transition team resources
10 Managing stakeholder–er expectations

Note: client = outsourcing organisation and service provider = supplier.
a These critical success factors and their ranking were established on the basis of the response to a questionnaire sent to 146 European-certified transition managers in Belgium, France, Germany, the Netherlands, the UK and Sweden in 2009. The authors thank Accenture for providing them with the mailing list used.

7.3.1 Success factor 1 – understanding contractual agreements

In multisourcing engagements, it is important to ensure a good understanding of the contractual agreements, including the scope of service provisioning. As there are multiple suppliers, the responsibilities of each of them have to be clearly demarcated. To this end, operating-level agreements between the suppliers involved are needed in addition to their service-level agreements (SLAs) with the outsourcing company.[33] Such operating-level agreements detail the responsibilities of the suppliers involved as well as the governance of their relations with the outsourcing organisation. The focus in operating-level agreements is on collaboration, including the processes and alignment of tooling, such as IT service management tooling. Typically, operating-level agreements do not include additional responsibilities for parties, while they do provide guidance and a frame of reference for the individual suppliers and the outsourcing organisation and enable a collaborative and cohesive way of working.

Outsourcing contracts can never be fully descriptive. Wareham et al.[34] and Beulen and Ribbers[35] therefore applied Tirole's[36] incomplete contract theory to IT outsourcing. Governance has to be implemented in the transition phase. The contracts must include procedures on how to deal with unforeseen events which are not detailed in the contracts. As there are multiple suppliers, the governance and contractual provisions require substantial management attention, as there are many dependencies.

7.3.2 Success factor 2 – setting up a joint steering committee

Parallel transitions are very dynamic, and there are many dependencies between an outsourcing company and its suppliers. Even in regular outsourcing engagements, a steering committee is required[37]; this is all the more important in parallel transitions. In order to manage the transition adequately, joint steering committees are needed. In these committees, all parties and stakeholders are represented. Transition managers from both the suppliers (which are responsible for the individual transitions) and the outsourcing organisation can address their questions and concerns in the committee's meetings. As all parties and stakeholders are represented, the committee can make all required decisions. By applying this approach, delays are avoided. Acting fast and decisively contributes significantly to the transition success. Parallel transitions typically display a layered structure of steering committees. The layered structure can best be aligned to the contract structure and the service delivery dependencies and/or domains, for example, by combining all application transitions in a single steering committee to facilitate coherence in the multiple transitions in the application domain.

7.3.3 Success factor 3 – managing dependencies between transitions

A parallel transition is a programme of multiple transition projects run in parallel. This transition requires multi-project planning, as described by Payne[38] and by Levy and Globerson.[39] In parallel transitions, the dominant dependency challenge is the availability of knowledge-givers and knowledge-takers. Knowledge-givers have to balance between ensuring the continuity of the IT provisioning and transferring knowledge to the IT professionals of the new suppliers. Knowledge-takers must be made available for receiving the knowledge, which means that they have to be recruited from or freed up from other projects. Insufficient availability results in delayed transition projects and may well have consequences for other transition projects. Managing these dependencies in a parallel transition is not easy.

Proper documentation by the incumbent supplier or the internal IT department of the outsourcing company reduces the dependencies in a transition. Also, the increasing standardisation of IT services (in general) and cloud services (in particular) reduces dependencies. However, the increased need for faster enabling of new functionalities significantly increases the dependencies in parallel transitions. Changing suppliers is not an accepted excuse for delays in enabling new functionalities in most outsourcing organisations.

7.3.4 Success factor 4 – ensuring clear and regular communication

In addition to joint steering committee(s), communication on the operational level is essential for parallel transition success. Also, communication between on-site and offshore teams is important. In offshore outsourcing, time zone differences, language barriers and cultural differences have to be bridged.[40,41] Technology can facilitate communication, with teleconferences, video conferences, collaborative tools, etc. In terms of meeting frequency, typically there will be daily update meeting for individual project, alignment meetings between transition projects at least weekly, and a bi-weekly overall steering committee as the duration of transitions has been shortening for decades.

Being sensitive to the meetings' participants' organisational differences will significantly contribute to the success achieved, as well. One can add to this setting the expectation that any participant in any meeting behaves and operates in accordance with contractual commitments combined with the best interest of the outsourcing organisation. Any individual participant who is not obedient to these ground rules needs to be expelled from the transition project.

7.3.5 Success factor 5 – ensuring commitment

Project management literature indicates that management sponsorship is a prerequisite for success. Lucier and Torsiliera[42] and Ruggles[43] have linked management sponsorship with knowledge management. In parallel transitions, senior managers from both the outsourcing organisation and their suppliers have to provide active support to transition projects, in addition to joining the steering committees. Senior managers can show their commitment by attending additional transition project meetings, such as the kick-off meeting, for example, or by periodic internal communication about the importance of a successful transition. Of course, consensus between the senior managers of all parties involved is essential. This consensus does not come about naturally, as involved suppliers are also competitors with potentially conflicting interests. This contradiction needs to be addressed in contracts as well as in transition meetings and steering committees.

7.3.6 Success factor 6 – implementing transition governance, monitoring and reporting

In order to manage transitions successfully, both the outsourcing company and their suppliers must develop and implement an appropriate governance model in order to conduct the day-to-day activities efficiently and to monitor the transition project progress. This model must ensure clarity in the roles and responsibilities of the involved organisations and define the communication, control and reporting structure.[44] Having a joint steering committee – a success factor in itself – significantly contributes to transition governance.

In terms of monitoring and reporting, most suppliers implement specific tooling to report transition progress, including transition issues. Automating the monitoring and reporting of transitions is extremely helpful in parallel transitions, as the volumes of issues to be resolved and dependencies in parallel transitions are significant. In order to manage the issues and dependencies, traditional project management tools are instrumental. Alignment on tooling prior to the start of a transition is essential for the implementation of a proper transition governance in parallel transitions.

7.3.7 Success factor 7 – conducting a comprehensive due diligence

During contract negotiations and prior to the supplier's final offer, a thorough due diligence must be carried out. By conducting a due diligence, suppliers make sure that they have a thorough understanding of the services outsourced and the dependencies involved within the outsourcing organisation, along with any associated challenges and risks. This essential activity is intended to discover any information gaps that might influence or disrupt the outsourcing relation.[45] A due diligence also provides a starting point for the transition planned. It can also be used to define the actions that must be included in the transition, such as base-lining and implementing measure and/or tooling to ensure compliance.

The due diligence is a formal step in contracting. By conducting a due dil-igence, suppliers waive their right to adjust the contractual commitments due to a difference in understanding related to the service delivery commitments. This clarity is not only important for the outsourcing company, but also for the suppliers. Conducting a due diligence is more difficult in parallel transition due to the increased number of suppliers and dependencies; however, it is not only important but necessary to have a successful start of the outsourcing relationship.

7.3.8 Success factor 8 – approving the transition's planning, deliverables and budget

A transition is a critical and complex stage in the outsourcing project. There-fore, its planning and preparation is important for achieving a successful out-sourcing relation.[46] This means that the outsourcing organisation and their suppliers must define the appropriate overall methodology for the transition together – be it a "big bang approach" or the phased approach– and must then make a detailed plan for the knowledge transfer needed (covering elements such as who transfers what to whom), for pilot projects and transition budget tracking. Pilot projects may be used to establish the operational tasks that are to be transferred to the suppliers, after which more complex services follow. Budget tracking must include the costs of supplier personnel visiting client sites for knowledge transfer activities.

7.3.9 Success factor 9 – ensuring the capability and availability of the resources needed

All of the above are still not enough to ensure success if both organisations cannot devote a team of highly capable personnel to conduct the transition.[47] Transitions become less challenging when the outsourcing organisation and their multiple suppliers begin to align their operations and to work closely together to generate a combined output. Transitions are very dynamic, with continuous changes and a frequent need for quick fixes. The availability of both knowledge-givers and knowledge-takers is another important chal-lenge, particularly for outsourcing organisations, as they need to carry out their routine operational activities besides their involvement in the transition.

7.3.10 Success factor 10 – managing stakeholder expectations

Transitions involve many stakeholders, from the outsourcing organisation's business management and senior IT managers to their IT personnel working on the actual activities that are being outsourced. Since outsourcing means that jobs are rotating, transitions have to be monitored closely, in particular the involvement of stakeholders and their job security. Once the knowledge transfer for service has been completed, employment becomes less of an issue, though it is still important in the context of being a good employer.[48]

Senior managers are always closely involved during contract negotiations. Nevertheless, their main focus is the continuity of their business and on making sure that the business case for the outsourcing decision will be realised. Therefore, it is important to communicate regularly and meticulously about the progress of the transition project. Senior managers are important stakeholders, and their expectations must be managed carefully.[49] Dependencies in parallel transitions make this critical success factor even more important.

7.4 Objectives of contracting

The most important aim of a contract is detailing the agreements made between contracting parties. These agreements include descriptions of the services to be delivered, service levels and prices. Many context aspects are also included, such as liabilities, contract termination conditions, contract term and IP rights. Thus, contracts give both the outsourcing organisation and the supplier control over the partnership, which is important to ensure service delivery continuity.

Contracts should also provide the parties involved with mechanisms to change provisions in the contract. Such changes over the term of the contract may be necessary when the business management of one or more of the parties is replaced, or when unforeseen technological innovations occur. By including clauses on how to make changes to the contract, parties are provided with a common context for making contractual changes when needed.

Contracts also include mechanisms to enforce the commitments detailed in the contract. Outsourcing organisations and suppliers are aware that their partner may go to court in case of default. Awareness related to this option is generally sufficient to ensure that the parties deliver in accordance with their contractual commitments. Contracts are important in enabling governance in IT outsourcing partnerships.

7.5 Contract structure

Typically, traditional IT outsourcing contracts are drawn up on three levels: strategic, tactical and operational. These are illustrated in Figure 7.3. At the strategic level, there are framework agreements and transfer agreements; at the tactical level, service agreements, project agreements and secondment agreements; and at the operational level, SLAs and secondment contracts. In small-scale partnerships, the tactical and operational levels are frequently merged into one; these are also the two levels represented in supplier's service portfolios. The framework agreements define overall issues, such as liabilities, jurisdiction, payment terms, fee structures and the applied indexes. Liabilities should not be overlooked in contract negotiations.[50] A more complete overview of the major topics involved is presented in Table 7.3.

Transfer agreements are on the same level as the framework agreement. The transfer agreement formalises the transfer of the former's IT department staff, assets and service contracts from the outsourcing organisation to the

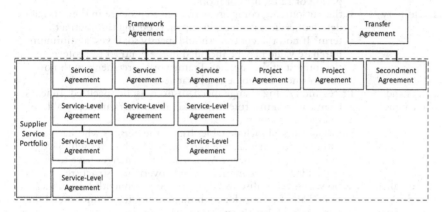

Figure 7.3 Contract structures for IT outsourcing partnerships.

Table 7.3 Major topics included in framework agreements (based on Beulen,[a] updated for third edition of this book)

Topic	Explanation
Objectives	The parties define the partnership objectives. Typically, the objectives are linked to the business strategy, the IT strategy and the IT sourcing strategy of the outsourcing company.
IT services	The IT services to be delivered are described. Details, however, are left to lower-level contracts, such a service agreements and service-level agreements. This offers the opportunity to differentiate by business process/department and/or by country – e.g. not all desktops require 24/7 support, and only some applications require 99.99999% availability.
Contract period	Most contracts have an agreed-upon contract term, typically three to five years, sometime supplemented with unilateral options for the outsourcing company to extend the contract by 12 or 24 months. For the initial term of long-term contracts, a break option can also be agreed upon, as an example, instead of a five-year term, a three-year and two-year term. In this example, the outsourcing organisation has the unilateral right to terminate the contract after three years. Break options provide leverage of the outsourcing company over a supplier, but most suppliers only take into account the term prior to the break option in offering their pricing and terms and conditions.

(Continued)

Topic	Explanation
Contract period	The alternative is a contract with a period of notice; such permanent contracts are terminated only on the initiative of one of the parties. Termination by the supplier potentially jeopardised the business continuity for the outsourcing organisation. The termination risk can be covered by a notice period of 12 months or more.
Exclusivity	Is the outsourcing company permitted to procure in the contract-detailed services from other suppliers during the contract term? If not, the contract should specify so; if yes, a minimum purchase value may be included in the contract to protect the interest of the supplier. Framework agreements with no commitment are not a good practice.
Prices and changes	Prices and pricing change mechanisms must be specified. Indexes from national institutes or market researchers are acceptable change mechanisms.
	Contracts should include tables listing the persons who have the authority to make change agreements. Such tables will have to be updated regularly. Authorising the changes have to be embedded in the contract-agreed governance structure.
Governance and reporting	Who will meet to discuss what, and how frequently? Again, it should also be clear, for both the outsourcing company and the supplier, who has the authority to make decisions.
	The content and formats of service delivery reports should be agreed upon. IT service management tooling, such as ServiceNow and BMC, are instrumental in reporting on the performance as well as tracking issues in the service delivery.
Liabilities and damages	These subjects require careful agreements, including but not limited to maximum liability per occasion, for direct and consequential damage.
	Damages and how to deal them must also be defined. There are obligations for both parties, including immediately informing the other party and fully cooperating with the other party to minimise the impact of the occurrence and the associated damage.
Contract termination	Termination conditions must be agreed upon. It is advisable to stay close to current legal terminology, such as reasonableness and fairness, and to define these as concrete as possible.
	Clauses should be included on the possible termination consequences of ownership changes concerning one or more of the parties involved – for example, consequences for the outsourcing contract if business processes are sold to parties with other outsourcing relations.

a Beulen, E. (2002). *Uitbesteding van IT-dienstverlening* (pp. 58, 59). Den Haag: Ten Hagen & Stam (in Dutch).

supplier. Transfer agreements are therefore linked to framework agreements, but with a few important differences: transfer agreements concern a single transaction, whereas framework agreements cover the full contract term. Also, transfer agreements have no direct link to the service provisioning.

Below the strategic level of framework agreement and transfer agreements is the tactical level. The service agreements form the body of the contract and include descriptions of the services. These agreements are based on the suppliers' service portfolios describing the services offered by the suppliers. Portfolios enable the supplier to deliver their services in a flexible, cost-effective way. Deviating from the services offered in the portfolio jeopardises achieving these advantages.

Project and secondment agreements also belong to the tactical contract level. Since every project is unique, project agreements must be made for every individual project. Project agreements must include all specifications: milestones, conditions, resources allocated by the outsourcing organisation and the supplier. Secondment agreements are drawn up to enable outsourcing companies to use their supplier's resources against pre-agreed rates per hour, or alternatively per day. The secondment agreement also contains a well-defined list of functions, including minimum number of years of experience and minimal certification. Rates will be differentiated per country, and are potentially in local currency to cover both the outsourcing organisation and the supplier for the inflation risks. Also, updating the rates every 12 months is important, as typically pre-agreed indexes are used. These updates ensure competitive rates over the contract term.

Finally, at the operational contract level, there are SLAs. SLAs work out in detail of the requirements of service agreements with respect to the outsourced services: the levels at which these services are to be delivered (gold/silver/bronze). Here, similar to the tactical level, the service portfolio of the supplier provides guidance. Again, standardising service levels ensure economies of scale, resulting in cost-effective service provisioning.[51] Nowadays, IT service management tools are highly automated, and it is easy to set parameters in these IT service management tools.

7.6 Competitive pricing

Relationships between outsourcing organisations and suppliers will always contain a certain amount of tension. The outsourcing organisation's objective is to purchase their IT services as cost-efficiently as possible, but the suppliers' objective is to increase their profit margin on the delivered services. Both clients and suppliers tend to behave opportunistically when entering into a contract, and this can lead to mutual disadvantage.[52]

If outsourcing organisations push their suppliers too much on price, the business continuity of the suppliers is at stake. Also, outsourcing organisations have to understand that clients with the most favourable margins will be served first and best by suppliers. For low-margin contracts, typically suppliers will only deliver the services as detailed in the contract and do not go the extra mile. The level of flexibility that can be expected from suppliers which hold a low-margin contract is minimal. Coordination will in such circumstances require much more effort from the outsourcing company. This additional effort raises coordination costs and sometimes even endangers the partnership.

However, improving the effectiveness and efficiency of services always remains part of the supplier's responsibilities, and outsourcing organisations must specify this in the contracts.[20] Defining the fees for the full contract term saves significant coordination costs, as intermediate contract negotiations are not needed. That said, the outsourcing organisation and supplier have to agree on the anticipated efficiency profile. Competitive pricing can only be achieved if the contract period is 24 months or less. For longer IT outsourcing contracts, prices must be agreed for the first 12 months of the contract, followed by annual renegotiations. The renegotiations result in competitive prices, but the coordination costs involved are higher for both the outsourcing company and the supplier, due to annual renegotiations.

In practice, prices are often set for the entire contract period, with the option to benchmark them if one of the parties involved feels this is necessary. Benchmarking ensures competitive prices while keeping coordination costs down. However, benchmarking is not inexpensive either, since it requires the services of a third, independent benchmarking company, plus a lot of management attention from both parties. Such an arrangement stimulates the participants to reach an agreement by themselves, thus keeping costs low.[53] Sometimes, it can be difficult to establish competitive pricing even through a benchmark investigation.[20] For generic services such as desktop management, network management or mainframe processing, enough benchmarking data are available. However, some services are designed especially for the client, which means that there are few similar contracts available for benchmarking. Also, suppliers which apply financial engineering impact the feasibility to conduct a benchmark. Financial engineering can be related to including cost for salaries of transferred staff which are not competitive, hardware depreciations and amortisation of the transition costs in their fees. Doing so makes price calculations opaque. It is therefore better to include such costs in the transfer contracts and then charge net prices only for the services that can be tested against the market at any time. The benchmarking process is detailed in the below sub-paragraph.

7.6.1 Benchmarking

Benchmarking is a good mechanism to ensure competitive pricing over the contract term. A benchmarking clause allows both parties to involve an external benchmarking company to assess the prices agreed upon in the contract. Parties have to understand that involving an external benchmarking company is not only expensive – it also requires significant involvement of both parties to provide information to the external benchmarking company, as well as to discuss the outcome of the benchmarking engagement. Instead of actually involving the external benchmarking company, both parties can also mutually agree on an adjustment of the pricing for the services. Having the option of calling in an external benchmarking company is beneficial for concluding on mutually agreed pricing adjustments.

In agreeing on benchmarking, a large number of aspects need to be agreed upon. This includes agreement on the first opportunity to exercise the benchmarking right. Typically, this is not earlier than 12 months after contract signing, nor no earlier than six months after the planned date for transition completion. Furthermore, the peer group used by the external benchmarking company needs to be defined in terms of characteristics, such as size, geography, sector and number in the benchmark-involved peer companies. The number typically ranges from four to a maximum of six peer companies, to avoid the database of the external benchmark company having insufficient peer companies. The benchmark data have to be recent, ideally 12 months or less, though up to 18 months is acceptable.

Furthermore, it is important if a benchmark has to be conducted over the entire contract scope or for specific services. For outsourcing organisations, the latter is preferred.

The implications of the benchmark report also need to be agreed upon – when must the pricing be adjusted? Typically, a 10% difference from the benchmark is acceptable, if the competitive pricing is 80th percentile (top quartile), unless the pricing is over 88th percentile, in which case the pricing has to be adjusted. Also, the timing of the adjustment has to be agreed upon; typically, contracts include applying the adjusted pricing per the start of the benchmark engagement and with no retrospective adjustment. A delicate point is whether suppliers have to be granted the right to terminate the contract if they are not willing or able to offer their services at competitive pricing.

In principle, suppliers should have this right to terminate the contract if they cannot commit to the price adjustment, but the outsourcing company should be allowed to hold them liable for their cost related to the contract termination. These liabilities have to be specified as a separate liability category in the contract. Also, there needs to be a provision in the contract that enables a smooth handover to a new supplier or to the internal IT department of the outsourcing company.

Also, the benchmarking frequency has to be agreed upon; typically, this is a 12-month period, which safeguards parties from high external costs and efforts. Finally, since the costs of the benchmarking have to be agreed upon, it is most reasonable that the supplier pays the external benchmarking company if their pricing was not competitive. The outsourcing organisation pays the external benchmarking company if the pricing was competitive. This incentivises both parties to agree on an adjustment of pricing without involving an external benchmarking company.

7.7 Completeness of contracts

To have a complete contract which covers all circumstances, issues and questions that may arise during its term is illusional.[35] Attempts to prepare for a complete contract will never be successful. It simply requires too much effort from both parties – if it is even actually possible to foresee every future scenario. Transaction cost theory provides guidelines to prepare for suitable IT outsourcing contracts which have not described every detail of the service provisioning.[54] The degree to which completeness is possible for IT outsourcing contracts depends on the following factors listed by the transaction cost theory: asset specificity, uncertainty and measurement and transaction frequency.[55]

In many outsourcing contracts, there is very little opportunity to incorporate detail. Typically, contract negotiations take place under significant time pressure. A good practice is to include procedures for dealing with changes not covered by the contract.[56] Contracts can be set up using the "liaison model,"[57] according to which a pre-agreed procedure is used as the starting point for formulating amendments to the contract – a contract change management clause. Another approach is based on the concept of "ex-post negotiations."[58] However, in many circumstances, the costs of renegotiating parts of the contract are very high.[59]

Another important issue to consider when assessing a contract's completeness is the extent to which it matches the requirements of the business. For this purpose, a so-called balanced scorecard may be used. Balanced scorecards should not contain technical details, but be business-oriented. These balanced score cards serve as a dashboard for senior management and stakeholders.

7.8 Flexibility and adaptability in IT outsourcing contracts

If the outsourcing organisation operated in dynamic markets, the challenges of incomplete contracts for both the outsourcing company and the supplier increase.[60] Dynamics can also be triggered by the endorsement of new business strategies by the outsourcing organisation and/or by technology innovations. Adjusting for technology innovations is the most straightforward adjustment, which can be captured in a "technology refresh" clause. This clause stipulates that suppliers are obliged to use the latest technologies available for the delivery of their services. This stipulation is predominantly linked to the version of software (latest version – X in Y months after release of the latest version) and amortisation period per device type (servers X months and desktops Y months). The commercial impact on the contract must be agreed between parties. This will be dealt with in the contract change process.[61] Typically, the outsourcing company has the option to cancel or postpone a technology upgrade. However, not upgrading the technology will have a commercial impact, especially if the assets are owned by the supplier. If the assets are owned by the supplier, the price for the service has to be deduced by the part of the fees attributed to the depreciation of the asset after the initial agreed period. For services that do not upgrade, the technology typically increases the fees, as the capabilities to provide the service over time become legacy capabilities and scares – consider mainframe computer capabilities.

As a consequence of these dynamics, contracts must be flexible and adaptable, which puts an even greater stress on the importance of contract management.[62] Formal controls in IT outsourcing contracts such as activity and capability controls are important.[63] Changes in the partnership's context necessitate "relational contracting."[64] This means that as well as formal contacts, informal conferencing is an important element in managing IT outsourcing partnerships. Furthermore, relational contracts for IT outsourcing innovation are detailed in the previous chapter (Section 6.4) and can also be applied to IT outsourcing.

7.9 Defining responsibilities in contact management

Nowadays, most IT outsourcing partnerships involve more than one supplier, i.e. multiple sourcing. Cost savings are still an important argument to outsource IT,[65] but access to capabilities is presently more important. This access is not limited to innovative capabilities. Outsourcing companies develop an IT sourcing strategy to ensure a fit-for-purpose supplier landscape. The supplier landscape will be developed along three dimensions: technology, geography and organisational unit (division/department). Typically, the IT sourcing strategy is based on a combination of these three dimensions.

If technology is the dominant dimension, suppliers will be selected by technology, such as desktop, network and server management, or application development and management. For globally operating outsourcing organisations, there are only a few suppliers which can globally provide services. Alternatively, second-tier suppliers set up partnerships in countries/regions where they have no presence. However, setting up partnerships increases the risk profile for both the outsourcing company and the supplier, as well as increases the coordination costs for the supplier.

If geography is the dominant dimension, the concerns related to the footprint of suppliers can be addressed better, second-tier suppliers can be considered as potential suppliers for one or multiple geographies. Enforcing competition for most outsourcing organisations, except for global blue chip outsourcing organisations, is more achievable in the geographical dimension than the technology dimension. The organisational unit dimension ensures supplier proximity to the outsourcing company. If needed, bespoke services can be delivered more easily than in the other dimensions. However, in this dimension, the outsourcing company does not fully benefit from potential economies of scale.

In addition to setting the right IT sourcing approach, thereby ensuring that the contracted IT service is delivered in accordance with the terms and conditions and agreed-upon service levels, penalties are an important tool for contract managers of outsourcing organisations. Although penalties decrease knowledge-sharing willingness and affective commitment, however, penalties increase effort-related commitment.[66]

It is important to agree on a cap for accumulated penalties over time. Typically, rolling 12-month periods are applied. The cap of the accumulated penalties must be 10% at a minimum and must not exceed 15% of the total fees for the rolling period. The mechanism to apply penalties has to be balanced. A mechanism that is too aggressive leaves outsourcing organisations empty-handed for the months of the rolling period remaining after the penalty cap has been hit.

Some IT outsourcing contracts include earn-back provisions. A supplier can compensate a breach of the service level by good performance for that service in the months after the missed service level. Earn-back provisions will incentivise suppliers to provide services in accordance with the agreed service levels.

Furthermore, parties might consider introducing a bonus for good performance. A bonus is only sensible if there is a business benefit over performance for the outsourcing organisation. This is mostly limited to projects, typically when functionality is made earlier than planned available to the outsourcing organisation, and is very rarely relevant for running IT services.

7.10 Contracting cloud

Contracting cloud services is distinctly different from contracting IT services. Both cloud services and IT services are based on the service portfolio of a supplier, but the ability to adjust cloud services ranges from limited to none at all. Cloud service providers' offerings are fully based on a 1:N delivery model. Cloud service providers have 100% standardised their offerings and optimised and automated their service provisioning fully. Standardisation also includes contractual terms. Any adjustment will jeopardise their business model. As a consequence, contracting cloud services is quite straightforward. Outsourcing organisations can decide to procure standard cloud services at the standard commercial conditions offered by the cloud supplier. Outsourcing organisations need to compare the offers of different cloud service providers and the bespoke offerings/proposals for IT services of suppliers. This comparison increases effort in comparing the alternative offerings of cloud service providers but reduces the time required, in case the outsourcing company decides in favour of cloud services, to contract the services. Also, the time required to manage cloud services is significantly lower than for IT services. The cloud service model is a pay-as-you-go model; as a consequence, the outsourcing company has full insight into their costs. Tooling supports outsourcing companies and also ensures cost control. The biggest challenge in cost control of cloud services is that cloud services can be invoked by (many) representatives of the outsourcing company. Setting authorisations for cloud services usages in the outsourcing organisation is essential. However, many organisations still struggle with implementing the authorisations. As a consequence, outsourcing organisations face unexpected cost overruns for their cloud services.

In the selection of cloud service providers, outsourcing companies must understand that switching from one cloud service provider to another service provider is still not straightforward. The compatibility in Infrastructure as a Service (IaaS) is improving but still problematic. Changing from one Platform as a Service (PaaS) to another is even worse. The Software as a Service (SaaS) platform is the most feasible cloud service for switching cloud providers, as only the data have to be migrated, and the Application Programming Interfaces (APIs) have to be adjusted. Outsourcing organisations must not underestimate the effort and associated costs and risks of switching cloud service providers. Despite this supplier lock-in, outsourcing organisations can trust the competitiveness in the continuously growing cloud services market. In order to be attractive for new clients and to expand their business with existing clients, cloud service providers have to offer competitive prices to their new and existing clients. However, especially in IaaS and PaaS, market dominance is watched closely by regulators worldwide.

Another aspect outsourcing organisation needs to be mindful of is continuous consolidation in the cloud service provider landscape. Large cloud service providers are acquiring systematically innovative niche cloud service providers and incorporating their innovations in their cloud service offerings. On the one hand, this is in the interest of outsourcing organisations, as cloud service providers enrich their service offerings and take care of the integration of this functionality. On the other hand, outsourcing organisations which contract with acquired niche cloud service providers are confronted with a new owner. This change of ownership also might have an impact on functionality and might require migration of data and adjustments of APIs, as well as have commercial implications. This acquisition strategy of the large cloud providers contributes to the reluctance of regulators with regard to market dominance.

7.11 Contract termination

In IT outsourcing, outsourcing organisations will terminate the contract at some point in time. After the termination, the services might be transferred to a new supplier or to the internal IT department. The latter is also called backsourcing. Outsourcing companies have to understand that by their initial decision to outsource the IT service, the knowledge related to the provisioning of the IT services is no longer available in their organisation. Rebuilding capabilities requires not only time but also management attention. The risk profile of backsourcing is higher than the risk profile for contracting with a new supplier.

To ensure a controlled contract termination, proper contractual provisions need to be in place from day one. The provisions must include "exit clauses" as well as "handover assistance clauses."[67] These clauses define the responsibilities of both parties, the primary aim being to guarantee service delivery continuity during the transfer. Also, commercial arrangements must be agreed upon in the contract. Typically, the supplier is compensated for their efforts in transition services. The transition services fees must be capped. The

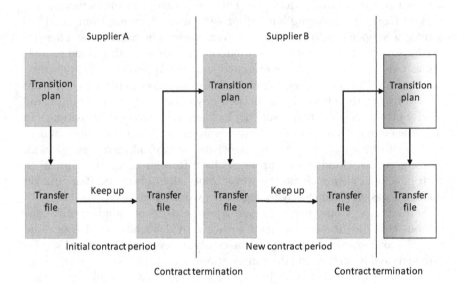

Figure 7.4 Transferring IT services delivery: transition plans and transfer files (Beulen, E. (2003). Lessons learned voor de beëindiging van uit bestedingscontracten. In van Bon, J. (Ed.), *IT beheerjaarboek 2003* (p. 154). Den Haag: Ten Hagen & Stam (in Dutch)).

supplier sets up a transfer file on the basis of the transition plan included in the contract (Figure 7.4). This file captures all the relevant aspects related to the contracted IT services. The supplier has the obligation to update this file over the contract term. To ensure the feasibly of an exit at any time, this file must be up to date at all times. Having an updated file is important, as exiting can be unpredictable. Exit can be initiated at any moment in time and can be related to contractual breach or be triggered by a specific contract termination provision. Outsourcing organisations have a unilateral right to excise the right to terminate the contract. Contractual breach includes severe and longitudinal missing of critical service levels and/or hitting the maximum cumulative penalty amount for missed service levels. Specific contract termination provisions are typically related to the financial position and the acquisitions or divestments of supplier.

7.12 Conclusions

Needless to say, transition projects enable a good start of the service delivery and require management attention of all parties. Parallel transitions are the norm. These complex transitions result in dependencies which must be managed carefully and jointly by the responsible suppliers and the outsourcing company.

Focusing on contracts is also important. A contract lays down the agreements made between the contracting parties. These agreements include descriptions of the services to be delivered, their service levels and pricing, along with the responsibilities and obligations of the contracting parties. Also, the contract structures have to match the partnership's context: the contract for a partnership with a limited scope and involving only one supplier will obviously be very different from global partnerships involving many suppliers. Typically, IT outsourcing contracts have three contract levels: strategic, tactical and operational. At the strategic level, there are framework agreements and transfer agreements, at the tactical level, service agreements, project agreements and secondment agreements and at the operational level, SLAs.

Whatever way any outsourcing contract comes to an end, both the outsourcing company and supplier must be prepared for the termination of the contract. Preparation begins prior to contract signing. The contract must include "exit clauses" and "handover assistance clauses." These clauses define the responsibilities of both parties and guarantee service delivery continuity during the transfer to either a new supplier or the internal IT department.

Appendix 7.1
Outsourcing contract clauses

Here, the contents of two kinds of contracts will be listed: those for service agreements and those for transfer agreements. Cloud suppliers have their bespoke contracts, which are cloud supplier-specific.

Service agreements

Preamble

The preamble to a contract defines the contract parties and their legal representatives. The names of the parties are given as registered by the Chamber of Commerce. The preamble also defines the objectives of the outsourcing organisation and the supplier.

Scope

The first clause of the contract contains descriptions of the services to be delivered by the supplier. These services must be described unambiguously. Full descriptions of the contracted services are typically moved to appendices. The description also includes an overview of those services; the outsourcing organisation will source from their own organisation or service, which will be delivered by other suppliers contracted by the outsourcing organisation.

The responsibility for any ongoing project transferred to the supplier must also be defined here. As part of due diligence, suppliers will audit the transferred project before accepting responsibility for completing the project.

Supplier preference

Two basic relationship types between outsourcing organisation and suppliers can be distinguished: preferred supplier and sole supplier relationships. Outsourcing contracts often include both types. Typically, the supplier is the sole supplier for the service defined in the contract, and the supplier is the preferred supplier for new services. The position of preferred supplier may be further defined as "first call," "last bid" or "first call and last bid." The latter of the three is the most favourable to the supplier, because it gives them a chance to revise their initial offer.

Performance reports and governance

The supplier has the obligation to report on the performance. Outsourcing agreements also require a strong governance structure. Thus, service levels and performances indicators, as well as the associated governance structure, need to be unambiguously described in the contract. For each governance meeting, the subjects to be discussed, the attending staff and the meeting frequency have to be defined in the contract. In most outsourcing relationships, governance meetings are structured on three organisational levels: strategic (typically twice per year), tactical (monthly) and operational (weekly) levels. Also, supplier performance reports provide input for the governance meetings.

Order of precedence

Outsourcing agreements include sub-agreements such as service agreements, service-level agreements, transition projects and project agreements. If staff or hardware and software are transferred from the outsourcing company to the supplier, transfer agreements must also be drawn up. The order of precedence for these contracts must be unambiguous. In many cases, transfer agreements prevail over service delivery agreements, as the transfer of staff, hardware and/or software is a precondition for the supplier to be able to deliver the contracted services. Service-level agreements and project agreements are of a lower precedence and are generally attached to service agreements.

Committed revenue

Some outsourcing contracts include revenue commitments. Often, such clauses are related to the risks the supplier takes by taking over staff from the outsourcing company. The revenue commitments typically reduce over the term of the contract. Revenue commitments are typically related to the IT spending agreed upon in the contract, not to IT spending related to contracted services.

Furthermore, committed revenue can be related to specific supplier investments for providing the contacted services to the outsourced organisation. Contracts will include a clear table, including the unamortised investments over time in order to enable a smooth process of contract changes.

Prices, benchmarking and payment

It is important to lay down unambiguously which service elements are included in contract price agreements. There are different pricing mechanisms, including price per unit, price bands and fixed prices. The clause must also define how the prices agreed upon are to be adapted during the contract period. Adaptation can be based on an annual indexation. In addition, benchmarking clauses can be added to the contract to ensure competitive pricing.

The third aspect to be laid down in this clause are payment terms. Typical payment terms range from 30 to 60 days. Some countries have strict regulations relating to maximum payment terms and the height of the interest percentage for late payment. The clause also needs to be clear about the impact of disputed invoices. It is a good practice that only the disputed amount of the invoice can be withheld.

Acceptance of deliverables and products

Apart from services, other products also may be delivered, such as software and hardware. In this clause, the moment of transfer from the supplier's ownership to that of the outsourcing company must be defined. It is reasonable to expect the outsourcing company to have completed the payment due before the property transfer takes effect. Payment does not lead to the waving of the rights of the outsourcing company. There might be a warranty applicable for the deliverables and/or products.

Data management and data retention

IT outsourcing relationships often involve the handling of business information on behalf of the outsourcing organisation. Parties need to agree on a data processing agreement. This details the obligations for both parties. These clauses are becoming very important due to increased regulations, such as GDPR and increased security treats. Often, suppliers need to certify their service delivery processes to meet contractual obligations.

Confidential information

The starting point is that all information is confidential, as well as the contact itself. For some information, the clause may include additional measures, such as penalties and contractual obligations, to safeguard the confidentiality of highly sensitive information.

Intellectual property

It is of essential importance to unambiguously define each of the contract parties' IP rights. In principle, rights reside with the supplier, unless the IP has been developed exclusively for the outsourcing company as well as developed at their costs. It is of course reasonable to prevent IP rights from threatening service delivery continuity, in case the outsourcing contract terminates. In case of contract termination, the supplier will have to make the IP available to the outsourcing company and their new supplier (internal or external), against reasonable costs. Typically, the IP is granted in the form of a licence to use, instead of transferring IP rights to the outsourcing organisation or their new supplier. Doing so enables suppliers to reuse their IP in delivering services to other clients.

Liability clauses

With respect to liability, a distinction must be made between direct and indirect damages. It is reasonable to include liability for direct damages in the contract. Such liability needs to be capped, prior to contract signing. Capping the liability ensures business continuity of the supplier; therefore, uncapped liability clauses should never be offered or be accepted. Often, the liability amount is capped at once or twice the annual contract fees.

Force majeure

Both parties may under certain circumstances claim force majeure, but this right may (by contract) be extended to their respective suppliers. Long-term force majeure may lead to contract termination. The consequences of contract termination must be defined clearly.

Early contract termination

Any service contract should include a limited list for contract termination, as well as of the consequences of such a termination. These consequences for the outsourcing organisation may differ widely: turnover compensation, profit compensation, cost refunds, etc. Likewise, the grounds for termination that are accepted as valid and their time horizons may also differ. Special circumstances, for instance, may cause the outsourcing organisation or the supplier to terminate the contract. Mergers and takeovers are among such circumstances, as are bankruptcy and the like.

Contract duration

The duration of the contract and the notification of termination (preferably by registered mail) must be detailed in the contract. Typically, the contract duration is three years or more. For outsourcing contracts for network services, the contracts will even be longer – five to ten years contract duration is not an exception.

Non-soliciting

None of the parties should recruit employees from the other party, since this puts service delivery and business continuity at risk. It is reasonable that this clause should continue in effect for a clearly defined period after the contract is terminated, which typically is set at six to twelve months.

Guarantees

Guarantees especially concern the software developed for the outsourcing organisation. Guarantee periods must be defined in this clause, which is typically three to twelve months. This clause is also defined as the acceptance procedure.

Disputes

Disputes should be handled at the appropriate management level, which are detailed in the governance section in the contract. Most of the disputes are settled between parties. When the dispute remains unresolved on the highest level, either arbitrage or judicial process remains as a next step. Either of the two has to be captured in the contract. Arbitrage is a cost-efficient and generally quick way to resolve the dispute. The applicable law and competent court are typically related to the country of the headquarters of the outsourcing company.

Transfer agreements

Preamble

The preamble to a contract defines the contract parties and their legal representatives. The names of the parties are given as they are registered by the Chamber of Commerce. The preamble also defines the objectives of the outsourcing company and their supplier. If the transfer involves employees, it is best to refer explicitly to the approval of the company's employee council. In some European countries, an employee transfer agreement must be explicitly linked to the service delivery agreement.

Assets and staff

This clause contains a list of the assets that are sold and/or staff and contracts and/or third-party contracts that are transferred by the outsourcing company to the supplier. This list must have been verified by the supplier's due diligence investigation. All assets must be physically labelled and the details of the transferred staff, including their labour conditions, have to be listed. Detailed lists are captured in appendices.

Price

The price of the transferred assets will be paid by the supplier to the outsourcing company. For the transfer of staff, the parties agree on the price for the transfer. This price can be either paid by the supplier, if the staff is competent, well trained and has a competitive salary. If the transferred staff has knowledge gaps or a compensation package which exceeds a competitive package, the outsourcing company will compensate the supplier. For both the transfer of the assets and the transfer of staff, these are typically one-off payments, due at contract signing date. By settling at contract signing, the assessment of the competitiveness of the service fees does not require a correction for charges related to the transfer of assets and/or staff.

Guarantees

The outsourcing organisation must safeguard their supplier from claims by third parties. Typically, this safeguarding is detailed in general protective clauses to cover taxes and social security costs, as well as specifics concerning the employees transferred (bonuses, pensions, holidays, homework, etc.). The supplier performs a due diligence on the assets and staff to be transferred prior to the signing of the transfer agreement.

Infringements

This clause lists the consequences of infringing on the guarantees made to one's partner. It is reasonable that the outsourcing company compensates for any infringements causing their supplier damage. Typically, these infringements are capped at an absolute amount, as it is the supplier that has conducted a due diligence prior to signing the contract.

Employees and working conditions

The contract should contain a list of activities, with detailed descriptions of the IT services that are to be delivered. Such a list will include estimates of the time needed per service per year. Formulated by the outsourcing company and checked and approved by the supplier in their due diligence investigation, the list is preferably included in the contract's appendices. The outsourcing organisation staff responsible for the execution of the listed activities will be transferred to the supplier. The transfer is detailed in a transfer protocol. This protocol records generic agreements concerning the transfer, as well as specific agreements made with the employees involved (on working hours, holidays and bonuses, for instance). Many countries include legislation related to the labour conditions for the transferred staff into the supplier organisation. These legal requirements may stipulate that the transferred staff's new employment conditions be at least equal to those of their former employer. This equality can be guaranteed by an employment condition comparison made in advance. When such a comparison is made, retirement conditions require extra attention, since these are typically not included in the legal equality requirements, even though they are a very important component of older employee's working conditions, in particular.

Third-party contracts

Transfer agreements should contain a list of relevant third-party contracts between the outsourcing company and third parties, not including the supplier, such as hardware maintenance and software licence contracts. If the list of novated contracts is extensive, it may be moved to the agreement's appendices; preferably, it is also included in the service agreement. If the contracts concerned are not transferred to the supplier, the management of the outsourcing organisation remains responsible. Novating contracts to a supplier requires a thorough investigation to assess if the contracts can be transferred to the supplier and/or are needed for the supplier to provide the contracted services.

Confidentiality

A transfer agreement is of another nature than a service agreement. The service agreement is a living document, which survives over the term of the contract. The transfer agreement is a transaction agreement which contains privacy-sensitive information and need be known only by the contract partners' senior managers. It is therefore advisable to keep transfer agreements confidential.

Disputes

Disputes should be handled on the appropriate management level, which are detailed in the governance clauses in the contract. Most of the disputes are settled between parties. When the dispute remains unresolved on the highest level, either arbitrage or judicial process have to be pursued. Arbitrage is a cost-efficient and generally quick way to resolve the dispute. The applicable law and competent court are typically related to the country of the headquarters of the outsourcing company.

Appendices

All lists – of assets, employees and contracts to be transferred – are best moved to appendices. This chapter should state clearly that such appendices are an integral element of the agreement.

Notes

1 See Lacity, M., & Hirschheim, R. (1995). *Beyond the information systems outsourcing bandwagon.* Chichester: Wiley & Sons; Saunders, C., Gebelt, M., & Hu, Q. (1997). Achieving success in information systems outsourcing. *California Management Review, 39*(2), 63–79; Cullen, S., & Willcocks, L. (2003). *Intelligent IT outsourcing, eight building blocks to success.* Oxford: Butterworth-Heinemann.
2 Whitten, D., & Wakefield, R. L. (2006). Measuring switching costs in IT outsourcing services. *The Journal of Strategic Information Systems, 15*(3), 219–248.
3 This paragraph is based on the paper 'Parallel transition in IT outsourcing' by Beulen, E., & Tiwari, V. (2010, March). Parallel transitions in IT outsourcing:

Making it happen. In Oshri, I., & Kotlarsky, J. (Eds.), *International workshop on global sourcing of information technology and business processes* (pp. 55–68). Berlin, Heidelberg: Springer and was subsequently published by Beulen, E., Tiwari, V., & Heck, E. (2011). Understanding transition performance during offshore it outsourcing. *Strategic Outsourcing: An International Journal*, 4(3), 204–227.

4 Cullen, S., and Willcocks, L. (2003). *Intelligent IT outsourcing, eight building blocks to success* (p. 151). Oxford: Butterworth-Heinemann.

5 See Gottschalk, P., & Solli-Saether, H. (2006). *Managing successful IT outsourcing relationships*. Hershey, PA: IRM Press; Tiwari, V. (2009). Transition during offshore outsourcing: A process model. In *ICIS 2009 Proceedings*, p. 33.

6 Beulen, E. J. J. (2008). Global Sourcing.

7 Williams, C., & Susanne Durst, S. (2019). Exploring the transition phase in offshore outsourcing: Decision-making amidst knowledge at risk. *Journal of Business Research*, *103*, 460–471.

8 Kotlarsky, J., Scarbrough, H., & Oshri, I. (2014). Coordinating expertise across knowledge boundaries in offshore-outsourcing projects: The role of codification. *MIS Quarterly: Management Information Systems*, *38*(2), 607–627.

9 Krancher, O., & Dibbern, J. (2020). Knowledge transfer in software maintenance outsourcing: The key roles of software knowledge and guided learning tasks. In Beulen, E., & Ribbers, P. (Eds.), *Information systems outsourcing* (pp. 147–181). Cham: Springer.

10 Ross, C., Pohlmann, T., & Ester, O. (2005). Confronting outsourcing myths. *Forrester Research Report*, December 13.

11 Lacity, M., & Willcocks, L. (2000). IT outsourcing relationships: A stakeholder perspective. In Zmud, R. (Ed.), *Framing the domains of IT management research. Glimpsing the future through the past* (p. 23). New York: Jossey Bass.

12 Tiwari, V. (2009). Transition during offshore outsourcing: A process model. In *ICIS 2009 Proceedings* (p. 33).

13 Carmel, E., & Tjia, P. (2005). *Offshoring information technology sourcing and outsourcing to a global workforce*. Cambridge: Cambridge University Press.

14 Szulanski, G. (1996). Exploring internal stickiness: Impediments to the transfer of best practice within the firm. *Strategic Management Journal*, *17*, 27–43.

15 See Cohen, M. D., & Bacdayan, P. (1994). Organisational routines are stored as procedural memory: Evidence from a laboratory study. *Organisational Science*, *5*(4), 554–568; Cyert and March (1963). See Cyert, R., & March, J. (1963). *A behavioral theory of the firm*. Bergen County, NJ: Englewood Cliffs.

16 Chua, A. L., & Pan, S. L. (2008). Knowledge transfer and organizational learning in IS offshore sourcing. *Omega*, *36*(2), 267–281.

17 Feeny, D., & Willcocks, L. (1998). Core IS capabilities for exploiting information technology. *Sloan Management Review*, *39*(3), 9–21.

18 Oshri, I., Kotlarsky, J., & Willcocks, L. (2007). Managing dispersed expertise in IT offshore outsourcing. *Management Information Systems Quarterly Executive*, *16*(2), 53–65.

19 Williams, C. (2007). Transfer in context: Replication and adaptation in knowledge transfer. *Strategic Management Journal*, *28*(9, September), 867–889.

20 Lacity, M., & Willcocks, L. (2000). IT outsourcing relationships: A stakeholder perspective. In Zmud, R. (Ed.), *Framing the domains of IT management research. Glimpsing the future through the past* (pp. 355–384). New York: Jossey Bass.

21 Cullen, S., & Willcocks, L. (2003). *Intelligent IT outsourcing, eight building blocks to success*. Oxford: Butterworth-Heinemann.

22 McGowan Poole, C. D. (2019). It outsourcing, knowledge transfer and project transition phases. *Vine Journal of Information and Knowledge Management Systems*, *50*(2), 219–246.

23 Currie, W., & Willcocks, L. (1998). Analysing four types of IT-outsourcing decisions in the context of scale, client/server, interdependency and risk mitigation. *Information Systems Journal, 8*(2), 119–143.

24 See Ward, J., & Peppard, J. (2002). *Strategic planning for information systems* (3rd ed.). Chichester: John Wiley & Sons; Jeffery, M., & Leliveld, I. (2004). Best practices in IT portfolio management. *MIT Sloan Management Review, 45*(3), 41–49; Cullen, S., Seddon, P. B., & Willcocks, L. P. (2005). IT outsourcing configuration: Research into defining and designing outsourcing arrangements. *The Journal of Strategic Information Systems, 14*(4), 357–387; Harries, S., & Harrison, P. (2009). IT value: The challenges of implementing portfolio management. *Information Systems Control Journal, 1*, 22–25.

25 Levina, N., & Su, N. (2008). Global multisourcing strategy: The emergence of a supplier portfolio in service offshoring. *Decision Sciences, 39*(3, August), 541–570.

26 See Cohen, L., & Young, A. (2005). *Multisourcing: Moving beyond outsourcing to achieve growth and agility.* Boston: Harvard Business School Press; Sharma, A. (2009). Challenges with multi-sourcing. *IDC report*, # AU22120RQ, January.

27 Maltus, R. (2009). Understanding outsourcing evaluation, selection and transition costs to lower risk. *Gartner research note*, G00167572, May 11.

28 Ridder, F. (2009). How to achieve efficient and effective multisourcing? *Gartner research note*, G00168520, June 23.

29 See Walden, E. (2005). Intellectual property rights and cannibalization in information technology outsourcing contracts. *Management Information Systems Quarterly, 29*(4), 699–720; Qiu, L. (2006). A general equilibrium analysis of software development: Implications of copyright protection and contract enforcement. *European Economic Review, 50*(10), 1661–1682; Sharma, A. (2009). Challenges with multi-sourcing. *IDC report*, # AU22120RQ, January.

30 IS is the abbreviation of Information Systems. In this book, the authors do not differentiate between IS and Information Technology (IT).

31 Blumenberg, S., Wagner, H. T., & Beimborn, D. (2009). Knowledge transfer processes in IT outsourcing relationships and their impact on shared knowledge and outsourcing performance. *International Journal of Information Management, 29*(5), 342–352.

32 Lin, M., Chau, M., Cao, J., & Nunamaker, Jr., J. F. (2005). Automated video segmentation for lecture videos: A linguistics-based approach. *International Journal of Technology and Human Interaction, 1*(2), 27–45.

33 See Heiden, G. van der, & Maurer, W. (2009). Defining operating-level agreements to enhance performance when outsourcing. *Gartner research report*, G00163282, August 10; Pultz, J., Scott, D., Cappuccio, D., Coyle, D., & Adams, P. (2009). Recommendations from IT I&O leaders workshop. Gartner publication, *G00166045*, April 16.

34 Wareham, J., Bjørn-Andersen, N., & Neergaard, P. (1998). Reinterpreting the demise of hierarchy: A case study in information technology, empowerment and incomplete contracts. *Information Systems Journal, 8*(4), 257–272.

35 Beulen, E., & Ribbers, P. (2003). IT outsourcing contracts: Practical implications of the incomplete contract theory. In *Proceedings HICSS-36 Conference*, Hawaii. New York: IEEE, 0–7695–1874–5/03.

36 Tirole, J. (1989). *The industry of organisations.* Cambridge MA: MIT Press.

37 See Weill, P., & Ross, J. (2004). *IT governance, how top performers manage IT decision rights for superior results.* Boston MA: Harvard Business School Press; Hirschheim, R., Heinzl, A., & Dibbern, J. (2006). *Information systems outsourcing, enduring themes, new perspectives and global challenges* (2nd ed.). Berlin: Springer-Verlag.

38 Payne, J. (1995). Managing of multiple simultaneous projects: A state of the art review. *International Journal of Project Management, 13*(3), 163–168.

39 Levy, N., & Globerson, S. (1997). *Improving multi-project management by using a queuing theory approach* (pp. 40–46). Philadelphia, PA: Project Management Institute.

40 See Carmel, E. (1999). *Global software teams: Collaborating across borders and time zones.* Hoboken, NJ: Prentice Hall; van Fenema, P. (2002). *Coordination and control of globally distributed software projects* (No. EPS-2002–019-LIS).

41 Beulen, E. (2012). I'm working while they're sleeping: time zone separation challenges and solutions. *Strategic Outsourcing: An International Journal, 5*(1), 89–93.

42 Lucier, C., & Torsiliera, J. (1997). Why knowledge programmes fail. *Strategy and Business, 4,* 14–28.

43 Ruggles, R. (1998). The state of the notion: Knowledge management in practice. *California Management Review, 40*(3), 80–89.

44 Mähring (2002); Choudhary and Sabherwal (2003). See Carmel, E. (1999). *Global software teams: Collaborating across borders and time zones.* Hoboken, NJ: Prentice Hall; Lacity, M., & Willcocks, L. (2000). IT outsourcing relationships: A stakeholder perspective. In Zmud, R. (Ed.), *Framing the domains of IT management research. Glimpsing the future through the past.* New York: Jossey Bass; Mähring, M. (2002). IT project governance: A process-oriented study of organizational control and executive involvement. *SSE/EFI Working Paper Series in Business Administration* (p. 15); Choudhury, V., & Sabherwal, R. (2003). Portfolio of control in outsourced software development projects. *Information Systems Research, 14*(3), 291–314.

45 See Kern, T., & Willcocks, L. (2000). Exploring information technology outsourcing relationships: Theory and practice. *The Journal of Strategic Information Systems, 9*(4), 321–350; Cullen, S., & Willcocks, L. (2003). *Intelligent IT outsourcing, eight building blocks to success.* Oxford: Butterworth-Heinemann; Sparrow, E. (2003). *Successful IT outsourcing: From choosing a provider to managing the project.* London: Springer.

46 See Cullen, S., & Willcocks, L. (2003). *Intelligent IT outsourcing, eight building blocks to success.* Oxford: Butterworth-Heinemann; Sparrow, E. (2003). *Successful IT outsourcing: From choosing a provider to managing the project.* London: Springer; Carmel, E., & Beulen, E. (2005). Managing the offshore transition. In Carmel, E., & Tjia, P. (Eds.), *Offshoring information technology sourcing and outsourcing to a global workforce.* Cambridge: Cambridge University Press.

47 See Cullen, S., & Willcocks, L. (2003). *Intelligent IT outsourcing, eight building blocks to success.* Oxford: Butterworth-Heinemann; Sparrow, E. (2003). *Successful IT outsourcing: From choosing a provider to managing the project.* London: Springer.

48 See for further reading on knowledge transfer on an individual level Thakurta, R., Urbach, N., & Basu, A. (2018). Understanding technology transition at the individual level. *Pacific Asia Journal of the Association for Information Systems, 10*(3), 2.

49 See Lacity, M., & Rottman, J. (2008). *Offshore outsourcing of IT work: Client and supplier perspectives.* New York: Palgrave Macmillan; Carmel, E., & Tjia, P. (2005). *Offshoring information technology sourcing and outsourcing to a global workforce.* Cambridge: Cambridge University Press; Cullen, S., & Willcocks, L. (2003). *Intelligent IT outsourcing, eight building blocks to success.* Oxford: Butterworth-Heinemann.

50 Burden, K. (2006). Indemnities in IT and outsourcing contracts. *The Computer Law and Security Report, 22*(1), 68–72.

51 See Goo, J., Kishore, R., Nam, K., Rao, H. R., & Song, Y. (2007). An investigation of factors that influence the duration of IT outsourcing relationships. *Decision Support Systems, 42*(4), 2107–2125; Paschke, A., & Bichler, M. (2008). Knowledge representation concepts for automated SLA management. *Decision Support Systems, 46,* 1(12), 187–205.

52 Aubert, B., Patry, M., & Rivard, S. (2003). A tale of two outsourcing contracts: An agency-theoretical perspective. *Wirtschaftsinformatik, 45*(2), 181–190, 183.

53 Aubert, B., Patry, M., & Rivard, S. (2003). A tale of two outsourcing contracts: An agency-theoretical perspective. *Wirtschaftsinformatik, 45*(2), 181–190.

54 Klepper, R. (1995). The management of partnering development in I/S outsourcing. *Journal of Technology, 10*(4), 249–258.

55 See Coase, R. (1937). The nature of the firm. *Economica, 4,* 386–405; Williamson, O. (1975). *Markets and hierarchies.* New York: The Free Press; Aubert, B., Rivard, S., & Patry, M. (1996). A transaction cost approach to outsourcing behaviour: Some empirical evidence. *Information & Management, 30*(2), 51–64.

56 Gietzmann, M. (1996). Incomplete contracts and the make or buy decision: Governance design and attainable flexibility. *Accounting, Organisation and Society, 21*(6), 611–626.

57 Burnett, R. (1998). *Outsourcing IT – the legal aspects.* Aldershot: Gower.

58 See Hart, O. (1995). *Contracts and financial structure.* Oxford: Oxford University Press; Segal, I. (1999). Complexity and renegotiation: A foundation for incomplete contracts. *Review of Economic Studies, 66*(226), 57–82.

59 Parkhe, A. (1993). Strategic alliances structuring: A game theoretic and transaction cost examination of interfirm cooperation. *Academy of Management Journal, 4,* 794–829.

60 Shepherd, A. (1999). Outsourcing IT in a changing world. *European Management Journal, 17*(1), 64–84.

61 Turner, M., Smith, A., & Smith, H. (2002). IT outsourcing: The challenge of changing technology in IT outsourcing agreements. *The Computer Law and Security Report, 18*(3), 181–186.

62 Lacity, M., & Willcocks, L. (2003). IT sourcing reflections: Lessons for customers and suppliers. *Wirtschafsinformatik, 45*(2), 115–125.

63 Langer, N., & Mani, D. (2018). Impact of formal controls on client satisfaction and profitability in strategic outsourcing contracts. *Journal of Management Information Systems, 35*(4), 998–1030.

64 Kern, T., & Willcocks, L. (2000). Exploring information technology outsourcing relationships: Theory and practice. *The Journal of Strategic Information Systems, 9*(4), 321–350.

65 Lacity, M., & Willcocks, L. (1998). An empirical investigation of information technology sourcing practices: Lessons from experience. *Management Information Systems Quarterly, 22*(3), 363–408.

66 Fehrenbacher, D. D., & Wiener, M. (2019). The dual role of penalty: The effects of it outsourcing contract framing on knowledge-sharing willingness and commitment. *Decision Support Systems, 121,* 62–71.

67 See Shepherd, A. (1999). Outsourcing IT in a changing world. *European Management Journal, 17*(1), 64–84; Cullen, S., & Willcocks, L. (2003). *Intelligent IT outsourcing, eight building blocks to success* (p. 151). Oxford: Butterworth-Heinemann.

8 Governance of IT outsourcing

The increasingly dominant influence of IT services results in a growing importance of IT governance. IT governance frameworks such as COBIT, ISO17799/ISO27001, ITIL, ISO/IEC 20000 and CMMi provide support for suppliers setting up IT governance structures. Besides formal governance mechanisms, the factor "trust" plays an important role. Governing complex client/supplier relationships requires critical structures and processes. How do contracts and trust relate? What applies – "the presence of good trust reduces the importance of contracts," or "trust is fine but good control is better"? Organisations increasingly function in networks and ecosystems. IT outsourcing in the context of a business ecosystem impacts the required co-ordination effort.

8.1 Introduction

Corporate governance has been an important subject of discussion and research for decades.[1,2] Recently, the interest in IT governance, which may be considered a special kind of corporate governance, is also growing. The relation between the two will be discussed in Section 8.2. IT governance is the implementation of enterprise governance for IT by the outsourcing organisation and will be defined in Section 8.3. Suppliers and outsourcing organisations are obviously both responsible for ensuring good IT governance; nevertheless, it is the outsourcing organisation which retains final responsibility. Several frameworks, some of them developed especially for the purpose of IT governance, will be discussed in Section 8.4: COBIT, ISO17799/ ISO27001, ITIL/BS15000 and CMMi. Such frameworks help outsourcing organisations and suppliers set up their IT governance structure and processes. This section ends with an overview of the steadily growing number of laws and regulations concerning IT governance. Achieving good governance is not just a matter of formal rules; good interpersonal relationships and trust are equally important. Section 8.5 presents a discussion on the impact of trust, which continues in Section 8.6 with a discussion on relational governance.

Section 8.7 analyses the necessary structures and processes to adequately govern complex outsourcing relations. Little research has been done on

DOI: 10.4324/9781003223788-8

governance in the face of change and uncertainty. Section 8.8 considers the impact of a dynamic/turbulent environment on business governance. For this, let's look for a basis in theory and discuss developments in practice.

This discussion continues in Section 8.9 with an analysis of how formal contracts and relational governance relate to each other: are they mutually exclusive or mutually supportive? The chapter concludes in Section 8.10 with a discussion of governance of IT outsourcing within the context of a business ecosystem. Section 8.11 closes with a conclusion.

8.2 Corporate governance versus IT governance

Corporate governance may be defined as the organisational expression of the company's business objectives, a structure that therefore includes the means of attaining those objectives as well as guidelines for performance monitoring. Good corporate governance provides incentives for the company's board and managers to pursue objectives that are in its own and its stakeholders' interests. It therefore also facilitates effective monitoring, thus encouraging companies to use their resources more efficiently.[3] An important goal of corporate governance is to prevent conflicts of interest between the company's employees (including its managers) and its stockholders.[4,5] It is, therefore, a subject that remains important.[6,7]

To set up a properly functioning corporate governance structure, the integrated enterprise risk management (ERM) framework, developed by the Committee of Sponsoring Organisations of the Treadway Commission (COSO),[8] may be used. This framework describes the essential concepts, principles and components of ERM and it applies to all organisations, regardless of size. In a world of heightened concern and with many people focusing on risk management, the framework provides boards of directors as well as managers with a clear roadmap for identifying risks, avoiding pitfalls and seizing opportunities to grow stakeholder value. To this end, the framework consists of a process that is implemented by the organisation's Board of Directors, managers and other personnel, and that is applied in strategy setting for the whole of the enterprise. It is designed to enable the organisation's staff to identify potential events that may affect the organisation, to manage the risks involved such that they remain within the limits of its risk appetite, and to provide reasonable assurance regarding the achievement of the organisation's objectives (see www.coso.org).

IT governance may be considered a special kind of corporate governance which should be embedded in corporate governance.[7] Its importance increases because IT services are becoming more dominant and because IT services and business management are increasingly integrated. In order to set up a good IT governance structure, it must be well anchored in the organisation's corporate governance set-up. According to the strategic alignment model,[9,10] this connection should be achieved on the strategic organisational level.

The question of how large organisations manage the complexity from global business operations and IT infrastructures remains one of the most pressing issues facing management. Traditionally, research on IT governance has focused on the design of decision-making structures for the control of IT.[11] Most of this literature about how to organise IT focused on choices between centralisation, decentralisation and federal models.

These studies indicate that a federal IT governance structure, i.e. a hybrid design of centralised infrastructure control and decentralised application control, is the dominant model in many contemporary enterprises. However, in current hypercompetitive environments and with the emergence of new electronic network organisations, the classical hierarchical design of IT governance becomes obsolete and inadequate to deal with the information-processing and coordination demands posed.[11] Later, the focus shifted to coordination, by introducing the issues of relational architectures and integration architectures as building blocks for the organising logic for IT activities.[11] The governance problem is pertinent when IT and its department form a legal part of the (business) organisation, and it is even more complex when IT is largely outsourced to one or more suppliers. The latest development in IT governance is the recognition of the importance of accountability. Financial scandals have caused authorities to issue stricter laws and regulations. A well-known example of the latter is the Sarbanes Oxley Act (USA, 2002). Governance of IT outsourcing relationships has to result in realising the mutually set goals of the relationship. This situation differs from insourcing and as a result is more complex, as there is no common hierarchy (the companies are legally and economically independent of each other), and their respective goals may not be aligned. An example of the latter is the cost-saving goal of the outsourcing organisations versus the return-on-investment goal of the suppliers. IT outsourcing partnerships involve an allocation of responsibilities to either the supplier or the outsourcing organisation. This split of course also influences IT governance, even though this always remains the outsourcing organisation's responsibility. Outsourcing organisations should ensure that their outsourcing contracts contribute to the realisation of their IT governance objectives.

In fact, one might say that meeting the outsourcing organisation's IT governance objectives is just one more of the requirements that suppliers must meet and that outsourcing organisation must therefore monitor. This monitoring is the task of the outsourcing organisation's Information Management. Naturally, if the outsourcing organisation's IT services are insourced rather than outsourced, this responsibility remains, but in such circumstances, it concerns the outsourcing organisation's internal IT department rather than an external supplier. Because of the link between corporate and IT governance, outsourcing organisations outsourcing their IT services to partners must give their suppliers insight into their corporate governance structure. Doing so requires trust. In reality, few companies like sharing such information with outsiders, so the increasingly strong link between corporate and IT governance effectively renders IT outsourcing partnerships less attractive. At the very least, IT governance requires the partners to set up extra organisational structures and processes, in order to realise a good alignment between the business and IT.

8.3 IT governance definitions

Many definitions of IT governance have been presented (see Table 8.1). As the demands made on outsourcing organisations changed, so did these definitions. The most important of them will be briefly discussed here. At first, only the locus of IT decision-making in the organisation was included.[12] Then, decision-making processes were added[11]: which IT decisions should the outsourcing organisation's IT and business managers take, and which priorities should they define? The next addition was that the return on their

Table 8.1 Definitions of IT governance

Researchers	IT governance definition
Brown and Magill (1994)	IT governance describes the locus of responsibility for IT functions.
Luftman (1996)	IT governance is the degree to which the authority for making IT decisions is defined and shared among management, and the processes managers in both IT and business organisations apply in setting IT priorities and the allocation of IT resources.
Sambamurthy and Zmud (1999)	IT governance refers to the patterns of authority for key IT activities.
Van Grembergen (2009)	IT governance is the organisational capacity by the board, executive management and IT management to control the formulation and implementation of IT strategy and in this way ensure the fusion of business and IT.
Weill and Vitale (2002)	IT governance describes a firm's overall process for sharing decision rights about IT and monitoring the performance of IT investments.
Schwarz and Hirschheim (2003)	IT governance consists of IT-related structures or architectures (and associated authority patterns), implemented to successfully accomplish (IT-imperative) activities in response to an enterprise's environment and strategic imperatives.
IT Governance Institute (2004)	IT governance is the responsibility of the Board of Directors and executive management. It is an integral part of enterprise governance and consists of the leadership and organisational structures and processes that ensure that the organisation's IT sustains and extends the organisation's strategies and objectives.
Weill and Ross (2004)	IT governance is specifying the decision rights and accountability framework to encourage desirable behaviour in using IT.
De Haes and Van Grembergen (2020)	Enterprise governance of IT, a concept that addresses the definition and implementation of processes, structures, and relational mechanism that enable both business and IT people to execute their responsibilities in support of business/IT alignment and the creation of value from IT-enabled business investments.

IT investments should be monitored.[13] It was then stressed that companies should ensure the organisational capacity to formulate and implement an IT strategy, in order to align IT and business.[9,14]

Meanwhile, two interesting observations were made. The first is that the set-up of a company's IT governance structure depends to a large degree on its environment, which means that there is no one way of doing it right. A more dynamic environment requires a more flexible IT governance structure, for example. The second observation concerns the importance of the IT organisation for the company.[15]

Finally, the importance of accountability was recognised.[16] In this area, laws and regulations clearly influence the way in which IT governance is implemented.

8.4 IT governance frameworks

In IT governance structures, several mechanisms may be distinguished: decision-making structures, alignment processes and communication approaches. In outsourcing situations, communication is of prime importance. After all, external suppliers are involved who, because of their greater distance to the outsourcing organisation's business management, are always behind with respect to the information they need to do their job well. Only good communication can provide them with this information.

To set up an IT governance structure, several frameworks are available: COBIT, ISO17799/ISO27001, ITIL, ISO/IEC 20000 and CMMi. These will now be discussed briefly.

8.4.1 COBIT

COBIT, or "control objectives for information and related technology," is an IT control framework first issued in 1996 by ISACA.[17] The latest release of the framework is COBIT 2019. The framework promotes process focus and process ownership. In COBIT 2019, there is a greater emphasis on security, risk management and governance. This emphasis is required for governing today's rapidly scalable multi-cloud environments. COBIT 2019 aims to re-shape this changed landscape.

8.4.2 ISO17799/ISO27001

British Standard 7799 (BS7799) was first formulated in 1995, and finalised in 1999. On the basis of this standard, ISO issued ISO 17799 in December 2000: the "information technology code of practice for information security management." Implementing this standard, which is meant for suppliers, requires substantial effort, as does maintaining it.[18] Nevertheless, it is a good standard with which to improve IT service delivery.[19] Since the rise of the Internet, extra attention is paid to security, which has further increased the need for a code of practice.

The standard is organised into ten major sections, each covering a different area: business continuity planning; system access control; system development and maintenance; physical and environmental security; compliance; personnel security; security organisation; computer and network management; asset classification; and control and security policy. For security, the ISO/IEC 27001 standard is the international standard on how to manage information security, initially published in 2005 and then revised in 2013.

8.4.3 ITIL and ISO/IEC 20000

The Information Technology Infrastructure Library (ITIL) was developed by the British Central Computer and Telecommunication Agency (CCTA). Since April 2001, it is distributed by another government agency, the Office of Government Commerce (OGC) (see www.ogc.gov.uk). ITIL consists of seven categories: managers, service support, service delivery, software support, networks, computer operations and environmental issues. Although it covers a number of areas, its main focus is on IT service management (ITSM). This, in turn, is subdivided into service support and service delivery, which together encompass ten disciplines that are responsible for the provision and management of effective IT services. Since 2019, there is a new release of ITIL, version 4. ITIL 4 includes an operating model for the delivery of tech-enabled products and services. ITIL 4 also supports new service management concepts for agile software development, DevOps and Lean. ITIL 4 is a framework for "service management" as opposed to "IT service management," including good service management practices in the business domain.

On the basis of ITIL, British Standard 15000 (BS15000) was developed (see www.bs15000.uk.org). This provides a certification programme for suppliers. Its formal part, BS15000–1 (which is the actual standard), consists of ten sections: scope, terms and definitions, requirements for a management system, planning and implementing service management, planning and implementing new or changed services, service delivery processes, relationship processes, resolution processes, control processes and release processes. BS15000–2 then consists of a code of practice, providing support to organisations that are to be audited against BS15000–1 or that are planning service improvements. The BS15000 was in 2005 replaced by the ISO/IEC 20000. The ISO/IEC 20000 is the first international standard for service management.

8.4.4 The Capability Maturity Model for integration

The Software Engineering Institute (SEI) is a federally funded research and development centre sponsored by the US Department of Defense and operated by the Carnegie Mellon University (see www.sei.cmu.edu/cmmi). In 2000, the Capability Maturity Model (CMM) was used to develop a model that focuses on integration: CMMi. It enables suppliers to improve the quality of their product and services development and maintenance processes (SEI

2002). The model consists of five maturity levels, each of which is coupled to several process areas; it also contains generic goals and practices (SEI 2002).

8.5 The impact of trust[20]

Trust between individuals and between organisations has become an important issue in management in general and Information Management in particular, as digital transformations further increasing the need to collaborate in organisations, with partners and suppliers. The existence of trust is an important condition for effective collaboration. As research also shows, the absence of trust can hardly be compensated for by formal agreements and rules. So, trust has to be worked on. In this section, first discussed is a definition of trust and the different levels of trust that exist. It is then stipulated that trust is a condition for the effective functioning of an organisation, i.e. for performance. The chapter will then go into the question of whether and how trust can be built up. Finally, this chapter will address the role and significance of trust in outsourcing relationships.

8.5.1 Trust defined

Trust plays a pivotal role in business and sustainable interpersonal relationships. Trust is essential in nearly all circumstances where human beings and/ or organisations are dependent on each other. High interdependence requires increased trust. Mutual trust is a precondition for interorganisational cooperation.[21] In particular, collaboration in the primary activities of the value chain requires sharing confidential planning information. Trust is a prerequisite for sharing. Also, collaboration between firms in product development constitutes a key strategic activity and will not happen without mutual trust. In the absence of trust, any collaboration is hindered. The collaboration includes shielding important information and setting up controls and procedures to protect the interests of the parties. In essence, trust is an important coordination mechanism.[22]

In business, trust can be defined as the expectation that the other (person or organisation) will behave in a mutually acceptable and predictable manner; also, explainability is becoming more and more important. This includes the expectation that neither party will take advantage of the other's vulnerabilities.[23] In a business environment[24] characterised by turbulence and complexity, sustainable joint competitive success is widely perceived as being dependent on the existence of trust between the parties commonly engaged in business. Handling turbulence requires swift and pro-active actions, which can only be developed if there is close to blind faith in the other. Equally, when facing complex managerial problems (e.g. in business and IT, in the context of digital transformations), no one has, nor can have, a full view on the situation at hand and potential future developments/scenarios. As a result, the views and opinions of those implicated in the problem situation should be trusted. Simon and March labelled the situation that occurs under these circumstances as "uncertainty absorption."[25]

Trust is a concept with many dimensions. Trust is based on the expectation that the parties concerned are competent, open, caring and reliable.[26,27] In case of interorganisational trust, e.g. between a supplier and the outsourcing organisation, trust also encompasses contractual trust.[23] Competence-based trust refers to the skills and capabilities of the other person or organisation in a specific domain, service or product: Is the other capable of doing what one says one will do? It is based on the perception that one can rely on activities, deliverables and processes performed by the other.

Openness-based trust is founded on perceived honest, morally sound behaviour by parties. Openness impacts the willingness to share information, insights and knowledge. Caring-based trust refers to the belief that the other party will support the other's interests. This goes beyond the basic expectation that the other will refrain from opportunistic behaviour by taking unfair advantage; the other party is also expected to be concerned that the other party's interests will not be damaged.[26]

Reliability-based trust refers to the expected consistency in behaviour, based on experience with and commitments and promises made by the business partner. Personal and not just organisational integrity and reliability are foundations for reliability trust within and between organisations.[28] However, the company culture of parties also contributes to this foundation. Finally, contractual trust refers to the question of whether the other party will carry out the contractual agreements.[24] The applicable jurisdiction is also important as this impacts the enforceability of the contractual commitments.

These trust dimensions also suggest a hierarchy.[23,29] Advanced levels of trust depend first and foremost on the existence of competence-based trust and, in interorganisational settings, also on contractual trust. If one of the parties proves not to be able to do and deliver what was promised or does not live up to one's contractual obligations, there is no basis for advanced levels of trust. However, next to competence, openness/transparency (demonstrating moral responsibility and positive intentions) is necessary for the other party to accept a potentially vulnerable position.[28]

For true business–IT partnerships, business trust in IT requires a foundation of proven competency and openness.[30] When occurring on an operational management level, the system availability competency and responsiveness to incidents as agreed is the dominant trust dimension. Similar for the tactical and strategic managerial levels, where the freedom for IT to act as a credible partner depends upon the ability to deliver the services and support the business objectives. On higher strata, the additional dimensions of trust, including caring and reliability, become more important. Next to organisational trust, person-based trust is a foundation for a true business–IT partnership. These conditions also apply to the business, seen from the perspective of IT, as trust is a relational concept. For the business–IT relationship to function well, it is pivotal that trust is reciprocal.

8.5.2 Trust improves business performance

There is a general belief that trust improves business performance. Let us understand how. First, trust reduces the coordination costs, as it is a coordination mechanism in and of itself. Trust reduces the need for extensive procedures and protocols, for negotiations to reach a mutually supported solution for specific problems as well as a reduced need to strictly monitor behaviour and its outcomes during the collaboration. Also, under conditions of change, all possible future contingencies need not be anticipated, because one can rely on fair and balanced adjustments and judgement when necessary. Second, trust is expected to contribute to joint innovation and learning. Under conditions of trust, unconstrained information and knowledge–sharing are possible, as the other(s) are not expected to use it for their own benefit at the expense of the one from whom the party received this information. In other words: no opportunistic behaviour!

8.5.3 Can trust be built?

According to a well-known and unfortunate saying, trust comes by foot and leaves by horse. Establishing trust takes time and is based on past experience of trustworthy behaviour. Apparently, losing trust goes faster. Although there is considerable disagreement among theorists whether trust can be built actively, it is, however, believed that an organisation can adopt and manage practices to promote and establish trust between parties.

The different dimensions of trust can be improved by a set of interdependent and mutually enforcing governance and policies. First, proven competency through past performance is a key condition for business and IT functions to gradually develop and establish reciprocal trust. The credibility of the other, in this respect, improves with competent behaviour through the course of time; it will be built by demonstrated capability in the past to solve problems, by interpersonal skills and by consistent professionalism.[28] Also, processes are important in enabling to build trust as they contribute to the performance and competencies of parties.

Performance not only relates to competent execution of responsibilities, but also to the ability to collaborate in open, caring, and reliable ways. This implies that both IT and business functions should be able to apply the right tools, dashboards and techniques to ensure the business gets the services that it needs. However, this is not enough. A good functioning of the informal organisation, through socialising and team development, has proven to be a prerequisite for a seamless collaboration.

Related to the latter is a second policy: open communication about goals, commitments and intentions. Communication has to take place regularly and planned for each level and must be embedded in organisational processes and procedures.

Third, various organisational measures can help overcome the barriers of differentiation and different mental models. They include promoting working in (joint) teams, encouraging collective training and learning experiences, job rotation, co-location, etc.[31] IT staff should develop a competent understanding of the (client) business side of IT, while business managers should understand how IT brings value to the business. The effects of (absence of) physical proximity should be well understood. For instance, having IT expertise concentrated in a shared service centre or distant service supplier is an impediment for effective communication and does not contribute to the establishment of trust. However, technology (such as video conferencing and collaboration tools) contributes to bridging the gap.

Finally, measuring is important. Organisations promoting trust should actively measure and monitor objectively the level of existing trust. Several consulting companies, such as Gartner, offer tools with which such measurements can be facilitated. These tools generally resemble balanced scorecards. An alternative formal tool is the Organisational Trust Index (OTI) developed by researchers at the University of Colorado.[32] It is based on the trust dimensions discussed above and assists managers in determining the level of existing trust in their organisations. Organisation can use the outcomes to implement additional measures such as boot camp sessions and/or replacing staff members.

8.5.4 *Trust in outsourcing relations*

In general, from a trust perspective, outsourcing forms a bigger challenge than in-house production and delivery. Companies have their own P&L statements and are driven by them. Opportunistic behaviour lurks behind every potential outsourcing agreement. Not everyone is equally honest. Some people or organisations try to exploit situations to their own advantage. Not everybody does, of course, and not all of the time. However, the problem is that some people or organisations do some of the time, and when one does business, it is difficult to distinguish between the honest and the dishonest. As a result, most transactions involve numerous inspections, controls, certifications and the like, even if the partner involved is considered perfectly trustworthy. Once the contract has been signed, the outsourcing organisation must ensure that the tasks being paid for are carried out in one's own best interests. The supplier, however, has a major information advantage, so these actions are difficult to assess from the outsourcing organisation side. Suppliers may boost their own profits, for example, by spending less time or utilise fewer resources than agreed. Monitoring is one way of countering this risk, but it is costly since one must set performance standards and measure the actual work performed or have it audited by an independent authority. Another method to combat this problem is to align the supplier's interests with those of the outsourcing company by introducing positive enforcement measures, such as incentive schemes, for example.[33]

The occurrence of opportunism will therefore increase costs. This is especially important when there are few potential partners. These partners will care less about their reputations, as there are few alternatives to which their clients may turn to if they are not satisfied. The fact is that outsourcing companies can never fully and accurately judge the quality of their potential suppliers, nor their true intentions. Therefore, it is important that they mitigate the risks involved in the selection stage by gathering as much independent information about their potential suppliers as possible. Sources for such information include market research and current and former clients, who are familiar with the supplier's track record, and sometimes independent authorities or institutes, who may carry out benchmarking activities.

A targeted policy aimed at promoting confidence in an outsourcing relationship comprises several components. Of primary importance is a mutually agreed method of transparent conflict resolution, whereby both parties view the decision process to be fair and just. This type of atmosphere supports feelings of fair treatment. Communication is a key in building trust, as two-way communication has been widely identified as a major contributing factor in trusting relationships. For example, suppliers must provide clear and understandable reports on the services they have delivered; outsourcing organisations should give clear feedback on their supplier's performance. Essentially, this is a matter of communication hygiene, and it applies to the parties' formal communication protocols. With respect to informal communication, trust may be generated through consultation prior to more formal discussion formats. In addition to trust between organisations and groups, trust must also be established between individuals. Both suppliers and outsourcing organisations must get a feel for which personal profiles best fit the management of their relationship, and staff in both organisations need to take the time to get to know each other. Trust also plays a role in reporting. Reports should not only concern the services delivered but the degree of trust between partners as well. It goes without saying that these measures also apply when IT service delivery is the responsibility of an internal department; however, as said before, outsourcing makes it more difficult.

8.6 The need for relational governance[20]

A general conclusion of the discussion in this chapter is that relationships are a foundation for strategic IT management.[29] Effective relationships are needed both within the organisation – between business functions and IT, and with external organisations, as far as IT services are outsourced. Relationships are critical to making the organisational machinery work properly; they are also necessary for the creation of an organisation-wide "shared view" and to jointly implement successful digital transformations. This "shared view" among business and IT functions concerns the direction into which the business ought to develop, and how IT should support or enable this. Relationships are needed at all planning levels:

- the strategic level, to establish the long-term view
- the tactical level, to assure the availability of the right IT services in the upcoming planning period

- the operational level, for solving problems in the actual service delivery
- between planning levels, to assure proper alignment between planning and operations

There is probably an inverse relationship between the planning level and the difficulty in establishing effective relationships: the lower the planning level, the more difficult it gets, and the more effort it requires. It is easier to achieve agreement among the members of a senior management team than among all concerned on an operational level.

Organisational relationships can be established by formal measures and structures.[34,35] There are different ways to establish organisational relations that do not mirror the established hierarchy. Cross-departmental horizontal and lateral direct contacts between managers jointly affected by a problem may be stimulated and should not be hindered by unnecessary procedures and regulations. If more frequent meetings and negotiations are necessary, this requires committees and task forces, with a formal charter and way of working. The responsibility to handle frequent communication between parts of the organisation may be assigned to specific liaison roles or departments. An example of this organisational form in European firms is the Information Management department that interfaces between business functions and IT. Special linking roles may facilitate communication, in particular between parts of the organisation that are highly differentiated in knowledge bases, cultures and environments. Again, in a European company, the CIO often acts as a managerial linking role between IT and the business functions.

Formal arrangements are a necessary condition for effective relationships; however, they are not sufficient.[36] On a person-to-person basis, open, participative and collaborative relationships are needed too. Without them, the organisation deteriorates to a malfunctioning machinery, with bad coordination and probably no shared views to be established. The so-called "relational mechanisms"[37] are instrumental in creating these conditions. Examples are offering the possibility of job rotation (IT staff working in the business units and vice versa), co-location (physically locating business and IT people close to each other), cross in company training, informal meetings between IT and business staff. Southern Californian Edison (SCE), a Californian Utility company, was known for these practices. They applied job rotation, e.g. IT management assuming the final responsibility for a part of the business, IT staff was forbidden to speak "IT-language" outside the IT department, etc. From this follows that when for efficiency reasons IT is organised in a shared service centre, additional complementary measures are needed to allow for better integration of business and IT and thus compensate for the additional "distance" created.

As argued extensively, trust is a "glue" that makes all of this work or, if, absent – distrust will function like "sand" in a complex machinery in delivering the services and even more in delivering digital transformations. The machinery slows down and in the end stops functioning. Already discussed were the foundations of trust between business and IT. The proposition that is taken here is that organisational trust, and in particular business-IT trust, should be an active management concern for the senior management team. Trust should be operationalised, objectives should be formulated, plans and actions should be in place to promote trust and finally trust should be measured on a regular basis. Decisions about who to place in particular positions should be also based on existing trust between the employees that have to work together. The composition of team, no matter on which level, is critical.

Good formal arrangements complemented by measures to support good person-to-person working relations, like mentioned above, are required for an effective business-IT relationship. This is true under conditions of change and uncertainty, as well as under more stable conditions. The external conditions do not make a difference here, as this book's authors have shown in earlier publications.[38] However, this being said, conditions of turbulence put much more stress on the relationship. There is need for mutually supported interpretations of (near) future uncertain events and their business and IT impact, and there is not much time to plan and organise.

Concluding "relational governance" is a senior management responsibility. Relational governance encompasses practice-based measures, as discussed, sanctioned by management to promote a desired collaborative organisational behaviour.

8.7 Critical structures and processes for governing complex client/supplier relationships[20]

Outsourcing IT creates relationships between the outsourcing organisation and suppliers. Making these relationships work is a critical condition for effective outsourcing. Already in 1995, McFarlan and Nolan recognised the problems created by a rapid-changing environment and suggested clients and their suppliers to form strategic partnership alliances.[39] This issue has become even bigger nowadays due to the rise of digital transformations. Outsourcing relations differ with respect to their complexity and therefore the management attention they need. Complex IT outsourcing relations obviously must be much more closely monitored than small IT projects or commodity services. Also, there is a relationship between the services needed and the sourcing types chosen, on the one hand, and the level of experience required for the relationship's management on the other.[40] Generally, the higher the degree of client-supplier interdependence and the more complex the IT services involved, the higher the level of experience needed.[41]

For successful outsourcing partnership relationships, it is critical that strategies, tactics and operations of outsourcing organisations and service suppliers are well aligned. Alignment requires governance, to be defined as conditions that must ensure that the right decisions are being made and executed.[42]

This book's research has yielded the identification of three interrelated factors that are critical for a successful IT outsourcing relationship: (1) a clear strategic positioning, (2) formal organisational arrangements that allow for adequate collaboration and (3) the presence of trust.

8.7.1 Clear strategic positioning

The business needs a clear vision on what it wants to accomplish with IT. Business strategies and IT strategies are closely related, and need to be integrated to enable digital transformation. Shaping the business and IT strategies is a matter of co-creation between business and IT and is an integral responsibility of the senior management team.

In the case of outsourcing of IT, the need for clear strategic positioning of both the outsourcing organisation and the suppliers is unanimously supported by the case studies. The outsourcing organisations should have a clear view with respect to their use of IT, IT services and role these play in their company. Clear IT strategies show service suppliers the direction in which their clients intend to move. Formulating this strategy remains the responsibility of the outsourcing organisation, and as such, is never a candidate for outsourcing. The contribution of the business, and in particular that of the CEO, is indispensable. Also, senior business managers should be highly involved in developing the IT strategy. The pressure to do so grows as IT services and business processes are becoming increasingly interdependent and intertwined. In the case of outsourcing parts of the IT operations, if the company cannot provide unambiguous requirements and/or has no clear IT strategy, many suppliers will react to a request for proposal with a no-bid response. On the other side, suppliers, both internal and external, must be able to show their clients and potential clients what IT services they can deliver and how. This is detailed in service catalogues and account plans. This includes their plans for the future, which form the basis of any business-IT partnership.

8.7.2 Formal organisational arrangements

Formal organisational arrangements and governance for managing and monitoring the IT (out)sourcing relationship are essential. These include structural provisions to support communication and collaboration between the outsourcing organisation and suppliers, such as the organisation and location of the IT functions, outlining clearly defined roles and responsibilities, and the diversity of IT/business committees needed to support the IT (out)sourcing relationship.[43]

Structural provisions are necessary on both sides of the relationship. Client organisations must adequately structure their Information Management function, which represents their demand management, service delivery and contract management and constitutes the interface between the business processes and the IT suppliers. The role of the Chief Information Officer (CIO) and the information managers is key in this regard. They are ultimately responsible for the company's IT strategy and the optimal use of the IT services delivered.

Information managers typically report to the CIO; their main responsibility is to ensure that the information needs of the business are met by the IT services provided. They form the link between the divisions/business units/ departments and their suppliers. Keeping internal and external IT suppliers on track is a challenging task and requires significant coordination, alignment and consultation, especially with regard to the delivery of diverse IT services by multiple service suppliers. Under conditions of change and turbulence, information managers have to contribute to the flexibility of services provided. The organisational embedding of information managers has to be adapted, so that hierarchically they report to business managers, while reporting functionally to the CIO. By being embedded in and maintaining close relationships with the business, they can react quickly and ensure adequate and up-to-date service delivery. However, success depends on communication skills and collaboration of the staff directly involved.

The IT suppliers, be it an internal department or external suppliers, have to carefully structure contract and account management (CAM), which operates as the counterpart of the Information Management function of the outsourcing organisation. It is important that outsourcing organisations and service suppliers can contact each other easily. Account management is about maintaining and building one's relationship with the client. The suppliers must build a network of relationships within the outsourcing organisation's organisation as well as staying ahead of the developments in their industry.[44] The suppliers' contract managers represent an additional major contact for the outsourcing organisation next to their dedicated account managers.

Contract management involves optimising the contractual agreements between supplier and outsourcing organisation. It also requires managing the IT professionals who execute the work and the resources/assets such as infrastructure and networks, as well as taking care of the administrative aspects of the relationship, including (service-level) reporting. As a result, suppliers have to make allowances for substantial costs involved in contract management.[45] These findings are supported by all the interviews. With respect to structuring CAM, all the experts interviewed agreed: "The structure of the CAM must mirror the structure of the outsourcing company." In all of the cases studied except for one, there is a mirrored structure with a consensus that this contributes to successfully managing IT outsourcing partnerships. In the exception case study, the CAM was part of a larger CAM organisation, which was responsible for a large number of complex IT outsourcing partnership contracts. This resulted in a relative limited attention from the CAM for this IT outsourcing partnership. This negatively impacted the relationship. As the responsible manager from the client said:

> The responsibilities for the CAM and the service delivery are embedded in one role. This results in possible conflicts of interest. The contract manager is responsible for customer satisfaction, and the service delivery manager [for] utilising the service delivery capabilities.

Another important point of attention for CAM is the continuity of personnel in CAM positions. Changeover results in discontinuity in the management of the partnership and endangers the continuity of service delivery and jeopardises trusts.

Organisational and governance arrangements also include a diversity of business/IT committees and coordinating roles to support communication and collaboration between the outsourcing organisation and suppliers at different levels. It is essential that senior managers of both suppliers and the outsourcing organisation can easily contact one another. This does not only relate to the CIO – the outsourcing organisation's business managers must also have an easy access to the suppliers' senior managers. As such, these organisational arrangements facilitate active participation, alignment and co-operation between stakeholders, a strategic dialogue and shared learnings.[43]

Planned and regular communication between the outsourcing organisation and the IT suppliers is essential in establishing flexible partnership relationships.[46] The communication structure of most is organised on three management levels. There is a steering committee at the strategic level, which includes senior management and IT management for the outsourcing organisation, and senior management and account management for the IT service supplier. Meetings typically take place once or twice a year. At a tactical level, there is a need for a monthly service review meeting to monitor overall ongoing performance and to anticipate the outsourcing organisation's future requirements/demand. Here, service supplier's performance is discussed on the basis of regular reporting and related to service-level management processes. At the operational level, daily discussions with the information managers concerning operational issues are taking place.

A key element in communication between suppliers and the outsourcing organisation is reporting. In order to track service delivery, the IT suppliers must report on a regular basis regarding the IT services delivered to the outsourcing organisation and the service level at which they were delivered.[45,47] Often, this requires monthly reporting.[48] Inadequate reporting will hinder the IT outsourcing relationship. Currently, integrate cloud service management tooling, such as ServiceNow and BMC, provide reporting across the entire IT landscape and include the service provisioning of all involved suppliers. The cloud tooling also enables the communication and collaboration between the outsourcing organisations and their suppliers as well as between suppliers. Reporting should not focus on technical details, but should inform business managers in business terms, such as balanced scorecards and dashboards.

8.7.3 Trust

As said before, and as a key theme of this section, managing the business–IT relationship is not a matter of the "hard side" only. Much attention must be paid to the "soft side," especially trust between the outsourcing organisation and their suppliers is of utmost importance. Such trust has to be created and maintained at all organisational levels as between the involved individuals. Open formal and informal communication through the structures discussed above is instrumental to this.

A purposeful organisational policy, which contributes to the creation of mutual trust, is establishing relational mechanisms at all levels.[49] The objective of relational mechanisms is to facilitate open two-way communication, active collaboration, alignment and knowledge-sharing. This may be achieved by measures like physically locating business and IT staff close to each other, cross-training about the value-adding role of IT in the business and informal meetings between business and IT management. Of course, this will challenge the "comfort zone" of all concerned. All these measures can only be effective if and only if they are actively endorsed by the senior management teams of both the client and the suppliers. They need to set the example. Again, the case of outsourcing is no different, only more difficult. Both outsourcing organisation and external suppliers have to actively assess how and what relational mechanisms can improve the collaboration on both organisational levels and the personal level.

While these measures are worth pursuing under all circumstances, they are especially required under dynamic environmental conditions, which impose flexible adaptation by both the outsourcing organisation and suppliers. Trust provides the glue for a flexible relationship between the organisations concerned, allowing them to sustain the relationship over the strategic planning horizon.[50]

8.8 Governing agile complex outsourcing organisation and supplier relationships[20]

Already discussed is how dynamics and uncertainty determine the functioning and management of an organisation. In particular, the need for the presence of dynamic capabilities was addressed. It is clear that this does not leave the design of governance unaffected either. Many of the governance frameworks assume a stable situation and do not address the question of how the need for change should be detected and implemented.

Agile IT governance is a relatively new research topic and, henceforth, not much literature can be found,[51] but there is growing interest for agile IT governance.[52] Vejseli et al. conducted research in the German, Swiss and Austrian banking industries on how emerging digital innovations are recognised and embedded in existing structures.[53] Using structures, processes and relational mechanisms as the foundation, their interviews with 33 top executives show that with regard to agile governance structure elements, process elements, and relational elements are mentioned. With regard to "structures," 13 banks mentioned the dimensions "digital transformation units," "short and flexible decision paths" and "interdisciplinary teams." Executives from 11 banks mentioned "lean project structures." Commonly, the creation of a digital transformation unit was also mentioned as a means of improving communication and collaboration. With respect to processes, agile practices are mentioned, such as scrum, design thinking and lean approach. The importance of fast and agile decision-making processes is recognised by respondents as important to be able to respond to unexpected events. With respect to relational mechanisms, external collaboration is mentioned. Internally, transformational leadership and transparent communication are particularly important. Ultimately, they arrive at the following effective agile IT governance mechanisms for agile organisations, as detailed in Table 8.2.

Not all management situations lend themselves to an agile approach. Stable market situations, clear expectations about what is expected (and the certainty of stability therein) and familiar work situations with clear specifications are among other conditions in which agility is not expected to work. In these, traditional management structures and processes will be more effective. However, almost all organisations must be able to deal with both situations simultaneously. In other words, organisations must be ambidextrous: they must have the ability to simultaneously perform two conflicting activities.[54] Literally, the term ambidextrous means "on both sides" (ambi) and "right-handed" (dextrous).

Ambidexterity in particular is increasingly important to the IT capability. Digitalisation is changing the way companies create and capture value and bring about innovation. Since IT is the foundation of digital transformations and innovations, a company's IT function plays an important role in supporting these digitisation initiatives. The IT function, that can sense relevant developments and act accordingly, is thus best suited to produce digital

Table 8.2 Most effective agile IT governance dimensions

	Most effective agile IT governance dimensions
Structures	Interdisciplinary and self-organised project teams
	Short and flexible decision path
	Project organisations with product owner
	Innovation lab
	Transformation board/innovative board
	Multidisciplinary transformation/innovation committee
Processes	Using agile practices (e.g. Scrum, DevOps, Design thinking)
	Trial-and-error processes
	Fast/agile decision-making processes
	Agile project and product management
	Change management processes
	Prototyping
	Co-creation workshops with clients
Relational mechanisms	Transformational leadership
	Open communication and participants
	Continuous employee training/cross-functional trainings on agile working
	Lean communication structures
	Empowerment of employees
	Management attention/management as example
	Cooperation and collaboration with start-ups
	Cooperation and collaboration with research partners

Source: Adapted from Vejseli et al., 2019.

innovation,[55] acting in close cooperation with the business functions, which are best placed to indicate where the added value of the innovation is the greatest.

The question is how to realise ambidexterity. Consulting firms are experimenting with various concepts. Gartner in particular is looking for the solution in the creation of two different organisational units: bi-modal IT.[56] They try to create space for innovation by setting up a group that can develop innovative IT initiatives and also has the necessary exploratory skills. This is Mode 2. The management of the existing IT environment is assigned to Mode 1, which continues to perform the basic functions of IT, delivering IT services in a predictable and reliable manner according to the wishes of the clients. In doing so, Mode 1 delivers the successful innovations to Mode 2.[57] The general aim is to increase innovation and the agility of IT service delivery.

According to the concept of fit,[58,59] the characteristics of an organisation should be aligned with each other and with its ultimate task.[60] Bi-modal IT helps to create units that are well-equipped for their specific task. Working on a stable platform and delivering services according to plan require different structures, culture, competences and management than working on successful innovations.

Bi-modal IT requires the shaping of IT services to be either agility-oriented or efficiency-oriented, thereby bringing new demands to an organisation's adoption strategies. How to structure it is a debate: e.g. Horlach et al. distinguish five different types of bi-modal IT organisations.[61]

Already discussed is the ladder of IT services provided to business functions. One can add to that perspective the discussion of Modes 1 and 2. Clearly, the services that belong to the operational and tactical levels belong in principle to Mode 1, the strategic services to Mode 2. Again, the distinction between levels is gradual not sharp. Depending on the innovativeness of new developments, they can be included either in the strategic or in the tactical level. Less fundamental changes could be classified as Mode 1.

An organisation thus faces two completely different situations under which IT services are developed and offered: focused either on efficiency and reliability or on agility and innovation. This implies that the governance approach should also be different. Efficiency-oriented IT (Mode 1) requires governance that ensures efficiency and reliability; innovation-oriented IT (Mode 2) requires a governance approach that focuses on agility and realising innovation.

In other words, the vision of a generally applicable governance approach must give way to a situation-specific approach. In a recent study, Gartner introduced the concept of adaptive governance.[62] Adaptive governance is defined as "the organisational capability that determines the governance style that will deliver the required business outcomes in a given context."[62] They distinguish four different styles, including "control based" and "agility based." Control-based governance is mainly about following procedures

Table 8.3 IT capability in Modes 1 and 2

The IT capability	The business contribution	IT's contribution	Bi-modal IT
Strategic planning	Strategic innovation	Strategic Innovation	MODE 2
	Business change	Business change	
	Business outcome & programme selection	Business outcome & programme selection	
Tactical and operational planning	Benefit realisation & project development	Benefit realisation & project development	
	Information & process requirements	Software configuration & development	Mode 1
	Service requirements	Service Design	
Operational execution	Utilisation of information services in business processes and management	Service delivery	

and rules and meeting compliancy requirements. A governance style that is more focused on achieving business goals is outcome-based governance. For outsourcing,[63] control-based and outcome-based governance broadly corresponds to the philosophy and measures described in Section 8.7. Agility-based governance corresponds in philosophy to what is described by Vejseli et al. Agile-based governance evolves to autonomous-based governance in case of extreme innovation challenges. These may occur due to the exponential developments of various forms of IT, e.g. the Internet of Things and algorithmic machine-to-machine decision-making.

8.9 Contracts versus relational governance

Managing the outsourcing relationship is inherently problematic and characterised by a tension between control and trust. Outsourcing organisations and suppliers are not only contractually but also socially related to each other. These two types of relationships also represent two streams in research.

The outsourcing contracts play an important role during the period that the outsourcing relationship is in effect.[64] They constitute the foundation for transferring responsibility. Contracts include the agreements that form the basis for executing the IT service. Typical components are the general conditions, agreements concerning the scope, the service levels and costs associated with the specific services to be provided.[65] In addition, contracts will include agreements concerning intellectual property rights (IPR), which are important when licences are transferred from the outsourcing organisation, and software is developed by the IT supplier on behalf of the outsourcing organisation during the course of the contract. Especially in the case of a digital strategy, which encompasses business process outsourcing (BPO), this is an important issue.[64] The IPR in principle belongs to the outsourcing organisation. However, BPO makes it essential for IT suppliers to own the IPR, while in the case of transferring to another IT supplier, the outsourcing organisation must be able to continue to use the software licences whose IPR remains with the incumbent supplier.[64]

As Lacity and Hirschheim formulated, "If a company decides to outsource, the contract is the only mechanism to ensure that expectations are realised."[66] The outsourcing reality must be seen as a success by both the outsourcing organisation and supplier. Consequently, the basic premise must be that the supplier and the outsourcing organisation are always ready to help one another and are willing to cooperate at all levels to make the relationship a success. Facing uncertainty and change, parties that wish to enter into an agreement together are not able to predict all the future situations that may occur as a result of the transaction they want to conclude. As a consequence, they are not able to describe all possible future scenarios as part of the contracts they negotiate. This does not concern questions of uncertainty in relation to the contracting parties involved, but uncertainties concerning the transaction itself.

In this context, the outsourcing literature has studied the incomplete contract theory developed by Nam et al.[67] Attempts to include all possible future scenarios into an outsourcing contract require intense efforts from both the outsourcing organisation and the suppliers, and may well be an impossible task. When preparing IT outsourcing contracts, the question is to what extent both parties are prepared to attempt to be complete. The degree to which this is possible for IT outsourcing contracts depends on characteristics of the transaction involved: asset specificity, uncertainty and measurement, and frequency of the transaction.[68] Moreover, in many outsourcing situations, the opportunity to include details into the contract is very limited. This is related to the time pressures that often exist to come to an agreement and the costs associated with the preparation of the outsourcing contract. Management may deem it essential for certain services to be quickly available.[64]

Contracts form a safety-net upon which the parties eventually may rely. Especially under uncertain and changing conditions, the future IT services needs of the outsourcing organisations are elements that cannot be defined when a contract is signed. Consequently, parties need to agree on procedures for dealing with changes that are not covered by the contract. These procedures need to enable a rapid resolution of the problem at hand, which saves costs and ensures that any damage to the image of both the supplier and the outsourcing organisation is avoided or minimised.[64] In short, the right governance must ensure that parties are willing and able to collaborate in a positive way. This type of governance is called "relational governance."

Social intervention plays a role in compensating the efficiency and technical limits of formal contracts. Relational governance comprises a social component by emphasising trust and commitment. Relational governance refers to unwritten enforcement of obligations, promises and expectations through social processes.[69] These processes promote a flexible behaviour to adapt to unforeseen events, solidarity and open information exchange. Key characteristics of relational governance are expected and accepted behaviour, harmonious conflict resolution and mutual dependence. Empirical research shows that relational governance is associated with trust, which improves performance in interorganisational exchanges.

Do these two types of governance form substitutes or are they complements?[70] The opinion of substitutes is found in expressions like "trust is good, but control is better" and more positively formulated as "trust in the relationship avoids complex contracts." Recent research has clearly shown that whether to craft formal contracts or to apply a more socially oriented relational governance in outsourcing is not a matter of either/or. Both are recognised to be complements to each other, as was empirically shown.[69,70] Greater levels of relational norms were employed as contracts became increasingly customised; also, more complex contracts were developed with greater levels of relational governance. Clearly stated contractual terms and processes, and the presence of accepted and expected relational norms together provide confidence and trust to organisations to cooperate.

8.10 Governance of IT outsourcing in business ecosystems

Single sourcing, which involves all IT services from one supplier, is giving way to multiple sourcing, which involves several suppliers in the provision of IT services. Plugge et al. define multisourcing as "a one-to-many relationships, in which one client uses multiple suppliers while the division of labour is jointly negotiated and understood by all parties to the agreement."[72] Multiple sourcing solves the problem of high dependence on one supplier. By using different suppliers, one can also have the benefits of specialisation. In addition, in the case of a digital strategy, a digital platform forms the basis for different applications that are then delivered by different suppliers. However, these benefits of multiple sourcing come at a price. Multiple sourcing creates a networked organisation, possibly with the characteristics of a business ecosystem. Collaboration between the different suppliers who may also be competitors of each other requires strong governance mechanisms.[73]

Service coordination and governance require extra attention. Section 8.7 discussed critical structures and processes required in the case of a complex outsourcing situation. Important are a clear strategic positioning, formal organisational arrangements and trust.

The implication of the multiple sourcing situation for these factors is discussed below. However, these are implications for the known factors; after a thorough analysis of the current literature, Herz et al. conclude that the current literature on IT governance mechanisms to a large extent can be applied to multisourcing.[74]

It will be clear that a clear strategic positioning of all parties involved is crucial for successful collaboration. However, this also implies that expected services from each of the IT suppliers involved must be clear and accepted from the outset. If ambiguities or vagueness exist in this respect, this can immediately or in the near future lead to disrupted relationships between the suppliers involved and with the customer.

Formal organisational arrangements are particularly necessary for the creation of consultation structures. These are crucial for operational and tactical issues that will arise concerning the service, as well as if the cooperation takes on a long-term strategic character. The composition of these bodies, the consultation agenda and the consultation frequency are established. In addition to these regular meetings, it must be clear to everyone how ad hoc issues are handled. Other formal organisational structures[75] for multiple sourcing mentioned by Herz et al. are IT steering committee, multisourcing project committee, and general and multisourcing specific reporting structures.

An important question here is how the responsibility for services provided is arranged. An interdependency between the suppliers can lead to the performance of one supplier being negatively influenced by one or more of the others. Control by the client of each individual supplier, assuming a dyadic relation, can then become problematic. The other possibility is that overall responsibility for the overall performance of the services rests with the group of suppliers. Collective formal control is likely to be particularly effective for achieving coordination among suppliers and, thus, high joint performance. When clients specify and monitor joint procedures, they are urging suppliers to interact, share information and help each other.[75] In this case, close coordination between the suppliers is important, which necessitates good consultation.

Finally, trust between the parties is crucial. Trust that what has been agreed can be delivered, trust that there are no hidden agendas and trust that in case of unexpected problems they will help each other. Trust is important between customer and supplier, but in the case of multisourcing also between the involved suppliers themselves. It is clear that this makes achieving and maintaining a situation of good mutual trust more complex. An important instrument to achieve trust, besides simply performing well on the contract, is open communication. The consultation structures discussed in the previous paragraph obviously contribute significantly to this.

Earlier it was pointed out that formal governance is a necessary but not sufficient condition for an effectively functioning organisation. There must be room for developing good interpersonal relationships horizontally, diagonally and vertically. The idea is that lines of communication are open and easily accessible. This presupposes trust. Although relational governance is thus of great importance in the situation of outsourcing in general, and the existence of a business ecosystem in particular, Krancher et al.[75] following Bapna et al.[76] suggest that relational governance relational models might not be feasible for multiple suppliers.

8.11 Conclusions

Corporate governance may be defined as the organisational expression of the company's business objectives, a structure that therefore includes the means of attaining those objectives as well as guidelines for performance monitoring. IT governance is the implementation of governance for IT by the outsourcing organisation. Suppliers and outsourcing organisations are obviously both responsible for ensuring good IT governance; nevertheless, it is the outsourcing organisation which remains finally responsible. IT governance frameworks such as COBIT, ISO17799/ISO27001, ITIL/BS15000 and CMMi provide support for outsourcing organisations and suppliers setting up IT governance structures and processes. Financial scandals such as that involving the American utility company Enron have caused authorities everywhere to issue stricter laws and regulations, both on a national scale and internationally. Of course, IT governance is influenced by these developments too, since all these laws and regulations aim to increase companies' financial transparency, and to allow senior managers to be held personally responsible for any transgressions. The effects of business and technology drivers on business models in general and on supplier–buyer relationships in particular form the subject of various organisation theories. Several approaches are discussed in the economics and organisation literature. The most important of these for this book's purposes are the theory of competitive strategy, the resource-based view and the theory of transaction costs.

Formal regulations are not sufficient for good governance. Effective relations between suppliers and outsourcing organisations depend on good interpersonal relations and mutual trust. This raises the question whether good interpersonal relationships can substitute for good contracts, or, conversely, good contracts can compensate for the lack of good relationships and trust.

Little research has been done on governance in the face of change and uncertainty. This issue was addressed in Section 8.8. The time is past when governance could be captured in generally applicable rules. The task of management is to adapt the governance used to the conditions under which an organisation operates. In this respect, governance aimed at complying with rules and ensuring efficient operations is different from governance aimed at facilitating agility and innovation.

Finally, organisations increasingly function as part of a broader network, with the characteristics of a business ecosystem. This requires a greater degree of coordination between the outsourcing organisation and the various suppliers. Moreover, it also requires clear coordination between the different IT suppliers in the ecosystem. This necessarily increases the coordination effort within the overall network.

Notes

1 Beulen, E. (2006). Governance in IT outsourcing partnerships. In *Strategies for information technology governance* (pp. 310–342). Igi Global.

2 Beulen, E., & Ribbers, P. (2007, January). Control in outsourcing relationships: governance in action. In *2007 40th Annual Hawaii International Conference on System Sciences (HICSS'07)* (pp. 236b–236b). IEEE.

3 OECD (2015). *Principles of corporate governance*. Paris: OECD. http://www.oecd.org/corporate/principles-corporate-governance/ – accessed 10 March 2021

4 Berle, A. A., & Means, G. C. (1934). *The modern corporation and private property*. New York: Macmillan Co.

5 Fama, E., & Jensen, M. (1983). Separation of ownership and control. *Journal of Law and Economics, 26,* 301–326.

6 Gugler, K., Mueller, D., & Yurtoglu, B. (2004). Corporate governance and globalization. *Oxford Review of Economic Policy, 20*(1), 129–156.

7 Van Grembergen, W., & De Haes, S. (2009). *Enterprise governance of information technology: Achieving strategic alignment and value.* New York: Springer Publishing Company, Incorporated.

8 https://www.coso.org/Documents/2017-COSO-ERM-Integrating-with-Strategy-and-Performance-Executive-Summary.pdf – accessed 10 March 2021. COSO is a voluntary private-sector organisation dedicated to improving the quality of financial reporting through business ethics, effective internal controls and corporate governance. The members of COSO are the American Institute of Certified Public Accountants, the American Accounting Association, Financial Executives International, the Institute of Management Accountants and The Institute of Internal Auditors. COSO was originally formed in 1985 to sponsor the National Commission on Fraudulent Financial Reporting, known as the Treadway Commission, an independent private-sector initiative which studied the causal factors that can lead to fraudulent financial reporting and developed recommendations for public companies and their independent auditors, for the SEC and other regulators, and for educational institutions. COSO then published Internal Control – Integrated Framework, also authored by PricewaterhouseCoopers. (www.coso.org).

9 Parker, M. M., Benson, R. J. with Trainor, H. E. (1988). *Information economics – linking business performance to information technology.* Hoboken, NJ: Prentice Hall.

10 Henderson, J., & Venkatraman, N. (1993). Strategic alignment: Leveraging information technology for transforming organisations. *IBM Systems Journal, 32*(1), 4–16.

11 Sambamurthy, V., & Zmud, R. (1999). Arrangements for information technology governance: A theory of multiple contingencies. *Management Information Systems Quarterly,* 23(2), 261–290.

12 Brown, C., & Magill, S. (1994). Alignment of the IS functions with the enterprise: Toward a model of antecedents. *Management Information Systems Quarterly, 18*(4), 371–403.

13 Weill, P., & Vitale, M. (2002). *Place to space, migrating to eBusiness models.* Boston, MA: Harvard Business School Press.

14 Parker, M. M., Trainor, H. E., & Benson, R. J. (1989). *Information strategy and economics.* Hoboken, NJ: Prentice-Hall, Inc.

15 Canadian Institute of Chartered Accountants, & Canadian Institute of Chartered Accountants. Information Technology Advisory Committee. (2004). *20 questions directors should ask about IT.* Toronto: Canadian Institute of Chartered Accountants.

16 Weill, P., & Ross, J. (2004). *IT governance, how top performers manage IT decision rights for superior results.* Boston, MA: Harvard Business School Press.

17 ISACA (the Information Systems Audit and Control Association) was founded in 1967 (www.isaca.org).
18 Thorp, C. (2004). Implementing ISO17799: Pleasure or pain? *The Information Systems Control Journal, 4,* 25–26.
19 Eloff, M., & von Solms, S. (2000). Information security management: A hierarchical framework for various approaches. *Computers & Security, 19*(3), 243–256.
20 An earlier version of this section has been published in Benson, R. J., & Ribbers, P. M. (2020). Strategic Sourcing in turbulent times – the Impact of Trust and Partnership. In Beulen, E., & Ribbers, P. M. (Eds.), *The Routledge companion to managing digital outsourcing* (4–40). London: Routledge.
21 Ibrahim, M., & Ribbers, P. (2006, January). Trust, dependence and global interorganizational systems. In *Proceedings of the 39th Annual Hawaii International Conference on System Sciences (HICSS'06)* (Vol. 8, p. 186a). New York: IEEE.
22 Lane, C. (1998). Introduction: Theories and issues in the study of trust. In Lane, C., & Bachmann, R. (Eds.), *Trust within and between organizations: Conceptual, issues and empirical applications* (p. 334). New York: Oxford University Press.
23 Sako, M. (1998). Does trust improve business performance. In Lane, C., & Bachmann, R. (Eds.), *Trust within and between organizations: Conceptual, issues and empirical applications* (pp. 88–117). New York: Oxford University Press.
24 See discussion on incomplete contract theory in: Goo, J., Kishore, R., Rao, H. R., & Nam, K. (2009). The role of service level agreements in relational management of information technology outsourcing: An empirical study. *MIS Quarterly, 33,* 119–145. and in: Beulen, E., & Ribbers, P. (2003, January). IT outsourcing contracts: practical implications of the incomplete contract theory. In *Proceedings of the 36th Annual Hawaii International Conference on System Sciences, 2003* (pp. 10–pp). New York: IEEE.
25 March, J. G., Simon, H. A., & Guetzkow, H. S. (1958). *Organizations.* New York: Wiley.
26 Mishra, A. K. (1996). Trust in organizations: Frontiers of theory and research. In Kramer, R. M., & Tyler, T. (Eds.), *Organizational responses to crisis: The centrality of trust* (pp. 261–287). Beverly Hills, CA: Sage.
27 Ibrahim, M., & Ribbers, P. M. (2009). The impacts of competence-trust and openness-trust on interorganizational systems. *European Journal of Information Systems, 18*(3), 223–234.
28 Blomqvist, K., & Ståhle, P. (2000, September). Building organizational trust. In *16th Annual IMP Conference, Bath, UK* (pp. 7–9).
29 Benson, R. J., Ribbers, P. M., & Blitstein, R. B. (2014). *Trust and partnership – strategic management for turbulent times.* New York: Wiley CIO Series.
30 Ibrahim, M., Ribbers, P. M., & Bettonvil, B. (2012). Human-knowledge resources and interorganisational systems. *Information Systems Journal, 22*(2), 129–149.
31 Peppard, J., & Ward, J. (2016) The *strategic management of information systems – building a digital strategy.* (4th ed.). New York: Wiley.
32 Shockley-Zalabak, P., Ellis, K., & Winograd, G. (2000). Organizational trust: What it means, why it matters. *Organization Development Journal, 18*(4), 35.
33 Baron, R.A. (1999). *Behavior in organizations.* Toronto: Pearson.
34 Galbraith, J. (1977). *Organization design.* Boston, MA: Addison-Wesley.
35 Daft, R. L., & Lane, P. G. (2007). *Understanding the theory and design of organizations.* Mason, OH: Thomson South-Western.
36 Kude, T., Lazic, M., Heinzl, A., & Neff, A. (2018). Achieving IT-based synergies through regulation-oriented and consensus-oriented IT governance capabilities. *Information Systems Journal, 28*(5), 765–795.
37 Van Grembergen, W. (Ed.). (2012). *Business strategy and applications in enterprise IT governance.* Hershey, PA: IGI Global.

38 Peterson, R., Parker, M., & Ribbers, P. (2002). Information technology govern-ance processes under environmental dynamism: Investigating competing theo-ries of decision making and knowledge sharing. *ICIS 2002 Proceedings* (p. 52).

39 McFarlan, F. W., & Nolan, R. L. (1995). How to manage an IT outsourcing alliance. *MIT Sloan Management Review, 36*(2), 9.

40 Currie, W., & Willcocks, L. (1998). Analysing four types of IT-outsourcing de-cisions in the context of scale, client/server, interdependency and risk mitigation. *Information Systems Journal, 8*(2), 119–143.

41 Willcocks, L., & Choi, C. J. (1995). Co-operative partnership and 'total' IT out-sourcing: From contractual obligation to strategic alliance?. *European Management Journal, 13*(1), 67–78.

42 Haes, S. D., & Grembergen, W. V. (2015). *Enterprise governance of information tech-nology achieving alignment and value.* Berlin: Springer.

43 De Haes, S., Van Grembergen, W., Joshi, A., & Huygh, T. (2019). *Enterprise gov-ernance of information technology: Achieving alignment and value in digital organizations.* Berlin: Springer Nature.

44 Verra, G. J. (2003). *Global account management.* London: Routledge.

45 Cullen, S., & Willcocks, L. (2003). *Intelligent IT outsourcing: Eight building blocks to success.* Oxford: Butterworth-Heinemann.

46 Lee, J. N., & Kim, Y. G. (1999). Effect of partnership quality on IS outsourcing success: Conceptual framework and empirical validation. *Journal of Management information systems, 15*(4), 29–61.

47 Palvia, P. C. (1995). A dialectic view of information systems outsourcing: Pros and cons. *Information & Management, 29*(5), 265–275.

48 Wallace, W. (2000). Reporting practices: Potential lessons from Cendant Corpo-ration. *European Management Journal, 18*(3), 328–333.

49 Van Grembergen, W., & Haes, S. de (2008). *Enterprise governance of information technology: Achieving strategic alignment and value.* Berlin: Springer.

50 Sabherwal, K. (1999). The role of trust in outsourced IS development projects. *Communications of the Association for Computing Machinery, 42*(2), 80–86.

51 Aguillar, D. A., Murakami, I., Junior, P. M., & Aquino, P. T. (2017, September). IT governance program and improvements in Brazilian small business: Viability and case study. In *2017 Federated Conference on Computer Science and Information Systems (FedCSIS)* (pp. 961–964). New York: IEEE.

52 Sommer, A. F., Dukovska-Popovska, I., & Steger-Jensen, K. (2014, September). Agile product development governance–on governing the emerging scrum/stage-gate hybrids. In *IFIP International Conference on Advances in Production Man-agement Systems* (pp. 184–191). Berlin, Heidelberg: Springer.

53 Vejseli, S., Rossmann, A., & Connolly, T. (2019). IT governance and its agile dimensions: Exploratory research in the banking sector. In *Proceedings HICSS-52 Conference, Hawaii.* New York: IEEE.

54 Raisch, S., & Birkinshaw, J. (2008). Organizational ambidexterity: Antecedents, outcomes, and moderators. *Journal of Management, 34*(3), 375–409.

55 Leonhardt, D., Haffke, I., Kranz, J., & Benlian, A. (2017). Reinventing the IT function: The role of IT agility and IT ambidexterity in supporting digital busi-ness transformation. In *Proceedings ECIS 2017,* Madrid. Trier, Germany: DBLP.

56 Haffke, I., Kalgovas, B., & Benlian, A. (2017). Options for transforming the IT function using bimodal IT. *MIS Quarterly Executive, 16*(2), 101–120.

57 Jöhnk, J., Oesterle, S., Winkler, T. J., Nørbjerg, J., & Urbach, N. (2019). Juggling the paradoxes–governance mechanisms in bimodal IT organizations. In *Proceed-ings ECIS 2019,* Stockholm. Trier, Germany: DBLP.

58 In organisation theory, Mintzberg speaks of the congruence hypothesis. This indicates that an effective structuring of an organisation requires a close fit

between the design of the organisation and its environmental characteristics on the one hand and of its structural characteristics among themselves on the other. The basis for this rests in the contingency theory.

59 Mintzberg, H. (1993). *Structure in fives: Designing effective organizations.* Hoboken, NJ: Prentice-Hall, Inc.

60 Miller, D., Kets de Vries, M. F., & Toulouse, J. M. (1982). Top executive locus of control and its relationship to strategy-making, structure, and environment. *Academy of Management Journal, 25*(2), 237–253.

61 Horlach, B., Drews, P., Schirmer, I., & Böhmann, T. (2017). Increasing the agility of IT delivery: Five types of bimodal IT organization. In *Proceedings HICSS-50 Conference,* Hawaii. New York: IEEE.

62 MacDorman, J., Gulzar, R. (2017). Adaptive IT governance. https://www.gartner.com/en/documents/3714223/adaptive-it-governance - accessed 31 March

63 Mao, H., Gong, Y., Liu, S., Zhang, Y., & Li, K. (2019). Adoption and risk management of bimodal IT outsourcing service: Review and directions for future research. *International Journal of Internet and Enterprise Management, 9*(2), 144–159.

64 Beulen, E., & Ribbers, P. (2003). IT outsourcing contracts: Practical implications of the incomplete contract theory. In *Proceedings HICSS-36 Conference,* Hawaii. New York: IEEE, 0–7695–1874–5/03.

65 Wheeler-Carmichael, G. (2002). With this contract I the wed: A look at the legal process involved in IT outsourcing. *Montgomery Research Europe,* ISSN, 1476-2064.

66 Lacity, M. C., & Hirschheim, R. A. (1995). *Beyond the information systems outsourcing bandwagon: The insourcing response* (Ser. Wiley series in information systems). New York: Wiley.

67 Nam, K., Rajagopalan, S., Rao, H. R., & Chaudhury, A. (1996). A two-level investigation of information systems outsourcing. *Communications of the ACM, 39*(7), 36–44.

68 Aubert, B. A., Rivard, S., & Patry, M. (1996). A transaction cost approach to outsourcing behavior: Some empirical evidence. *Information & Management, 30*(2), 51–64.

69 Goo, J., Kishore, R., Rao, H. R., & Nam, K. (2009). The role of service level agreements in relational management of information technology outsourcing: An empirical study. *MIS Quarterly, 33,* 119–145.

70 Poppo, L., & Zenger, T. (2002). Do formal contracts and relational governance function as substitutes or complements?. *Strategic management journal, 23*(8), 707–725.

71 See also: Qi, C., & Chau, P. Y. (2012). Relationship, contract and IT outsourcing success: Evidence from two descriptive case studies. *Decision Support Systems, 53*(4), 859–869.

72 Dibbern, J., Goles, T., Hirschheim, R., & Jayatilaka, B. (2004). Information systems outsourcing: A survey and analysis of the literature. *ACM SIGMIS Database: The DATABASE for Advances in Information Systems, 35*(4), 6–102.

73 Plugge, A., & Janssen, M. (2020). Governing and orchestrating relationships in outsourcing with multiple vendors. In Beulen, E., & Ribbers, P. M. (Eds.), *The Routledge companion to managing digital outsourcing* (159–176). London: Routledge.

74 Herz, T. P., Hamel, F., Uebernickel, F., & Brenner, W. (2012, January). IT governance mechanisms in multisourcing—A business group perspective. In *2012 45th Hawaii International Conference on System Sciences* (pp. 5033–5042). New York: IEEE.

75 Krancher, O., Oshri, I., Kotlarsky, J., & Dibbern, J. (2018). How formal governance affects multisourcing success: A multi-level perspective. In *Proceedings ICIS 2018,* San Franciso, Atlanta, GA: AIS.

76 See also: Bapna, R., Barua, A., Mani, D., & Mehra, A. (2010). Research commentary—Cooperation, coordination, and governance in multisourcing: An agenda for analytical and empirical research. *Information Systems Research, 21*(4), 785–795.

9 Governance factors

To ensure that IT outsourcing relations are properly contracted and governed, both the outsourcing organisation and the suppliers have to put effort in the relationship, in addition to implementing specific measures in their own organisation. What governance factors are required to ensure outsourcing success?

9.1 Introduction

In order to structure governance of IT sourcing relationships, a descriptive framework is presented that has three dimensions: that of the outsourcing relationship, that of the supplier and that of the outsourcer-supplier relationship as a whole. In each of these dimensions, four governance factors are distinguished. Reference theories discussed in Chapter 2 help to distinguish relevant governance factors for each of the three components.

It is important to start with a detailed discussion of outsourcing organisation-side governance factors. Outsourcing organisations must set up the governance of their IT outsourcing partnerships on the basis of those measures and organisational elements that allow them to control the outsourcing relationship. These measures and elements are their governance structure's control aspects, which surpass the service levels agreed upon and focus on the organisational structures of their suppliers. These governance factors define how the outsourcing organisation can align its business and IT services and how it can manage its suppliers. The first outsourcing organisation's governance factor is having a clear IT strategy,[1] which is linked to the competitive strategy of Porter.[2] The outsourcing organisation has to determine the competitive strategy first. The second governance factor is the embedment of IT in the business, to ensure that IT is well supported. The business managers and IT managers have to collaborate. The resource dependency theory provides insights into the fundamental motivations for actions.[3,4] The third governance factor is the presence of a Chief Information Officer (CIO), whose tasks include attaining the alignment of IT and the business. The fourth factor concerns information managers, who contribute to the management of the outsourcing activities. The third and fourth governance factors – a clear demand management structure on the strategic and

DOI: 10.4324/9781003223788-9

tactical levels – are linked to the resource-based view because they relate to competencies the outsourcing organisation must possess.[5,6]

Within the context of an outsourcing partnership, it is the supplier who must take care of the actual delivery of the IT services contracted. Suppliers should also strive to control their relationships with their clients; their governance structure must be set up on the basis of measures and organisational elements that allow them to do so. In the supplier's case, however, the emphasis of these control aspects is of the manner in which they can best meet the information needs of their client. The four supplier-side governance factors are a clear and consistent market position, a front office, a back office and the availability of IT professionals. For suppliers, it is important to know the market, what their vision for the future is and which IT services they should have in their portfolio. They themselves must also know the sectors and segments of which their market is composed. This market includes the geographical scope within which they can deliver their services. These governance factors are embedded in the detailed theories, as detailed in Chapter 2. The first governance factor, a clear and consistent market position, is linked to the institutional theory.[7] What is the strategy of the suppliers towards the market? The implementation of the front and back offices is related to organisational theories. The effectiveness of the decision-making process is key.[8] The resource-based view supports the fourth governance factor, the availability of IT professionals. What core competence do the IT professionals need? Now is the time to take a closer look at these factors.

Finally, there are four governance factors that concern the outsourcing relationship as a whole. That is, the factors are intended to give both the outsourcing organisation and supplier control over their partnership. The emphasis of these control aspects is of the manner in which their collaboration and the allocation of responsibilities are defined. First of all, the responsibilities of each of the partnership's participants must be clear, without any ambiguity. The outsourcing contract plays an important role here. However, having a contract is not enough. Participants to a partnership must continuously keep each other's interests in mind: trust is an important factor in realising IT partnership governance. Finally, steering organisations are needed in order to generate such trust. Most of the relationship governance factors are linked to the agency theory, as there is information asymmetry between the supplier and the outsourcing organisation.[9] The insights of the resource-based view contribute to the implementation of the responsibilities and steering organisations.[5,6] The insights of the transaction cost theory contribute to the governance "contracts."[10,11] The coordination costs of outsourcing contracts are substantial, and the fourth governance factor, steering organisations, is part of the coordination costs.

9.2 A descriptive framework

The literature on IT outsourcing contains several contributions to the question of how to manage IT outsourcing relationships. An IT outsourcing relationship is characterised by the outsourcing organisation, the supplier and the existence of a relationship. The outsourcing organisation and the supplier(s) are bound by a (contractual) agreement regarding the provision of IT services.

9.2.1 The organisations involved

The outsourcing organisation is the organisation that decides to start a long-term contractual relationship with one or more suppliers to provide all or part of its IT services. The supplier is responsible for the delivery of the IT services to the outsourcing organisation. In selecting a supplier, the outsourcing organisation must choose a supplier with a profile that fits the requested IT services.[12] A proper supplier selection adds value.[13]

9.2.2 The relationship

Outsourcing organisations and supplier(s) engage in relationships. The characteristics of these relationships may vary considerably, depending on the type and level of responsibilities outsourced to the supplier. In particular, the type of outsourcing decisions and the type of services offered will impact the relationship. Moreover, these relationships may change over time. With respect to the type of outsourcing decisions, two choices must be made. The first choice is between outsourcing the entire IT service and partial outsourcing, also referred to as "total outsourcing" and "selective sourcing," respectively.[14] Next, a choice must be made between outsourcing to a single supplier or to multiple suppliers, referred to as "single sourcing" and "multiple sourcing."[14]

9.2.3 A descriptive model

The foregoing discussion provides the building blocks for the conceptual model that helps to explain governance of outsourcing relationships (as detailed in Figure 9.1). First, the three components of the model that are involved in the governance are the outsourcing organisation, the supplier(s) and the relationship between them. Next, reference theories discussed in Chapter 2 help to distinguish relevant governance factors for each of the three components.

From the competitive strategy theory, the resource-based view and the resource dependency theory, it can be gleaned that strategic positioning, which identifies critical internal resources and capabilities and defines external resources on which the firm depends, is critical in governance. Having a clear IT strategy, which includes a sourcing strategy, is obviously a key governance factor for the outsourcing organisation, as is having *a clear market position* for the supplier.

From the economic theories, in particular transaction cost economics and agency theory, one learns that formal arrangements for managing and

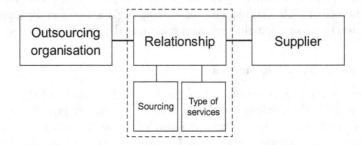

Figure 9.1 Conceptual framework to manage IT outsourcing relationships.

monitoring the relationship are essential. Formal organisational arrangements are necessary at both the outsourcing organisation and the supplier's side of the relationship and also with respect to the relationship itself. On the one hand, the outsourcing firm has to structure the information systems function that represents their demand management. The supplier, on the other hand, has to structure their interface with the supplier, e.g. through contract and account management (CAM) which operates as the counterpart of the outsourcing organisation's Information Management, and their back-office processes, in particular consistent service delivery processes. Formal arrangements regarding the relationship are the existence of adequate contracts and organisational arrangements that support communication and reporting. From the social/organisational theories, one learns that formal arrangements are necessary but not sufficient conditions for effective governance. Relationships based on shared understanding and commitment between people and organisations are essential. It is worthwhile to propose the existence of trust between the parties involved as an essential element of governance. Some authors even see trust as an outcome measure of a successful outsourcing relationship.[15,16,17] The descriptive model proposed based on the foregoing discussion is represented in Figure 9.1. Outsourcing organisations and suppliers may use the governance factors presented here to provide substance to their IT outsourcing partnership. While these factors do not constitute a comprehensive inventory of all measures that should be adopted, they do point to specific organisational elements that outsourcing organisations and suppliers can implement. This model is thus meant for both parties to outsource partnerships, parties who can use these governance factors to improve their relationships further.

The governance factors for each of these dimensions are summed up in Table 9.1, and then discussed more fully in the next sections. There, four aspects of each of these factors will be identified and discussed. In this section, only a brief introduction of the management model's dimensions and governance factors will be presented.

Table 9.1 IT outsourcing management model's dimensions and governance factors

Dimensions	Governance factors
Outsourcing organisation	A clear IT strategy
	The embedment of IT in the business
	A Chief Information Officer (CIO)
	Information managers
Supplier	A clear and consistent market position
	A front office
	A back office
	The availability of IT professionals
Relation	Unambiguously defined responsibilities
	Contracts
	Trust in the partnership
	Conferences

9.2.4 Governance factors for the outsourcing organisation

Outsourcing organisations must set up the governance of their IT outsourcing partnerships on the basis of those measures and organisational elements that allow them to control these relationships. These measures and elements are their governance structure's control aspects, which surpass the service levels agreed upon and focus on the organisational structures of their suppliers. They define how the outsourcing organisation can align its business and IT services and how it can manage its suppliers. Four such governance factors may be distinguished:

1   A clear IT strategy. By developing and implementing a clear IT strategy, the formulation of which is the responsibility of the organisation's information systems function, outsourcing organisations enable themselves to achieve good long-term alignment between IT and business processes. Doing so helps to focus on their outsourcing relationships: external suppliers can direct their efforts towards the realisation of this IT strategy, for both offer and delivery of IT services.

2   The embedment of IT in the business. The outsourcing organisation's senior managers must devote a significant part of their time and attention to the IT services that their organisation needs. The attention paid will contribute positively to the control achieved over the outsourcing organisation's IT outsourcing relationships. Since this embedment is important, so is the outsourcing organisation's internal communication about the objectives of the partnership.

3   A CIO. Being at the top of the IT hierarchy, the outsourcing organisation's CIO is accountable for all its IT services. The CIO's most important task is to promote awareness of the importance of IT.

4   Information managers. Information managers must ensure that the information needs of the business are met by the IT services provided by the organisation's suppliers. These managers thus constitute the organisational link between the outsourcing organisation's business units and their suppliers.

9.2.5 Governance factors for the supplier

Suppliers should also strive to control their relationships with their clients; their governance structure must be set up on the basis of measures and organisational elements that allow them to do so. In the supplier's case, however, the emphasis of these control aspects is on the manner in which they can best meet the information needs of their client. The four supplier-side governance factors are as follows:

1   A clear and consistent market position. It is important for suppliers to know the market, what their vision for the future is and which IT services they should have in their portfolio. Suppliers themselves must also know the sectors and segments of which their market is composed.

2   A front office. A front office is an important interface between suppliers and their clients. Outsourcing organisations use this interface as their point of contact with the supplier's back office. Effectively, this means that organisations use it to control their outsourcing relationships. The supplier-side counterpart of this activity is called their CAM. It focuses on making sure that the contracted agreements are met, which requires much internal alignment to ensure that the resources needed are actually available.

3   A back office. Back offices are responsible for the actual delivery of the IT services contracted.

4   The availability of IT professionals. In order to deliver the required IT services, the supplier must have IT professionals available. In view of scarcity on the labour market, suppliers must devote particular attention to their human resources, both in a quantitative and in a qualitative sense.

9.2.6 Governance factors concerning the relationship

Finally, this chapter distinguishes four governance factors that concern the outsourcing relationship as a whole. The emphasis of these control aspects is in the manner in which their collaboration and the allocation of responsibilities are defined. Agreements and contracts therefore play an important role here, but they are not sufficient if there is no trust between the parties. In order to achieve that, regular conferences are of essential importance.

In IT outsourcing partnerships, both parties' responsibilities should be defined unambiguously. Doing so is even more important if more than one supplier is involved in delivering the IT services that their client needs. That way, these suppliers have responsibilities to one another as well as to the outsourcing organisation. A distinction can be made, by the way, between responsibilities concerning the outsourcing organisation's business functions and those concerning their information functions. In all cases, the responsibilities of the suppliers need to be clear at all times. When there is more than one supplier, the responsibilities of the suppliers with respect to each other must be clear. The responsibilities of each supplier with respect to the outsourcing organisation need to be clear as well.

Clear responsibilities prevent suppliers from blaming one another or their client should anything go wrong. Efficient and effective IT outsourcing contracts greatly enhance the clarity and measurability of the agreements made. It is therefore important that the measurements made are expressed in terms that the business functions of the outsourcing organisation are able to recognise. Balanced scorecards work well to achieve this, and they are therefore often used. When formulating IT outsourcing contracts, the parties involved should not forget to provide the opportunity for adjusting the terms in order to adapt the contract to changing circumstances. Only then will the services provided remain aligned with the information needs of the outsourcing organisation.

Mutual trust between outsourcing organisation and supplier is important – not only during the selection process but also during the contract period, when the services agreed upon are delivered. Such trust has to be generated and maintained on a business level as well as between individuals.

Such open communication can be achieved if the outsourcing organisation and the supplier's staff on all organisational levels – strategic, tactical and operational – regularly confer on the issues at hand. To this end, the authority and responsibilities of every conference must be clearly delineated. One must also define clearly who participates in which conferences, as well as the frequency with which they are to meet. Naturally, these aspects depend to a certain extent on the partnership's dynamics. The following sections discuss the governance factors from the conceptual framework in more detail.

9.3 Governance factors – the outsourcing organisation

Outsourcing IT services does not mean that the outsourcing organisation is no longer responsible or can stop paying attention to them. It was concluded earlier that only operational responsibilities for IT services delivery can be outsourced. Even then, the outsourcing organisations must still manage their delivery. Four outsourcing organisation-side governance factors were identified: a clear IT strategy, the embedment of IT in the business, a CIO and information managers.

The first governance factor (a clear IT strategy) is linked to the competitive strategy of Porter (1980).[2] The outsourcing organisation has to determine the competitive strategy first. The second governance factor is the embedment of IT in the business, in which business managers and IT managers must collaborate. The resource dependency theory provides insights into the fundamental motivations for actions.[18,19] The third and fourth governance factors, a clear demand management structure on the strategic and tactical levels, are linked to the resource-based view because they relate to competencies the outsourcing organisations must possess.[5,6] These governance factors link to the core competences of the outsourcing organisation. These factors will now be discussed in detail. To get a better grip on the subject, four aspects are defined here that are important for achieving the desired results.

9.3.1 *A clear IT strategy*

An outsourcing organisation's IT strategy may be defined as their strategy with respect to IT, IT services and the role these play in the outsourcing organisation. For such a strategy to be any good, it must be well aligned with the business. Clear IT strategies show suppliers the direction in which their clients intend to move. Suppliers must therefore know and understand their client's IT strategies very well, for only then will they be able to deliver the services needed and anticipate future developments.

Having a clear IT strategy is not enough, however – it must also be implemented. To assess the extent to which implementation is done successfully, a balanced scorecard may be used (Figure 9.2). Balanced scorecards allow input from both the IT and the business sides with which to keep the IT outsourcing partnership on the right track (Table 9.2).[20]

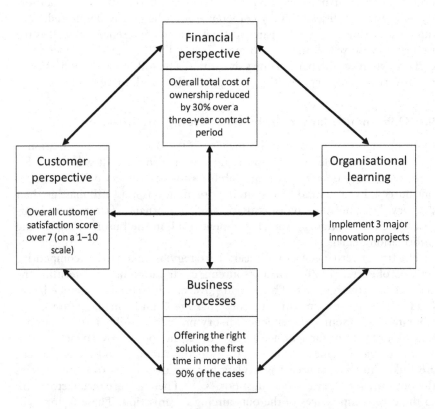

Figure 9.2 An example of a balanced scorecard for IT outsourcing partnerships (Kaplan, R. S., & Norton, D. P. (1992). The balanced scorecard—measures that drive performance. *Harvard Business Review, 70*(1), 71–79).

Table 9.2 Governance factors and aspects – IT outsourcing (outsourcing organisation)

Governance factors for the outsourcing organisation	Governance aspects
A clear IT strategy	Aligning the IT and business strategies
	Aligning the IT strategy with that of the parent organisation
	Preparing for the organisation's business dynamics
	Involving external experts
The embedment of IT in the business	Appointing IT portfolio managers in the business
	Changing from a cost perspective to an added-value perspective
	Involving the supplier in product development
	Involving the business in the management of the partnership
Clear demand management structure on a strategic level: Chief Information Officer (CIO)	Developing the IT strategy
	Maintaining good relations with the business
	Knowledge of both the business and technology
	Reporting to the Board of Directors
Clear demand management structure on a tactical level: information managers	Implementing the IT strategy
	Maintaining good relations with the business
	Knowledge of both the business and technology
	Reporting to both the CIO and the business

9.3.1.1 Aligning the IT and business strategies

Aligning the IT and business strategies is of essential importance.[21] Although the IT strategy is derived from the business strategy, the influence is not just one-way. For example, new technologies will also have their effect on the outsourcing organisation's business strategy. The increasing interaction between business and IT renders a proper alignment increasingly important. IT executives can no longer afford to focus on IT only; they must also be involved in corporate planning. Likewise, outsourcing contracts must also be used to promote organisational systems integration, and internal coordination mechanisms should facilitate systems consistency as well as decrease transaction costs.

9.3.1.2 Aligning the IT strategy with that of the parent organisation

When procuring IT services, especially in larger organisations that encompass several divisions, the centralisation or decentralisation of IT strategy present is an important factor. Centralised purchasing of services improves the negotiating position vis-à-vis the supplier. In addition, centralisation makes it easier to coordinate the technical and other standards to be used, which benefits interoperability. The real cost advantages, however, are gained in maintenance. Standard interfaces make this much cheaper to do than when there is an array of different, customised links between the information systems of several divisions and business units. However, in strongly diversified organisations, alignment is difficult to achieve.

9.3.1.3 Preparing for the organisation's business dynamics

Mergers, acquisitions, divestments and the rise of network organisations cause ever-increasing business dynamics.[21] These dynamics, in turn, influence IT services delivery and IT strategies. When organisations merge or are bought, their information systems must be coupled and realigned with those of their new colleagues. Divestments, however, require disentanglement. Such changes usually come unexpectedly, with very little time between the announcement and their becoming effective. It is therefore wise for outsourcing organisations to organise their IT services such that their constituent parts can be disconnected easily from one another or integrated with those of other organisations. This implies strategic choices for proven technology and limited IT services integration. Also, the interfaces between information systems preferably should be standard products.

9.3.1.4 Involving external experts

Defining and implementing an IT strategy is quite a challenge. It takes highly qualified personnel to do so – staff which not all outsourcing organisations have. External experts can be involved temporarily, such as in times of peak activity or when some very specialised expertise is required. Even in large organisations, the CIO and the CIO's information managers' work volume fluctuates intensely. Temporarily hiring experts is then a fitting solution.

To prevent conflicts of interests from arising, outsourcing organisations would do well to hire independent experts rather than consultants working for suppliers who deliver IT services or who may do so in the future. This explains why freelancers and specialised firms are well represented in this field. In all cases, the supplier retains final responsibility for the decisions taken, no matter how many external experts they hire.

9.3.2 The embedment of it in business

Aligning IT and business strategies is a necessary condition for success. In addition, the need to do so grows as IT is increasingly interwoven with both primary and supportive business processes. That said, there are many more aspects in which alignment can be attained, such as the outsourcing organisation's organisational set-up and the distribution of responsibilities, among other things. There should be a dialogue between the organisation's business people and their IT staff.[21]

9.3.2.1 Appointing IT portfolio managers in the business

All organisations of some size have IT departments, which include their CIOs and information managers. Since the 1980s, however, researchers have pointed out the need to make business managers responsible for IT as well.[22,23] An effective way to change this is by appointing IT portfolio managers in the organisation's business units. These IT portfolio managers are business managers and members of their units' management teams, but they are also the IT department's contacts. By formally appointing IT portfolio managers, clear communication lines between the IT department and the business are established.

9.3.2.2 Changing from a cost perspective to an added-value perspective

The role of IT changes, and the way of looking at it should therefore also change. The most important value that suppliers can provide in outsourcing relationships is introducing new technologies. Since suppliers work for multiple clients, they can invest in research into new developments and their potential much more effectively and efficiently than internal IT departments.

9.3.2.3 Involving the supplier in product development

In good outsourcing relationships, suppliers can contribute in an early phase of their clients' development processes. Suppliers can delegate specialists to their customers' development teams. This is done more frequently, since marketing a new product or service makes increasing demands on the information provision processes involved: applications must be adapted or even set up from scratch, and extra hardware may have to be bought. Unless this is done properly, it may unnecessarily increase the time-to-market.

9.3.2.4 Involving the business in the management of the IT partnership

Business embedment can be improved by appointing IT portfolio managers among the business managers. This is not only important during the IT strategy development process. Once IT services have been outsourced, the business should also be involved in the management of the outsourcing partnership and in assessing the quality of the services provided. Again, this task lies primarily with the IT department, but this does not relieve the business managers of their responsibility for it.

In many organisations, several managers are involved in running IT outsourcing relationships. First is the CIO, of course. Since the costs and investments associated with IT outsourcing are substantial, the Chief Financial Officer (CFO) is often also involved. Then there is the procurement department, who generally support their organisation's IT department in the management of the outsourcing relationship. Care must be taken during negotiations, however, since their lack of IT knowledge may cause them to focus too much on cost decreases, instead of on increasing the value added by the supplier. Typically, outsourcing organisations involve external consultants to contract IT outsourcing.[24]

9.3.3 Clear demand management structure on strategic level: Chief Information Officer

The CIO is the highest-ranking employee in the organisation who spends 100% of the time on information systems. All information managers report to the CIO. CIOs are responsible for the development of their organisation's IT strategy and for optimising the use it has of the IT services delivered – the outsourcing organisation's side of IT services delivery. This means, among other things, that if the organisation also has an internal IT department, the CIO cannot be its manager, for such a manager is responsible for the execution of IT services delivery – that is, the supplier side.

Combining the two functions would cause a conflict of interests, so organisations with internal IT departments must appoint a separate IT director. IT directors focus on maximising the use made of their department's services production capacity, in terms of IT professionals, hardware and software. For CIOs, internal capacity is of less interest. New technologies, for example, will therefore more usually be introduced on the initiative of CIOs than of IT directors, for doing so may make it more difficult to recoup the costs of previous investments. Of course, their generally stronger technical background means that IT directors can and therefore will advise their organisation's CIOs about such new technologies. They are better able to judge the effects on IT services delivery. CIOs and IT directors must therefore collaborate closely, certainly when new technologies are introduced. For CIOs to be effective and develop a robust IT strategy, they must keep their position for a relatively long period. Unfortunately, this is not always the case. For a positive contribution, CIOs should stay in their post for five years at least.

9.3.3.1 Developing the IT strategy

CIOs working on their organisation's IT strategy must take care to ensure support for it in the organisation. This means that they must collaborate with the organisation's business managers to decide on how IT is to be used. Considering the business dynamics most organisations are involved in, their IT strategy will have to be updated every year. With respect to long-term views, CIOs must often perform a balancing act between standardisation, which reduces total costs of ownership, and flexibility, which contributes to the optimum match with the information needs of the business. This requires substantial analytic acumen.

9.3.3.2 Maintaining good relationships with the business

For outsourcing organisations, it is very important that their general business strategy and their IT strategy are well aligned.[21] CIOs play an important role here. They must therefore prove their own added value to the business, by lowering the IT services costs, for example, or by showing the advantages of new technologies. The CIO must spend a lot of time and attention on relationships with an organisation's business managers in order to further strengthen those relationships.

9.3.3.3 Knowledge of both the business and technology

There is much discussion on the degree of technological knowledge CIOs should have. If they have too much, they may lose themselves in the details and neglect setting and guarding long-term policies. However, the advantage of profound knowledge is that it renders the CIO capable of judging the technical possibilities and their implications. It is obvious, therefore, that CIOs must have thorough technological knowledge. This is even more important in those many organisations where CIOs have rather few staff and resources to do research – they must simply be able to do that themselves. The need to have business knowledge is much less disputed. Attracting professionals with a "double competency" is both very important and at the same time very difficult, as these people are hard to find.[25]

9.3.3.4 Reporting to the Board of Directors

To enable the CIO to function properly, the CIO position must be located at the proper organisational level. Generally, however, IT is the responsibility of the board as a whole.

Anyone who would like to be an entrepreneur – and this should include all board members – simply must have IT knowledge. Maybe the service aspects can be left to the CIO, but the understanding of what IT can do for the business should become an integral part of entrepreneurship. Positioning CIOs outside the board also prevents them from being used as a scapegoat for anything in the field of IT that does not go as planned. CIOs should report to a member of the Board of Directors. The trend seems to be in the direction of reporting to the general manager and away from reporting to the director of finances or the chief operations manager.[26]

9.3.4 Clear demand management structure on tactical level: information managers

Information managers are responsible for linking the IT function with the business in order to implement their organisation's IT strategy. Theirs is mostly a bridging task involving relationships at the tactical level; they report to the CIO and the business managers. Information managers have a difficult job, since the resources with which to do it are not part of their own organisation but of the organisation's internal IT department or the external suppliers, or both. Thus, information managers depend on others for the ability to carry out their tasks.

Like the CIO, information managers must be permanent staff. The continuity needed requires that they do their job for several years, with little personnel or job rotation. Implementing an IT strategy is not a matter of a few months, but a continuous activity.[20]

9.3.4.1 Implementing the IT strategy

While the CIO is responsible for developing the organisation's IT strategy, it is the information managers who implement it.[20] Apart from their strategy implementation task, information managers must keep an eye on changes in the business and the organisation's business processes. Business dynamics may profoundly influence the IT strategy and even cause it to be changed.[21] Information managers can provide their CIO with bottom-up assistance.

9.3.4.2 Maintaining good relationships with the business

Today's business is very dynamic. Organisations, who can handle these dynamics well, sometimes called adaptive enterprises,[27] are more successful than those who cannot. Nowadays, the adaptive organisations are indicated as agile organisations.[28] Implementing agility at scale is also critical.[29] That said, doing so makes major demands on their IT services. Information managers contribute to the flexibility of these services. By maintaining good and trusted relationships with the business, suppliers can react quickly and ensure adequate, up-to-date service delivery.[21] It goes without saying that information managers must have excellent communication skills.

9.3.4.3 Knowledge of both the business and technology

To be able to bridge any gap between the IT department and the organisation's business management, information managers must have knowledge of both the business and technology. For many information managers, keeping both kinds of knowledge up to date is difficult. They do not work daily with technology anymore, so their knowledge slowly becomes outdated, making it difficult to follow and assess new technological developments. Attending seminars and regularly inviting experts are ways to stay up to date, but these activities require constant attention. With respect to business knowledge, information managers of course have contacts with organisation business managers, but this is not enough. A good idea is for organisations to include information managers in their management development programmes, rotating them with business managers and therefore stimulating some cross-fertilisation.

9.3.4.4 Reporting to both the CIO and the business

Positioning information managers in the organisation is a difficult matter for many outsourcing organisations. Organisations can have the information manager report to the CIO or to their business managers. Each option has advantages and disadvantages. A frequently chosen solution is to let information managers report to the CIO *and* the business. This contributes to the alignment between the business and IT that is to be achieved. An important question to answer in such cases is to whom the information managers will report hierarchically and to whom functionally. Centrally organised organisations will position information managers hierarchically as the CIO's staff, with functional accountability to the business managers. Less centralised organisations will include information managers in their business management teams hierarchically and let them report functionally to the CIO. Many organisations even seek an intermediate position between these two possibilities and opt for a small central staff of information managers reporting directly to the CIO, plus a number of information managers who are members of the business management teams. The intermediate positions secure a strong position for the CIO and yet stimulate maximum alignment with the business.

9.4 Governance factors – the supplier

In this section, four supplier-side governance factors that are important for IT outsourcing partnerships will be discussed in further detail:

- a clear and consistent market position
- a front office
- a back office
- the availability of IT professionals.

Within the context of an outsourcing partnership, it is the supplier who must take care of the actual delivery of the IT services contracted for. This supplier can be either an internal IT department or an external organisation, or both. For governance purposes, this makes no difference in principle, since all suppliers must implement governance to ensure proper service delivery.[30,31,32] The governance includes developments facing the outsourcing organisation (the external focus, from the supplier's point of view) and the manner in which the services will be delivered (the internal focus).[33]

The first governance factor, a clear and consistent market position, is linked to the institutional theory.[34] What is the strategy of the supplier towards the market? The implementation of the front and back offices is related to organisational theories.

The resource-based view supports the fourth governance factor, the availability of IT professionals. What core competence do the IT professionals need? Here, a closer look is taken at these factors. In addition, as done with the outsourcing organisation-side governance factors, each will be subdivided into several aspects, as listed in Table 9.3.

Table 9.3 Governance factors and aspects – IT outsourcing (supplier)

Governance factors	Governance aspects
A clear and consistent market position	A vision of the future
	Product portfolios
	Market segmentation
	Geographical scope
A front office	Senior management embedment of the partnership
	Account management
	Contract management
	Innovation management
A back office	The organisational embedment of the back office
	Service delivery management
	Process-based service delivery
	Audit processes
The availability of IT professionals	Sourcing portfolios
	Embedment transferred employees
	Attention for individual employees
	A planned approach

9.4.1 A clear and consistent market position

Suppliers must be able to show their clients and potential clients what IT services they can deliver and how. The description of the service includes their plans for the future, which form the basis of any IT outsourcing partnership. Naturally, communication about such a vision on the future is a two-way process: suppliers must be receptive to developments and opinions in their markets, and these suppliers must adapt their strategies and product portfolios as needed. A first selection of suppliers is often made on the basis of their profiles, derived from information such as their vision on the future, their product portfolio and the market segments in which they operate. Only suppliers who make the selection shortlist are sent a request for information or a proposal. Outsourcing organisations often hire external consultants to help the organisations make such shortlists. Suppliers must therefore also maintain good relationships with these consulting firms and keep them informed of supplier strategy and the IT services these suppliers can deliver, in order to be placed on a shortlist.

9.4.1.1 A vision of the future

The supplier's strategy is important to the outsourcing organisation. Having a clear vision on the future helps a supplier keep attuned to their client's needs. Suppliers who lack such a vision will have as much difficulty getting or renewing contracts as do organisations with bad financial results, for many CIOs and other senior managers will hesitate to let their IT services be provided by unstable partners.

9.4.1.2 Product portfolios

Suppliers use product portfolios to show which services they can deliver. Such a portfolio is not a static collection. The changes in the needs of their clients and potential clients force them to keep their portfolios up to date, as do technological developments. Interestingly, suppliers must manage their own IT needs as portfolios too and must decide which of them to insource and which to outsource.

Most suppliers offer integrated product portfolios, which means that they can fulfil most of their clients' information needs. This is especially true of commodity services such as desktop, server and network management. The differences between suppliers are generally found in the additional services they provide. These extras are often specific to certain industries and require specific knowledge and experience on the part of the suppliers. They offer them a chance to distinguish themselves from their competitors.

Another important difference between suppliers is whether they provide only services or hardware and hardware-related software as well. The so-called system integrators (such as Accenture, ATOS, Capgemini and Tata Consultancy Services) offer only services, which means that they can choose the hardware platform to be used on the basis of the situation's specific needs and thus achieve a close match with their clients' wishes. In addition, since system integrators are not the ones selling the hardware, they often manage to get good hardware prices for their clients. However, suppliers who also offer hardware and the software going with it, such as DXC and IBM, can make fully integrated offers. Outsourcing organisations doing business with them rarely get into hardware performance discussions, since these suppliers take responsibility for both application and hardware. That said, the prices of their services and hardware are not always clear, so their offers are less transparent, and outsourcing organisations have no choice in the hardware used.

9.4.1.3 Market segmentation

Since many IT services are commodities, such as desktop, server and network management, price is the most important sales argument. Nevertheless, the supplier's knowledge of a client's industry and the market developments in that industry can be used to offer extra added value and achieve a competitive advantage. Therefore, having such knowledge is essential. The supplier has to have both sector and domain knowledge and experience.[35]

Large suppliers are well represented in all major industries. However, representation alone does not suffice for delivering real added value in IT outsourcing relationships, which requires clear market positioning. The suppliers' market managers must use their knowledge of their client's industry to convince outsourcing organisations that the suppliers can be of real help.

9.4.1.4 Geographical scope

IT outsourcing partnerships increasingly have an international scope. Suppliers must therefore also deliver outside their own countries. To do so, they have a choice between relaying the work to subsidiaries or collaborating with other suppliers. Nowadays, many of the services to be delivered need not be executed on the spot. Remote service provisioning has been a serious possibility for decades now, causing the rise of offshore outsourcing. Most of the current outsourcing engagements are based on +80% offshore outsourcing. Subcontracting part of the IT services to local parties increases the risks for outsourcing organisations. Primary contractors must therefore assume end-to-end responsibility. Many suppliers therefore collaborate with subcontractors on the basis of framework agreements. This enables them to call in "trusted" subcontractors quickly and cost-effectively. A lack of such framework agreements increases the difficulty of arranging ad hoc solutions, thereby increasing the risk for outsourcing organisations.

9.4.2 A front office

A front office is the interface between an outsourcing organisation and a supplier. They strongly influence the effectiveness of the supplier and thereby the whole of the partnership's governance. Front offices include account management (which is responsible for relationship aspects) as well as contract and innovation management. These relational aspects must be executed on all three organisational levels (strategic, tactical and operational), while the people doing so are the hands and feet of the outsourcing partnership. For a successful operation, these responsibilities must be tightly aligned in order to ensure a quick, adequate reaction to questions and delivery problems. Of course, the partnership must be well anchored in the supplier's senior management efforts. This, too, will improve the supplier's agility and effectiveness.

9.4.2.1 Senior management embedment of the partnership

For the success of an IT outsourcing partnership, it is essential that the senior managers of both supplier and outsourcing organisation can easily contact one another. This does not involve the CIO only; the outsourcing organisation's business managers must also have a direct line to their supplier's senior managers. In case of trouble or otherwise, response times must be short.

Both parties must also be aware of one another's position. The supplier, for instance, usually has more information than the outsourcing organisation. Sharing it openly with their client is a good means of minimising distrust.[36,37]

While many suppliers' senior managers only pay attention during the selection phase, they would do better to stay in touch regularly during the whole of the contract period, even when everything is going fine. This kind of proactivity generates trust and contributes to the good governance of the partnership. Besides, suppliers may well be rewarded with an increase of their contract scope when new or extra work is to be done.

9.4.2.2 *Account management*

Account management is about maintaining and building one's relationships with the client. It involves building a network of relationships in the outsourcing organisation as well as staying ahead of industry developments.[38] The network can include risk and reward-based contracts in software.[39] The relationships to be built should include preferably not just a client's CIO and information managers, but also the business managers of outsourcing organisations. Unfortunately, not all outsourcing organisations allow their suppliers to build these relationships. Some are afraid that direct contacts between their suppliers and their business managers might influence the business managers' information service needs. CIO and information managers are quite capable of translating the needs of the business into terms that suppliers can work with. In such cases, getting permission to contact the client's business managers requires the time to gain the CIO's and information managers' trust. Letting the CIO or the information managers be present when suppliers meet their business managers is often useful; the business managers will then consider these contacts much less of a threat.

Apart from their knowledge of the client's industry and market, account managers must obviously know their own organisation's product portfolio very well. If they do not, their partnership can experience severe stress. In order to present their organisation's product portfolio well, account managers often bring along their service delivery managers, who are responsible for the actual delivery of the services contracted.

9.4.2.3 *Contract management*

In outsourcing partnerships, the supplier's contract managers represent a major contact for the outsourcing organisation, second only to account managers. Contract management means optimising the contractual agreements between supplier and outsourcing organisation. It involves managing the IT professionals who execute the work as well as taking care of the administrative aspects of the partnership, including reporting. With respect to invoicing, it is always wise to align with one's client, thus avoiding discussions and ensuring quick payment. These broad responsibilities have the consequence that suppliers make allowances for substantial costs for contract management.[33] In modern contracts, suppliers also track client satisfaction and profitability.[40]

While contract management is a front office task, service delivery managers are part of their organisation's back office. Contract managers act to increase customer satisfaction, and service delivery managers focus on efficiency and effectivity.

9.4.2.4 Innovation management

Many suppliers have a chief technology officer who represents their innovative efforts. However, this alone is not enough to ensure that clients always get true state-of-the-art technology. Suppliers should therefore set up innovation management teams, allocating innovation managers to clients. Those clients then have someone with whom they can discuss the potential offered by new technological developments and who is thus an important link to the outsourcing organisation's business managers.

Innovation managers draw the business managers' attention to new technologies, which has never been easy to outsource.[41] Even today, this is difficult when related to bounded rationality and IP (sharing).[42,43,44]

The discussions that follow often cause changes in delivered IT services. They can even cause changes in the client's business: business process redesign (BPR). Another of the innovation manager's tasks is ascertaining the proper alignment[45] between supplier and outsourcing organisation. Suppliers provide their account managers with essential support, enabling them to deepen the partnership with the client. Innovation managers offer their clients concrete proposals, often focused on value propositions rather than on technological products or services and frequently made in alliance with the supplier's partners. The innovation allows the supplier to distinguish itself from competitors and to add real value for the client.

9.4.3 A back office

Back offices take care of the actual delivery of IT services agreed upon in contracts between outsourcing organisation and supplier. Since delivery processes are the heart of the outsourcing partnership, outsourcing organisations must feel confident that their supplier's back office is up to the task. However, it is very difficult for outsourcing organisations to get a good idea of the capabilities of the supplier making them offers during the selection process.[46,47] It is therefore important that both outsourcing organisation and supplier carry out due diligence assessments before any contracts are signed.[35,48]

In practice, suppliers often set up a "pursue team" during the selection process, composed of senior IT professionals who must try to win the contract. Once successful, they tend to replace such seniors with more junior staff. It is therefore important that outsourcing organisations watch their interests closely and include their demands with respect to the team that will execute the services needed in the contract.

Another advantage of such contract clauses is that one is then more certain that the supplier will really be capable of delivering the services agreed.

9.4.3.1 The organisational embedment of the back office

Suppliers must make choices with respect to the execution of their IT service delivery. Efficiency and effectiveness are the objectives. A supplier's back office must be set up such that the office matches the supplier's service portfolio.

One of the choices to be made is between dedicated and non-dedicated resources. Allocating dedicated resources means that a close alignment can be achieved with the client's wishes, because the available knowledge of their business can be solidly anchored in the team of professionals carrying out the service delivery. However, dedicated resources do not allow much room for advantages of scale, while non-dedicated resources do. Generally speaking, the deciding factor is the character of the services rendered. For commodity services, non-dedicated resources are usually the right solution. The dedicated also enable the outsourcing organisation to contribute industry knowledge by allocating IT professionals with experience in the field.

Another choice concerns employees transferred from the outsourcing organisation to the supplier. Should they be directly integrated into the supplier's back office, or be maintained in a separate unit as a part of the outsourcing organisation?

Since outsourcing organisations usually outsource their IT services because they need a change, integration seems the best option. However, social obligations may point both ways.

9.4.3.2 *Service delivery management*

Service delivery managers face many developments, both in business and in technology. They must be able to act on anything and everything. Another aspect of their work is people management. Service delivery managers constantly face challenges in identifying, recruiting and retaining competent IT staff in order to acquire and possess the necessary skills to manage the outsourcing organisation's IT needs. Personnel management is key in the success of a service delivery manager.

A major focus of the job of service delivery manager is efficiency, but resources must also be made available for innovation. Most suppliers allocate a set percentage of their budget to innovation. By using that money to best effect, service delivery managers can ensure that the services delivered will also be valuable in the future. Thus, suppliers help secure their organisation's continuity.

9.4.3.3 *Process-based service delivery*

To deliver services effectively and efficiently, suppliers must define and implement standard processes: methodology development and dissemination. Having such standards shows clients and potential clients that one really can deliver as promised. Many outsourcing organisations demand process certification as part of their selection processes. However, certification also negatively impacts innovation.[49] The first step to such a process orientation is acquiring ISO 9000 related to quality management and ISO/IEC 17799 certificates related to information security. Implementing the Capability Maturity Model Integration (CMMi) for application development and maintenance and ITIL/BS15000 for infrastructure management (originated from CCTA 1993) and replaced by the ISO/IEC 20000, also important for process-based service delivery. Finally, Six Sigma (originally developed by Motorola), in combination with LEAN,[50] may also be implemented, with the aim of achieving focused improvements.[51] Six Sigma can also be helpful to increase the quality of service provisioning.[52]

9.4.3.4 Audit processes

It is essential that service suppliers implement audit processes. Suppliers can use these processes to show clients how IT service delivery processes have been set up. Also, some outsourcing organisations have legal obligations that are transferred to suppliers. These obligations usually involve privacy (in particular, being compliant with GDPR), information security (for example, in the financial services industry) or data reliability (for example, in the pharmaceutical industry). Setting up audit processes helps to cover the most important risks involved.[53] Therefore, audit processes receive increasing attention. In the US, the main audit processes are those of Sarbanes Oxley, HIPPA, Gramm-Leach-Billey, the DB Breach Security Notification Act (CA) and the USA Patriot Act. In the UK, the most important is the Organisations Bill, in Germany, the Cramme Code and in Switzerland, the Swiss Code of Best Practice. All other EU countries have their own regulations.[54]

Auditing processes involve three major matters: internal controls, compliance and calculations.[33] The ISAE 3402 is the *de facto* global standard regarding suppliers' special purpose reports on internal controls. Outsourcing organisations may require an ISAE 3402 certification from their supplier to be compliant. However, outsourcing organisations have to understand that the costs of a statement are substantial for both the supplier and the outsourcing organisation. Compliance with contract provisions and service-level agreements (SLAs) includes a broad range of subjects. Finally, there are similar benchmarks for contractual agreements on the calculation of charges and performance levels by suppliers.

9.4.5 The availability of IT professionals

There is a shortage of qualified IT professionals.[55] Keeping IT professionals for longer periods is difficult. There remains a shortage of those who have the right training and experience. This situation is caused by the rapidity of the technological developments in the field. IT professionals must keep up to date, which involves much training and a steady hand to guide careers.

9.4.5.1 Sourcing portfolios

For the execution of their IT services, delivery suppliers have a choice between onshore and offshore outsourcing, a special case of the latter being nearshore outsourcing.[56] Onshore outsourcing means that the services are delivered from the outsourcing organisation's countries of residence; offshore and nearshore indicate delivery from abroad, usually countries with lower wages such as Argentina, Brazil, China, India, the Philippines, Poland or Russia, the greatest advantage of course being a cost decrease.[57,58] The difference between offshore and nearshore outsourcing is the distance between outsourcing organisation and supplier. There are no fixed rules here, but for a North American, for example, outsourcing organisations delivery from Central America would be nearshore; from India, offshore.[59]

As not all services are equally suited to all three options, suppliers must carefully consider their distribution over their portfolio. Nearshore and off-shore outsourcing are usually only included in supplier's offers if their clients specifically ask for it. Nearshore and offshore outsourcing is caused by the allocation of profit and loss accountability: generally speaking, each country's operating organisation is held accountable for its results, and management teams in developed countries will therefore not like to see their revenue move to other countries even if it saves their clients costs.

9.4.5.2 Embedment of transferred employees

Outsourcing involves divestments on the part of the outsourcing organisation. If this includes the transfer of employees to a supplier, extra care must be taken with staff with a long tenure. The staff are very vulnerable and (when fired) may not easily be able to find new jobs. Nevertheless, in outsourcing, objectives often change, so suppliers will need to make the necessary changes to the IT delivery processes. These changes make it more difficult for older employees to keep up. It may be necessary to deploy staff other than the original staff now transferred to the supplier. However, management attention is required to ensure that the knowledge of all transferred staff members is captured.[60,61]

The changes in the way services are delivered frequently cause older employees who have been transferred to the supplier to leave as well, and before reaching normal retirement age. This problematic situation requires much attention and effort, for example, in the shape of training and coaching, to try and keep such staff employable.

9.4.5.3 Attention for individual employees

It is very important to pay attention to individual employees. They must feel at home with their organisation.[62] Of course, suppliers must also offer career opportunities, which includes training possibilities and is closely related to salary matters. The organisation's financial policies in this respect must therefore be flexible. Nonrecurring bonuses or temporary labour market surcharges may be granted in order to prevent the salaries of IT professionals rising permanently as a result of temporary conditions, which would make it difficult to readjust them once conditions are normalised. To ensure flexibility and yet not be ruled by temporary conditions, suppliers must be able to refer to their salary policies.

9.4.5.4 A planned approach

The predictability of resources needed for the mid- and long-term future is a supplier's issue which requires their serious attention. This is not easy and therefore requires a planned approach, including a so-called staff-disposition plan. Such plans are based on current capacity in terms of recognised (technical) competences, as well as the changes expected. The three kinds of change that are likely to influence the organisation's capacity are employee turnover (people resigning, being fired or retiring), training (increasing the depth or breadth of their knowledge) and recruitment.

Suppliers must realise that the continuity of their IT services delivery may be jeopardised if 20% or more of their IT professionals are replaced within 12 months. Such rapid changes cause a loss of tacit knowledge.[63] A similar problem is that of suppliers' internal dynamics. Quite contrary to their staff-disposition plans, often the best professionals are moved from one client to another in order to solve the problem of meeting contracted agreements. Again, continuity may be jeopardised.

9.4 Governance factors – the relationship

Four governance factors have been identified that concern the whole of partnership relations between outsourcing organisation and suppliers:

1 unambiguously defined responsibilities, for both the outsourcing organisation and their suppliers;
2 contracts, in which such responsibilities (as well as other aspects) are captured;
3 trust in the partnership, well embedded in both organisations;
4 steering organisations, set up to ensure the regular exchange of information and opinions.

These governance factors will be discussed here in further detail, divided (as in the previous chapters) into four governance aspects each, for extra clarity. Apart from the governance factors relating to outsourcing organisation and individual suppliers, attention must also be paid to the governance of their relationship as a whole.

First of all, the responsibilities of each of the partnership's participants must be clear, without any ambiguity. The outsourcing contract plays an important role here. However, having a contract is not enough. Participants to a partnership must continuously keep each other's interests in mind: trust is an important factor in realising IT partnership governance.[64] Finally, steering organisations are needed in order to generate such trust.

Most of the governance factors are linked to the agency theory, as there is information asymmetry between the outsourcing organisation and the supplier.[65] The insights of the resource-based view contribute to the

Table 9.4 Governance factors and governance aspects of IT outsourcing relationships

Governance factors	Governance aspects
Unambiguously defined responsibilities	Defining client-supplier interfaces
	Defining organisational responsibilities
	Optimising and updating organisational responsibilities
	Setting up procedures for responsibility transfer
Contracts	Defining the IT services unambiguously
	Defining a procedure for situations not described in the contract
	Structuring the contract into layers
	Defining a procedure for price changes
Trust in the partnership	Arranging for trust to be built continuously
	Ensuring personal trust between key staff members on both sides
	Measuring trust regularly
	Aligning frames of reference
Steering organisations	Steering organisations on the strategic organisational level
	Steering organisations on the tactical organisational level
	Steering organisations on the operational organisational level
	Ensuring coherence between the several conference levels

implementation of responsibilities and steering organisations.[66] The insights of the transaction cost theory contribute to governance "contracts."[10,11] The coordination costs of outsourcing contracts are substantial, and the fourth governance factor, steering organisations, is part of coordination costs. These four governance factors (clearly defined responsibilities, well set-up contracts, trust in the partnership and steering organisations) are listed in Table 9.4.

9.4.1 Unambiguously defined responsibilities

Even in IT partnerships that involve little complexity, it is important that everyone's responsibilities are completely clear. In reality, IT outsourcing partnerships often involve many participants, especially since most outsourcing organisations prefer having multiple suppliers. Coordinating all these suppliers therefore falls to the outsourcing organisation's IT department. But how can they guarantee optimum collaboration between all suppliers? For one, it is essential that the IT services are managed as a portfolio.[67] Outsourcing organisations have to closely monitor their suppliers' portfolios.[68] Another issue that must be considered here is suppliers who subcontract some of their activities to third parties. Doing so generally improves the flexibility of the set-up, but it requires much more of the supplier's management attention, and attention must also be paid from a partnership governance point of view. The most important matter is to have all parties work together smoothly – only this can lay the basis for a successful IT outsourcing partnership.

9.4.1.1 Defining client-supplier interfaces

Outsourcing organisations must define their information needs for themselves. The actual delivery of the services is then the responsibility of the suppliers, one of whom may be the outsourcing organisation's internal IT department.

Suppliers often attempt to support their clients' CIOs and information managers in their task of identifying information provisioning solutions. By involving their suppliers, CIOs and information managers may achieve advantages of scale. However, an important disadvantage of doing so is that some control over service delivery may be lost to those suppliers. Shifting such responsibilities may lessen the outsourcing organisation's grip on their suppliers.

9.4.1.2 Defining organisational responsibilities

When responsibilities are defined, the lines between outsourcing organisations and suppliers are usually pretty clear. Organisational responsibility must be defined. These responsibilities describe the situations in which the activities of different suppliers connect with one another. A good rule of thumb is to ensure as little interdependence between suppliers as possible. If one supplier provides network management services, for example, including the on-site services involved, it is best not to have another supplier, who works on server management, carry out on-site server tasks as well. The network management services supplier is in a better position to handle these activities too, since network disturbances and server disturbances are often directly related.

9.4.1.3 Optimising and updating organisational responsibilities

The nature and scope of IT service delivery change with time, as do organisation information needs. Organisational responsibility must therefore be optimised and updated regularly[69]; this is nowadays an integral part of governance in IT outsourcing relations.[70] For example, if a standard desktop environment is introduced, it may be wise to let a single supplier manage the environment entirely. One or more organisational responsibilities are then removed. Likewise, if a new server management system is introduced, a new supplier may be needed to implement that system; then, an extra organisational responsibility interface is added. In another vein, it is sometimes necessary to update one's organisational responsibilities because the suppliers involved do not perform as they should. The responsibility for delivering the IT services needed may then be transferred to another supplier, thus again causing changes in the organisational responsibilities. Situations such as the ones described here turn the updating of one's organisational responsibilities into a continuous process.

9.4.1.4 Setting up procedures for responsibility transfer

In the past, many outsourcing contracts were repeatedly renewed, which sometimes made them seem almost permanent. It is now understood that all contracts end at some point, so it is a good idea to be prepared for the transfer of responsibilities that must then take place. Transfer procedures should be set up, the main objective of which being to eliminate continuity risks to the service delivery. One of the aspects of such procedures is the thorough documentation of all activities that are to be carried out by the new supplier. The suppliers need this information in order to be able to carry out their tasks properly.

9.4.2 Contracts

In IT outsourcing partnerships, contracts are important instruments for both outsourcing organisations and suppliers. In these contracts, the agreements are laid down on the services to be delivered, the service levels and penalties expected and the consequent prices.[71] Contracts have been more fully discussed in Chapter 7, but here a few aspects are reiterated. For instance, outsourcing organisations should never simply accept a supplier's general terms and conditions. Especially considering payment terms, liability and intellectual property, the rule is to avoid the supplier's standard contract.[30] However, contracting bespoke services is different from contracting cloud services. The three aforementioned matters must therefore be thoroughly discussed before an agreement is reached.

Another important aspect of contract writing is the balance between business and technology perspectives. Too many technical details cloud the issue, since only a few people are then able to understand what the contract specifies – and these people are usually not the business managers whose information needs the contract is supposed to cater to. Business managers must be enabled to play their part in contract discussions.

9.4.2.1 Defining the IT services unambiguously

A first objective when writing outsourcing contracts is to define IT services unambiguously. The contract includes both the supplier's and the outsourcing organisation's tasks and responsibilities, which must be described in some detail. The service levels required must also be defined.[72] Many suppliers use sets of definitions to describe their work. Outsourcing organisations doing business with several suppliers may be confronted with a number of such sets, all of which are slightly different from the rest. Organisations would do well to make their own set(s) and require all suppliers to work on that basis rather than accepting any of the supplier's definition sets. An added advantage of doing so is that the outsourcing organisation then has more control over their suppliers.[73]

Since many services of the total delivery package are interrelated and interdependent, such relationships must also be laid down in the contract. Defining these interfaces will establish better understanding among the several parties of the interdependencies in the partnership as a whole.

9.4.2.2 Defining a procedure for situations not described in the contract

Business dynamics and the developments in the field of technology are such that there will always be unexpected situations. This unexpectedness of things may cause friction or even disputes between outsourcing organisations and their suppliers. All parties should then try to solve such matters in concert and avoid having to go to court over them. To facilitate such discussions, contract parties can include agreements on how to deal with situations not described in the contract. These agreements must define which people will contact one another; financial pointers may be included as well. The goal is always to prevent a situation getting in the way of service delivery. One possible solution must be kept in mind and should preferably be included in the contract: independent, binding arbitration. This means that a third party decides when the outsourcing organisation and its suppliers cannot find a solution to which all parties agree. Taking a decision is always better than letting the problem exist unresolved. If arbitration has been included in the contract before the partnership begins, a solution is all the more quickly found when a problem arises.

9.4.2.3 Structure the contract into layers

Business dynamics and technological developments do not influence all contractual agreements equally. Structuring the contract in several layers will accommodate the differences between the relatively stable aspects and those components that are more likely to need a change. Aspects that are unlikely to change much, like payment, jurisdiction and liabilities, may be laid down in framework agreements. Service agreements can then be used to define the IT services involved. Finally, SLAs contain the service levels and quantities to be delivered, as well as their price. Many suppliers work with service catalogues. These contain descriptions of the services they can deliver as a kind of menu from which to choose. These catalogues are used to set up service agreements and SLAs.

9.4.2.4 Defining a procedure for price changes

Cost-saving is one of the prime arguments for outsourcing. Establishing the right price level is therefore important, though it is not as easy as it may seem. During the selection and agreement phase, suppliers compete for the contract. However, once the contract is signed, there is no more competition.

Contracts must therefore contain clauses that ensure market conformity during their running time.

To this end, the initial price is often combined with an indexing mechanism, the advantage of which (from the outsourcing organisation's point of view) is that the costs of the services are highly predictable. That said, this set-up does not allow for adaptations as a result of price level changes in the IT outsourcing industry as a whole. Another possibility is the open-book approach. The supplier shows a client the costs made for the delivery of services; should these costs rise, the increase may be included in their prices. The disadvantage here is the lack of incentive for cost effectiveness. This approach therefore only works well for innovative projects. Finally, the contract may include a benchmarking agreement. A yearly benchmark then provides input for setting next year's prices. This ensures competitive pricing. To increase the benchmarking efficiency (and thus decrease its costs), the services delivered should be in accordance with the definitions as determined by the independent consultancy that executes the benchmark. For commodity services, this is usually not a problem, since most suppliers use almost the same definitions for them anyway. Nevertheless, benchmarking is always an expensive process. Many organisations devise a combination of indexing mechanisms and benchmarking: in principle, the prices of the services delivered are indexed every year, but if the fees in the industry as a whole deviate too much from the index, a benchmark is carried out and used as the basis for next year's prices.

9.4.3 Trust in partnership

Managing IT outsourcing partnerships is not a matter of the "hard side" only. Much attention must be paid to the "soft side," especially trust, which is of essential importance.[21,64,74] A lack of trust, by opportunistic behaviour, results in an accelerated failure-time.[75] Several kinds of trust may be defined: organisational trust, group trust and personal trust, among others.[76] All require attention if the partnership is to be a success. The major difficulties with trust are that it takes time to generate and that it is very difficult to measure. To give trust time to grow, suppliers and outsourcing organisations must begin by clearly expressing to one another that they will put effort into it. Then, trust-building is explicitly on the programme.

9.4.3.1 Arranging for trust to be built continuously

A first step towards generating trust is being open in one's communication. Suppliers must provide clear and understandable reports on the services they have delivered; outsourcing organisations should give clear feedback on their supplier's performance.[77] Essentially, proper reports are a matter of communication hygiene, and it applies especially to the parties' formal communication. With respect to their informal communication, much trust may be generated by consultation: before any formal communication takes place, the partners discuss matters informally. If new ideas and solutions can be tested and discussed first, before they are laid down and everybody reads about them in their formal communication, mishaps can be prevented. Care must still be taken, of course, but informal consultation generally brings the parties closer together.

9.4.3.2 Ensuring personal trust between key staff members on both sides

Trust between organisations and groups is important but not enough. For collaboration efforts to work, personal trust is needed, too.[76] The process of generating personal trust begins during the contract negotiation process. Both supplier and outsourcing organisation must get a feel for which personal profiles best fit the management of their partnership. Some researchers even advise outsourcing organisations to select the account manager they feel the most comfortable with.[30] Then, after the contract has been signed, the key people on both sides must take time to get to know each other. Sports and cultural outings are excellent opportunities to do so. Should the match be uncomfortable, it may at this point still be necessary to replace one or two individuals. Both parties must realise, however, that frequent personnel changes do not help generate personal trust, and personal relationships should always remain professional.

9.4.3.3 Measuring trust regularly

IT outsourcing partnerships involve much reporting. These reports should not only concern the services delivered but also the degree of trust between the partners. Reporting has long been a difficult subject to discuss, especially since most outsourcing organisations have thought of their outsourcing relations in terms of client–customer relationships rather than partnerships. However, for IT outsourcing to work well, relationships must go much beyond that. To measure trust, objective instruments should be used.

Several consulting organisations, such as Deloitte, Gartner, ISG and KPMG, offer tools with which such a measurement can be facilitated. These tools generally resemble balanced scorecards.[78] Once the degree of trust between the partners has been measured, the results must be used to increase it further. To this end, boot camp sessions can be effective, but it may also be necessary to replace some of the team's members.

Other soft elements that may be included in assessment scorecards used for IT outsourcing relationships are innovation or governance proposals. Innovation proposals contain suggestions for improving the service delivery; on the basis of a business case, the outsourcing organisation can decide to accept the offer or not. Bringing forward innovation is easier said than done,[79] and relational governance is required.[80,81] Since suppliers obviously have a commercial interest in these proposals, it can be difficult to assess the suppliers' value. Governance proposals may include agreements on support given by the supplier in professionalising their client's demand management. The supplier will not take over demand management as such, but they will contribute their knowledge and know-how to set it up to maximum effect. A difficulty in this respect is that it is hard for outsourcing organisations to estimate either the value of their supplier's contribution or the effects of such professionalisation efforts.

9.4.3.4 Aligning frames of reference

Apart from profit, turnover and market penetration goals, many organisations wish to act on their social responsibilities. Environmental care is one point of attention, and it may be explicitly included in the partnership contract. Laying down an environmental protection code helps the partners find their bearings in this field – not just the outsourcing organisation but also their suppliers.[82, 83, 84, 85] Such codes may include aspects like ink cartridge reuse, paper use (double-sided or single, recycling, etc.) and stimulating the use of public transport rather than private automobiles. In a similar vein, social policies with respect to employees may be included. Even though suppliers are unlikely to exploit their staff or use child labour, setting clear standards will help generate mutual understanding and trust.

9.4.4 Steering organisations

Since so many things must be aligned for a partnership to work well, all these matters must be discussed and then agreed upon. When the steering organisations to do so are set up, it is important that every issue is allocated to the right organisational level – strategic, tactical and operational. This means deciding who talks to whom and about what.[33] Of course, a properly functioning partnership requires that there be a well thought-through coherence between these levels – which procedure must be followed when no agreement can be reached on a certain level, and how are issues escalated to the level above? Finally, each organisational level has its own conference frequency. Strategic matters are usually discussed only a few times per year, while many operational issues require daily attention. The steering organisations discussed in full in the next four sections of this chapter are summarised in Table 9.5.

9.4.4.1 Steering organisations on the strategic organisational level

On the strategic level, three kinds of conferences are to be found: the IT board, the partner board and, when needed, the change advisory board. They meet once or twice a year.

Generally, only outsourcing organisation staff are present. These internal steering organisations are used to maximise the contribution of IT to the organisation's business processes. Aligning future business requirements and providing business managers with an overview of technical innovations

Table 9.5 Steering organisations on all three organisational levels, including the subjects discussed there and the people attending them.

Level[a]	Conference	Subjects discussed	Meeting frequency	Attendees – outsourcing organisation[b]	Attendees – supplier[c]
S	IT Board	Aligning future business requirements Providing business managers with an overview of technical innovations	Once a year	**Chief information officer** Information managers Business managers (including C-level)	Independent experts (only invited when necessary)
S	Partner Board	Joint strategic planning Resolving issues escalated from the tactical level Relation building	Once or twice a year	**Chief information officer** Information managers	**IT director/Account manager** Contract manager Service delivery manager
S	Change Advisory Board	Change request approvals	Every two months	**Information managers** Business analysts Business managers	**Contract manager** Service delivery managers
T	Service Portfolio Board	The appropriateness of new technologies	Twice a year	**Information managers** Service delivery supervisor Business managers	**Contract manager** Service delivery manager
T	Service Review Meeting	Service provider performance Improvement plans status	Monthly	**Service delivery supervisor** Information managers	**Contract manager** Service delivery managers
O	Service Meeting	Day-to-day service provisioning issues	Weekly	**Service delivery supervisor** Business analysts Business managers	**Contract manager** Service delivery manager
O	Change Control Meeting	Analysing the implications of implementing change requests Implementing approved change requests	Weekly	**Information managers** Business analysts	**Contract manager** Service delivery managers
O	Project Meeting	Day-to-day project execution issues	Weekly or daily	**Contract manager** Information analysts Business managers	**Project managers** Contract manager (Service delivery manager)

a S = Strategic level; T = Tactical level; O = Operational level.
b The meeting frequency depends on the size of the contract (here: annual contract values of more than ten million euros).
c The bold attendees are in charge for their respective companies.

therefore figure prominently on their agenda. Sometimes, IT boards are also used to get feedback from business managers on IT strategy drafts, prior to their endorsement. In all cases, the results of IT board discussions are captured in the organisation's IT strategy.

As the IT board's discussions involve the organisation's business strategy, usually no representatives of the organisation's suppliers are present. Resistance to sharing such strategic information with outsiders generally prevents their attendance, as do the suppliers' commercial interests. Only real experts with an in-depth knowledge of certain topics are sometimes invited, this being knowledge-based contribution by suppliers. However, even then there is a preference for independent consultants.

The primary task of partner boards is strategic planning, which involves senior managers from both the outsourcing organisation and their supplier, in order to implement visionary strategies. Partner boards are also the place where issues that are escalated from the tactical organisational level are decided. These issues are usually matters concerning service provisioning and mutual contractual obligations. After all, contracts provide guidance, but they do not cover everything. Both parties must work on this in good faith, and relationship-building is therefore an important aspect of the board's work, too.

Finally, the interests of both partners may be furthered by setting up a change advisory board, to which independent consultants are often invited. The rationale behind calling such a meeting is that the changes continually made in dynamic partnerships must be implemented with both sides' interests in mind, which requires the careful attention of a separate conference. Adding independent advisers on this strategic governance level ensures that changes in service provisioning and contractual obligations are made with integrity.

9.4.4.2 Steering organisations on the tactical organisational level

On the tactical level, there are three steering organisations as well: the service portfolio board, the service review meeting and the contract review meeting. They meet every month or, in the case of the service portfolio board, every two months. Issues that cannot be solved on this level are escalated to the strategic boards.

Service portfolio boards explore the appropriateness of new technologies; this act of exploration is also known as technology watch. The characteristics of the outsourcing organisation's production processes are therefore of prime importance to service portfolio board discussions, as are the organisation's configuration management and software control and distribution processes. On the basis of the outsourcing organisation's IT strategy, the supplier provides the board with feasibility studies and pilot projects for new technologies. The board then takes decisions on the implementation of such new technologies. Ideally, however, strategic guidance is not provided by the outsourcing organisation only: if the outsourcing organisation is willing to share not only their IT strategy but also their business strategy with their suppliers, the exploration of appropriate new technologies will be more effective. The initiatives of service portfolio boards have to be approved by their organisation's partner board; this escalation to the strategic organisational level is necessary because implementing new technologies involves substantial costs.

In service review meetings, the performance of the organisation's suppliers is discussed on the basis of reports for the previous month as well as on earlier periods, so that any trends can be discerned. Service-level management processes therefore play a major role here. If a supplier underperforms, improvement plans must be made, concerning among other matters incident and problem management processes. These plans must then be implemented by the supplier, a process that often requires a certain amount of change management. Consequently, the status reviews of such implementation plans and change management processes are discussed in service review meetings as well.

9.4.4.3 Steering organisations on the operational level

Finally, on the operational level, there are also three kinds of conference: service meetings, change control meetings and project meetings. These meetings have a weekly or daily frequency.

Unsolved issues on the operational level are escalated to the tactical level. In service meetings, day-to-day service provisioning issues are discussed. The partnership's service-level management process is therefore very important to these meetings. Since it is essential to keep track of all issues discussed, incident and problem management processes play a major role as well. Escalation to the tactical level, if necessary, is advanced to the organisation's service review meeting.

Change control meetings analyse the implications of carrying out any change requests made. Since the changes requested may be business-driven, business managers sometimes attend these meetings. To be able to make the analyses, the organisation's present mode of operations, its configuration management and its software control and distribution process are closely involved. On the basis of the outsourcing organisations analyses, change control meetings approve or reject implementation plans for changes, which means that the organisation's change management process is involved too. However, final and financial approval remains the responsibility of the organisation's partner board, as changes involve substantial costs.

Finally, in project meetings, day-to-day project issues are discussed, all of which must be kept track of as the partnership progresses. If any unsolved issues have to be escalated, it will be to the tactical-level service review meeting.

9.4.4.4 Ensuring coherence between the several steering organisations

Of course, for the partnership's success, it is important that this set of boards and meetings is formed into a coherent whole. Each conference's processes

and procedures must be aligned with those of the other steering organisations. The ITIL guidelines provide a good connection between the tactical
and operational levels, while the COBIT guidelines do so for the strategic
and tactical levels.

The size of the partnership naturally influences the steering organisations needed. For small-scale partnerships, strategic and tactical levels can be
merged. However, the operational level will always remain separate, since the
tasks on this level differ completely from those on the other levels.

9.5 Conclusions

An outsourcing situation calls for governance that considers the entire outsourcing: the situation of the outsourcing organisation, the situation of the
supplier and the relationship itself. The conclusions for each factor are summarised below.

9.5.1 Governance factors – the outsourcing organisation

Four outsourcing organisation-side governance factors of the conceptual
framework have been discussed in detail. The IT strategy should prepare
the organisation for business dynamics. For such a strategy to be any good, it
must be well aligned with the business. Clear IT strategies provide guidance
to suppliers. The increasing interaction between business and IT renders a
proper alignment increasingly important.

Achieving business–IT alignment and fostering the relationship between
business and IT requires appropriate structures and processes. Appointing IT
portfolio managers in the business and involving the business in the management of the IT partnership are important organisational measures to be
taken.

The CIO provides a clear demand management at the strategic level. The
CIO has knowledge of the business and technology. Their main responsibility is developing the IT strategy and ensuring the continuing support for
it in the organisation. CIOs should report to one of the Board of Directors'
members. The trend seems to be towards reporting to the general manager
and away from reporting to the director of finances or the chief operations
manager.

Information managers provide a clear demand management structure on the
tactical level. Their responsibility is the implementation of the organisation's IT
strategy. It goes without saying that information managers must have excellent
communication skills. They have to generate business support for the IT strategy, which is much more effective than forcing decisions on people.

9.5.2 Governance factors – supplier

Within the context of an outsourcing partnership, it is the supplier who must
take care of the actual delivery of the IT services contracted for. They must

therefore pay thorough attention to the governance of the partnership in order to guarantee delivery continuity. In this chapter, the four supplier-side governance factors are discussed.

Suppliers must be able to show their clients and potential clients what IT services they can deliver and how. The "what" and "how" include their plans for the future, which form the basis of any IT outsourcing partnerships, their current and near-future product portfolios and their targeted markets.

Front offices include account management (which is responsible for relation aspects) as well as contract and innovation management. These management tasks must be executed on all three organisational levels (strategic, tactical and operational), and the people doing so are the hands and feet of the outsourcing partnership. A successful front office organisation depends on the embedment of senior management in the partnership and a well-functioning account and contract management.

Since these delivery processes are the heart of the outsourcing partnership, outsourcing organisations must feel confident that their supplier's back office is up to the task. Important questions relate to the organisational embedment of the back office: are there dedicated or non-dedicated resources, and are transferred employees integrated in the partnership?

The rapidity of the technological developments in the field causes a shortage of qualified IT professionals. A well-balanced sourcing portfolio consisting of onshore, offshore and nearshore outsourcing should be matched with the outsourcing organisation's needs. It is important for the supplier to have a well-developed HR policy to bind their employees to the organisation. Staff-disposition plans are needed to plan the future availability of resources needed.

9.5.3 Governance factors – relationship

Attention must also be paid to the governance of the relation as a whole. Since such relations are the nucleus of IT partnerships, a breakdown into several governance factors is required.

The outsourcing organisations' information needs and the supplier's responsibilities must be completely clear. However, in multiple outsourcing agreements, determining the boundaries between individual suppliers' responsibilities is less straightforward. Organisational responsibility interfaces, which describe the situations in which the activities of different suppliers connect with one another, need to be established.

A first objective when writing outsourcing contracts is to define IT services unambiguously. This includes both the supplier and the outsourcing organisation's tasks and responsibilities. Contract parties should include agreements on how to deal with (unexpected) situations not described in the contract. Structuring the contract in several layers will accommodate the differences between the relatively stable aspects and those components that are more likely to need a change. Aspects that are unlikely to change significantly, like payment, jurisdiction and liabilities, may be laid down in framework agreements.

Trust should be purposefully managed. A first step towards generating trust is being open in one's communication. Since trust between organisations and groups is important but not enough, personal trust between key staff members on both sides must be ensured. Measuring trust on a regular basis, through, for example, a balanced scorecard, helps to facilitate intervention when lack of trust seems to emerge.

Steering organisations are needed to assure that the right issues are addressed on the right level and by the right people. The ITIL guidelines provide a good connection between the tactical and operational levels, while the COBIT guidelines do so for the strategic and tactical levels.

Notes

1 Lee, J. N., Park, Y., Straub, D. W., & Koo, Y. (2019). Holistic archetypes of IT outsourcing strategy: A contingency fit and configurational approach. *MIS Quarterly, 43*(4), 1201–1225.
2 Porter, M. (1980). *Competitive strategy.* New York: The Free Press.
3 Thompson, J. D. (1967). *Organizations in action: Social sciences bases of administrative theory.* New York: McGraw-Hill.
4 Pfeffer, J., & Salancik, G. R. (1978). *The external control of organizations: A resource dependence perspective.* New York: Harper & Row.
5 Barney, J. (1997). *Gaining and sustaining competitive advantage.* Reading, MA: Addison-Wesley.
6 Prahalad, C. K., & Hamel, G. (1990). The core competence of the corporation. *Harvard Business Review.*
7 DiMaggio, P. J., & Powell, W. W. (1983). The iron cage revisited: Institutional isomorphism and collective rationality in organizational fields. *American Sociological Review, 48*(2), 147–160.
8 Dyer, J. H., & Singh, H. (1998). The relational view: Cooperative strategy and sources of interorganizational competitive advantage. *The Academy of Management Review, 23*(4), 660–679.
9 Fama, E. F., & Jensen, M. C. (1983). Separation of ownership and control. *The Journal of Law & Economics, 26*(2), 301–325.
10 Coase, R. (1937). The nature of the firm. *Economica, 4,* 386–405.
11 Williamson, O. (1975). *Markets and hierarchies.* New York: Free Press.
12 Lacity, M. C., & Willcocks, L. P. (2001). *Global information technology outsourcing: In search of business advantage.* New York: John Wiley & Sons.
13 Das, A., & Grover, D. (2018). Biased decisions on IT outsourcing: how vendor selection adds value. *Journal of Business Strategy, 39*(5), 31–40.
14 Currie, W., & Willcocks, L. (1998). Analysing four types of IT-outsourcing decisions in the context of scale, client/server, interdependency and risk mitigation. *Information Systems Journal, 8*(2), 119–143.
15 Barthelemy, J. (2003). The hard and soft sides of IT outsourcing management. *European Management Journal, 21*(5), 539–548.
16 Langfield-Smith, K., & Smith, D. (2003). Management control systems and trust in outsourcing relationships. *Management Accounting Research, 14*(3), 281–307.
17 Delen, G. P., Peters, R. J., Verhoef, C., & van Vlijmen, S. F. M. (2019). Foundations for measuring IT-outsourcing success and failure. *Journal of Systems and Software, 156,* 113–125.

18 Thompson, J. (1967). *Organizations in action: Social sciences bases of administrative theory*. New York: McGraw-Hill.
19 Pfeffer, J., & Salancik, G. (1978). *The external control of organizations*. San Francisco, CA: HarperCollins.
20 Peppard, J., & Ward, J. (2016). *The strategic management of information systems – building a digital strategy* (4th ed.). New York: Wiley.
21 Benson, R. J., Ribbers, P., & Blitstein, R. B. (2014). *Trust and partnership: Strategic IT management for turbulent times* (Ser. Wiley cio series). New York: Wiley.
22 Gerrity, T. P., & Rockart, J. F. (1986). End-user computing: Are you a leader or a laggard?. *Sloan Management Review (1986-1998)*, *27*(4), 25.
23 Parker, M. M., Trainor, H. E., & Benson, R. J. (1989). *Information strategy and economics*. Hoboken, NJ: Prentice-Hall, Inc.
24 Erdogmus, T., Czermak, M., Baumsteiger, D., Kohn, D., Boller-Hoffecker, A., Schmidt, N., & Linden, R. (2018). How to support clients and vendors in IT outsourcing engagements: The different roles of third-party advisory services. *Journal of Information Technology Teaching Cases*, *8*(2), 184–191.
25 Sanz, L. F., Gómez-Pérez, J., & Castillo-Martinez, A. (2018). Analysis of the European ICT competence frameworks. In Ahuja, V., & Rathore, S. (Eds.), *Multidisciplinary perspectives on human capital and information technology professionals* (pp. 225–245). Hershey, PA: IGI Global.
26 Johnson, A. M., & Lederer, A. L. (2010). CEO/CIO mutual understanding, strategic alignment, and the contribution of IS to the organization. *Information & Management*, *47*(3), 138–149.
27 Haeckel, S. H. (1999). *Adaptive enterprise: Creating and leading sense-and-respond organizations*. Boston, MA: Harvard Business Press.
28 Tan, F. T. C., Pan, S. L., & Zuo, M. (2019). Realising platform operational agility through information technology–enabled capabilities: A resource-interdependence perspective. *Information Systems Journal*, *29*(3), 582–608.
29 Karimi-Alaghehband, F., & Rivard, S. (2019). Information technology outsourcing and architecture dynamic capabilities as enablers of organizational agility. *Journal of Information Technology*, *34*(2), 129–159.
30 Lacity, M., & Hirschheim, R. (1995). *Beyond the information systems outsourcing bandwagon*. Chichester: Wiley & Sons.
31 Feeny, D., Lacity, M., & Willcocks, L. P. (2005). Taking the measure of outsourcing providers. *MIT Sloan Management Review*, *46*(3), 41–48.
32 Lioliou, E., & Willcocks, L. P. (2019). Exploring outsourcing, governance, and discourse. In Lioliou, E. (Ed.), *Global outsourcing discourse* (pp. 1–19). Cham: Palgrave Macmillan.
33 Cullen, S., & Willcocks, L. (2003). *Intelligent IT outsourcing: Eight building blocks to success*. Oxford: Butterworth-Heinemann.
34 DiMaggio, P. J., & Powell, W. W. (1983). The iron cage revisited: Institutional isomorphism and collective rationality in organizational fields. *American Sociological Review*, *48*, 147–160.
35 Willcocks, L., Hindle, J., Feeny, D., & Lacity, M. (2004). IT and business process outsourcing: The knowledge potential. *Information Systems Management*, *21*(3), 7–15.
36 Aubert, B., Patry, M., & Rivard, S. (2003). A tale of two outsourcing contracts: An agency-theoretical perspective. *Wirtschaftsinformatik*, *45*(2), 181–190.
37 Vaia, G., DeLone, W., Arkhipova, D., & Moretti, A. (2020). Achieving trust, relational governance and innovation in information technology outsourcing through digital collaboration. In Agrifoglio, R., Lamboglia, R., Mancini, D., & Ricciardi, F. (Eds.), *Digital business transformation* (pp. 285–300). Cham: Springer.

38 Verra, G. J. (2003). *Global account management*. London: Routledge.

39 Ali, S., Li, H., Khan, S. U., Abrar, M. F., & Zhao, Y. (2020). Practitioner's view of barriers to software outsourcing partnership formation: An empirical exploration. *Journal of Software: Evolution and Process, 32*(5), e2233.

40 Langer, N., & Mani, D. (2018). Impact of formal controls on client satisfaction and profitability in strategic outsourcing contracts. *Journal of Management Information Systems, 35*(4), 998–1030.

41 Weigelt, C. (2009). The impact of outsourcing new technologies on integrative capabilities and performance. *Strategic Management Journal, 30*(6), 595–616.

42 Aubert, B. A., Kishore, R., & Iriyama, A. (2015). Exploring and managing the "innovation through outsourcing" paradox. *The Journal of Strategic Information Systems, 24*(4), 255–269.

43 Casas-Arce, P., Kittsteiner, T., & Martínez-Jerez, F. A. (2019). Contracting with opportunistic partners: Theory and application to technology development and innovation. *Management Science, 65*(2), 842–858.

44 Anand, K. S., & Goyal, M. (2019). Ethics, bounded rationality, and IP sharing in IT outsourcing. *Management Science, 65*(11), 5252–5267.

45 Broadbent, M., & Weill, P. (1997). Management by maxim: How business and IT managers can create IT infrastructures. *Sloan Management Review, 38*, 77–92.

46 Du, W., Pan, S. L., & Wu, J. (2020). How do IT outsourcing vendors develop capabilities? An organizational ambidexterity perspective on a multi-case study. *Journal of Information Technology, 35*(1), 49–65.

47 Wang, M. M., & Wang, J. J. (2019). How vendor capabilities impact IT outsourcing performance. *Journal of Enterprise Information Management, 32*(2), 325–344.

48 Burden, K., O'Conor, M., & Pithouse, D. (2019). *Negotiating technology contracts*. Croydon: Globe Law and Business.

49 Gopalakrishnan, S., & Zhang, H. (2019). The link between vendor certification and growth in IT outsourcing: A tale of two stories. *International Journal of Production Research, 57*(13), 4228–4243.

50 Blijleven, V., Gong, Y., Mehrsai, A., & Koelemeijer, K. (2019). Critical success factors for Lean implementation in IT outsourcing relationships. *Information Technology & People, 32*(3), 715–730.

51 Linderman, K., Schroeder, R. G., Zaheer, S., & Choo, A. S. (2003). Six Sigma: A goal-theoretic perspective. *Journal of Operations Management, 21*(2), 193–203.

52 Subramanian, G. H., Jiang, J. J., & Klein, G. (2007). Software quality and IS project performance improvements from software development process maturity and IS implementation strategies. *Journal of Systems and Software, 80*(4), 616–627.

53 Caplan, D. H., & Kirschenheiter, M. (2000). Outsourcing and audit risk for internal audit services. *Contemporary Accounting Research, 17*(3), 387–428.

54 McDonald, M. (2004). IT risk management: Strategizing the operational profile. In *Gartner conference* (p. 31), October–4 November, Cannes, France.

55 Fernandez-Sanz, L., & Castillo Martinez, A. (2018). Analysis of the European ICT competence frameworks. In Ahuja, V., & Rathore, S. (Eds.), *Multidisciplinary perspectives on human capital and information technology professionals* (225–245). Hershey, PA: IGI Global.

56 Lacity, M., & Rottman, J. (2008). Offshore outsourcing of IT work. In Lacity, M., & Rottman, J. (Eds.), *Offshore outsourcing of IT work* (pp. 1–53). London: Palgrave Macmillan.

57 Beulen, E., & Ribbers, P. (2003). International examples of large-scale systems-theory and practice II: A case study of managing IT outsourcing partnerships in Asia. *Communications of the Association for Information Systems, 11*(1), 21.

58 Beulen, E., & Ribbers, P. (2002, January). Managing an IT-outsourcing partnership in Asia. Case study: the relationship between a global outsourcing company

and its global IT services supplier. In *Proceedings of the 35th Annual Hawaii International Conference on System Sciences* (pp. 3122-3131). IEEE.

59 Carmel, E., & Agarwal, R. S. (2008). The maturation of offshore sourcing of information technology work. *MIS Quarterly Executive, 1*(2), 5.

60 Grimshaw, D., & Miozzo, M. (2009). New human resource management practices in knowledge-intensive business services firms: The case of outsourcing with staff transfer. *Human Relations, 62*(10), 1521–1550.

61 Krancher, O. (2020). Review of the literature and implications for digital business strategy and agility. In Beulen, E., & Ribbers, P. M. (Eds.), *The Routledge companion to managing digital outsourcing* (177–202). London: Routledge.

62 Pfeffer, J. (1998). Seven practices of successful organizations. *California Management Review, 40*(2), 96–124.

63 Nonaka, I., & Takeuchi, H. (1995). *The knowledge-creating company: How Japanese companies create the dynamics of innovation.* Oxford: Oxford University Press.

64 Ibrahim, M., & Ribbers, P. M. (2009). The impacts of competence-trust and openness-trust on interorganizational systems. *European Journal of Information Systems, 18*(3), 223–234.

65 Fama, E., & Jensen, M. (1983). Separation of ownership and control. *Journal of Law and Economics, 26*, 301–326.

66 Barney, J. (1991). Firm resources and sustained competitive advantage. *Journal of Management, 17* (1), 99–120.

67 Peppard, J. (2003). Managing IT as a portfolio of services. *European Management Journal, 21*(4), 467–483.

68 Murphy, M. D. (2015). Sourcing portfolio analysis: Power positioning tools for category management & strategic sourcing. *Strategic Outsourcing: An International Journal, 8*(2/3), 284–286.

69 Kern, T., & Willcocks, L. (2000). Exploring information technology outsourcing relationships: Theory and practice. *The Journal of Strategic Information Systems, 9*(4), 321–350.

70 Rosin, A. F., Stubner, S., Chaurasia, S. S., & Verma, S. (2019). Outsourcing, information symmetry and governance. *Journal of Enterprise Information Management, 32*(6), 993–1014.

71 Fehrenbacher, D. D., & Wiener, M. (2019). The dual role of penalty: The effects of IT outsourcing contract framing on knowledge-sharing willingness and commitment. *Decision Support Systems, 121*, 62–71.

72 Domberger, S., Fernandez, P., & Fiebig, D. G. (2000). Modelling the price, performance and contract characteristics of IT outsourcing. *Journal of Information Technology, 15*(2), 107–118.

73 Goo, J., Kishore, R., Rao, H. R., & Nam, K. (2009). The role of service level agreements in relational management of information technology outsourcing: An empirical study. *MIS Quarterly, 33*(1), 119–145.

74 Goo, J., & Huang, C. D. (2008). Facilitating relational governance through service level agreements in IT outsourcing: An application of the commitment–trust theory. *Decision Support Systems, 46*(1), 216–232.

75 Goo, J., Kishore, R., Nam, K., Rao, H. R., & Song, Y. (2007). An investigation of factors that influence the duration of IT outsourcing relationships. *Decision Support Systems, 42*(4), 2107–2125.

76 Fukuyama, F. (1995). *Trust: The social virtues and the creation of prosperity* (Vol. 99). New York: Free Press.

77 Langfield-Smith, K., & Smith, D. (2003). Management control systems and trust in outsourcing relationships. *Management Accounting Research, 14*(3), 281–307.

78 Purser, S. (2001). A simple graphical tool for modelling trust. *Computers & Security, 20*(6), 479–484.

79 Lai, E. L. C., Riezman, R., & Wang, P. (2009). Outsourcing of innovation. *Economic Theory*, *38*(3), 485–515.

80 Aubert, B. A., Kishore, R., & Iriyama, A. (2015). Exploring and managing the "innovation through outsourcing" paradox. *The Journal of Strategic Information Systems*, *24*(4), 255–269.

81 Kranz, J. (2021). Strategic innovation in IT outsourcing: Exploring the differential and interaction effects of contractual and relational governance mechanisms. *The Journal of Strategic Information Systems*, *30*(1), 101656.

82 DesJardins, J. (1998). Corporate environmental responsibility. *Journal of Business Ethics*, *17*(8), 825–838.

83 Kalsheim, J. P., & Beulen, E. (2013). Framework for measuring environmental efficiency of IT and setting strategies for green IT: A case study providing guidance to chief information officers. In Appelman, J. H. (Ed.), *Green ICT & energy* (pp. 77–96). Boca Raton, FL: CRC Press.

84 Beulen, E. (2015, February). The importance of IT energy efficiency in outsourcing decision making: A survey in the dutch outsourcing infrastructure market. In *Global Sourcing Workshop 2015* (pp. 240–250). Cham: Springer.

85 Sambhanthan, A., & Potdar, V. (2017). A study of the parameters impacting sustainability in information technology organizations. *International Journal of Knowledge-Based Organizations (IJKBO)*, *7*(3), 27–39.

10 Contracting and managing agile software development and DevOps

Contracting and managing agile software development and DevOps is distinctly different from contracting and managing traditional services. Organisations that have embraced agile software development have to also embrace infrastructure cloud services to enable DevOps. Infrastructure cloud services and DevOps are prerequisites for successfully managing agile software development. Many organisations are struggling with contracting and managing agile software development. No longer is there a fixed price contract. Furthermore, many organisations are not yet ready for DevOps, as their architecture and security are simply not at level. How can outsourcing organisations address these challenges successfully?

10.1 Introduction

In agile software development, requirements and solutions evolve through the collaborative effort of self-organising cross-functional teams. Adaptive planning, evolutionary development, early delivery and continuous improvement are key characteristics. Agile software development encourages rapid and flexible response to change. An agile project includes multiple releases, and each release includes multiple sprints. Each release delivers – independent from other releases – business functionality.

Agility facilitates digital transformations. In agile software development, the scope is not fixed on a detailed level and changes are embraced. A description of the high-level functionality from a customer value perspective is sufficient to kick off a software development project. Agile ways of working deliver incremental functionality per release, which consists of multiple two- to four-week sprints. Priorities are set per sprint, enabling new and revised requirements to be added at each sprint. This flexibility enables adoption to changed priorities or amended legislation. Furthermore, sprints ensure quality and timely completion of the project, as potential roadblocks are identified early. In waterfall, requirements are set at the start and are fixed, with milestones typically set every three to six months. Waterfall is too rigorous to facilitate digital transformations.

DOI: 10.4324/9781003223788-10

Also, the contractual obligations in agile software development are minimal, compared to 12 or more months of contractual commitments in waterfall projects. In the true spirit of agile software development, outsourcing organisations commit to completing a release, and are not obliged to order a next release. Additional business value drives the appetite to order the next sprint and/or release. Even outsourcing organisations that have to comply with European tendering regulations can sign framework contracts with no volume commitments. Contracting agile software development ensures budget control and maximises business value. However, in most organisations, agile software development is contracted based on time & materials (T&M). This results in an input obligation for the suppliers. As a consequence, all the risks related to software development are with the outsourcing company. In order to transform the input obligation into output obligations, contracting based on fixed price per story point is recommended. This requires implementation guidelines for contracting agile software development, which are detailed in Section 10.3.

10.2 Agile software development challenges

The challenges in agile software development are both in the design and build of the software and in the contracting. Agile software development is based on the Agile Manifesto.[1] In the manifesto, there are four values:

1 Individuals and interactions over processes and tools
2 Working software over comprehensive documentation
3 Customer collaboration over contract negotiation
4 Responding to change over following a plan.

The adoption of agility must not stop outsourcing organisations from focusing on business value.[2] The coordination of the autonomous teams is the biggest challenge in agile software development. Frameworks are required to align on priorities and to ensure that the functionality meets the business requirements.[3] There are a number of agile frameworks, including Scrum and Kanban for small-scale projects. There are three agile frameworks for large-scale projects: Scaled Agile Framework (SAFe),[4] Large-Scale Scrum (LeSS)[5] and Disciplined Agile Delivery (DaD).[6,7] The DaD is not as popular as SAFe and LeSS, but it has a goals-driven approach instead of a descriptive one.

Nevertheless, there are additional challenges in the area of architecture[8] and security.[9] Knowledge related to these two topics needs to be captured in the central centre of excellence of outsourcing organisation and decentralised in the agile software development teams. Architects and security specialists can be added (part-time) to agile team and/or the architectural and security knowledge of agile software team members can be upgraded. It is important to understand that both architectural and security requirements are non-functional requirements. Therefore, these requirements are vulnerable for de-prioritisation by product owners. Not meeting non-functional requirements results in technical debt.[10,11] As such, technical debt is not a problem, as it was a deliberate decision. However, technical debt needs to be managed, as it impacts the future ability of software development teams to deliver functionality. Although the focus of agile coaches is limited to process, collaboration and teamwork, agile coaches can be supportive in supporting agile teams in managing technical debt responsibly.

10.2.1 *Contracting*

In contracting agile software development, the biggest inhibitor is mixed teams.[12] Most organisations deploy agile software development teams with team members from their own organisation combined with team members from multiple suppliers. Due to this mix of team members, neither the outsourcing organisation nor any of the suppliers can reasonably sign up for an output obligation. Also, there is not a straightforward and unambiguous measure for agile software development productivity. In transitional software development, function points can be used to estimate the effort and to agree on the fees for software development. In agile software development, function points cannot be used as the primary contractual construct. This is a step back from the fixed price application development projects that outsourcing organisations were contracting in the past.

On top of this, in many organisations, the maturity of key roles in agile software development is still low. Outsourcing organisations predominantly struggle to put forward internal candidates for the product owner role, and the accountable business executive role often lacks experience. This issue is more problematic for smaller organisations (<250m Euro turnover).[12] In addition to mixed teams, many organisations are confronted with teams that are based in many geographic locations. Although during the pandemic, many organisations (including supplier organisations and individual professionals) have built up vast experience with remote working, the productivity of an agile team is negatively impacted by geographic dispersity. National culture and distributed teams reduce the agile software development productivity.[3] Smaller organisations typically leverage nearshore locations over offshore locations for their agile software development teams.

To resolve the above issue, outsourcing organisations have to follow contracting guidelines. The contract guidelines for agile software development are detailed in Section 10.3.

10.3 Agile contracting implementation guidelines

Agile implementation guidelines provide guidance to outsourcing organisations on how best to contract agile software development. The guidelines balance the interests of outsourcing organisations and suppliers.[13]

There are several agile roles to be considered here:

1   The accountable executive is, for lack of a better word, accountable. This person solves cross-function problems and drives decision-making.
2   The delivery manager is responsible for facilitating agile teams and taking pre-emptive action to remove IT and service excellence roadblocks, as well as engagement interlocks.
3   The product owner is responsible for sprints and release, shapes vision and objectives, oversees overall sprint/release delivery processes and is empowered with decision rights.
4   The scrum master manages sprint/release progress and clears obstacles.

10.3.1   Identify and appoint product owners and accountable executives to ensure governance and budget control

Product owners of outsourcing organisations drive the sprint and release planning in conjunction with the supplier's scrum master and agile development team, supported by the delivery manager from the outsourcing organisation. Also, alignment with the client architectural and security teams is essential prior to the start of a project, release or sprint, during sprints and at the acceptance of code.

In agility, governance is embedded at all times. In daily stand-ups, progress is monitored and priorities are set and the work for the day is agreed upon. A sprint will be concluded by a sprint demo and refinement session. Stakeholders will accept the work in the demo (Definition of Done). The refinement session prioritises and refines the tasks for the upcoming sprints and releases, including considering new items from the product backlog.

It is a good practice to implement agile programme governance and embed the accountable executive role at a senior level. Product owners are responsible and accountable executives are responsible for tracking the story points of the delivered and contracted functionality in order to ensure budget control. To ensure budgeting control, procurement will also be involved in monitoring and signing off on budget at the project level.

10.3.2   Start with time & material contracting, gather up metrics and grow agile capabilities to prepare for fixed prices per story point contracting

To gradually build up experience, most outsourcing organisations start to contract small agile T&M software development projects. It is a good practice to have a 12- to 24-month initial phase to gradually gather up metrics. It is important that metrics are put into context and discussed between the outsourcing company and the supplier. Documenting the context and the discussion contributes to a mutually agreed-upon additional reference point for fixed price story point contracts.

It is also critical to invest in parallel in building product owner and agile sourcing capabilities in all participating outsourcing organisations. Many organisations invest heavily in making their organisation more agile. Employing agile coaches is helpful to make organisations successful. Agile coaches are not embedded in the agile teams. Their focus is not on supporting individual team members or agile teams but rather on enabling the implementation of agile ways of working across the organisation and developing a collective agile mindset in the organisation. Agile coaches are also involved in the implementation of agile frameworks.

10.3.3 Step up to fixed price per story point contracting based on defined reference stories to ensure budget control

Story points require multiple reference stories in contracts on supplier level, not per project; typically, reference stories of 2, 3, 5, 8, 13 and 20 story points are included. Complexity, number of fields and interaction between fields are important drivers for the number of story points. If productivity is disputed, both parties can ex-post leverage function point metrics in order to evidence productivity. This ex-post measure ensures that the interests of both the supplier and the outsourcing organisation are protected, as function point metrics are fully objective and not disputable.[14] Parties have to understand that calculating function point metrics requires a significant effort and only should be applied if there are structural and significant disputes about the story point estimates of the supplier.

At the start of each sprint, the number of story points will be set by the supplier software development team. Reference stories are the starting point for the estimates. The estimates will be validated by the product owner and typically are supported by the central metrics team of the outsourcing organisation.

10.3.4 Contract based on framework agreements in order to minimise contracting effort and throughput time and maximise competitiveness

Due to the significant volume of required application development capacity and the time required to fully leverage agile development benefits, long-term framework contracts with selective suppliers are required. To begin with, it is a good practice to have a contracting framework agreement for three to five years with two to five suppliers, depending on the size and geographic spread of the outsourcing organisation. For governmental organisations in the European Union, it is a good practice to use the restricted procedure and award work based on mini-competitions.[15] However, this is also a good practice for any organisation. Pre-qualification will be based on supplier capabilities (including number of certified scrum masters) and project references. In the qualification, the fixed price per story point for contracting and hourly rates for reference will be decisive for ensuring competitive pricing. The framework agreements also include technical debt requirements, penalties for underperformance and service levels such as customer satisfaction, burn down/ burn up, velocity, escaped defects and resolution time of defects.

10.3.5 Reward projects to suppliers with the most experienced team to ensure quality

Successfully agile contracting on fixed price per story point requires that each agile team is staffed by a single supplier, not a mixed outsourcing organisation or supplier teams. In mini-competitions per project, suppliers are invited to comment on the project specifications and propose their development team by including CVs of all team members. Projects will be awarded based on commercial attractiveness and the average number of years of experience of the proposed team. It is a good practice to introduce a higher weighting for the years of experience for developers which have participated in earlier projects under the framework agreement, as past experience improves the software quality. Projects will be contracted by a Statement of Work under the framework agreement. As the legal terms and conditions are already agreed upon in the framework agreement, this approach enables contracting speed, which is essential in contracting agile software development.

10.3.6 Leverage agile management frameworks to facilitate large-scale software development programmes while ensuring governance

In order to ensure governance, consistency across large-scale software development programmes and preferably across departments is important. Off-the-shelf frameworks such as LeSS[16] and SAFe[17] facilitate software development by multiple agile teams, potentially from multiple suppliers, in a programme consisting of multiple projects. It is a good practice to work with a single supplier in a domain or geographic area in order to maximise the learning curves of individual agile teams as well as the supplier organisation.

Adoption of these off-the-shelf frameworks might be required in order to ensure that the frameworks are fit for purpose, but outsourcing organisations need to be careful with adjusting these frameworks. The supplier teams benefit from adhering to standards; adhering to client-specific standards potentially reduces the efficiency and effectiveness of the software development.

10.3.7 Track technical debt[18] to ensure software quality

In addition to thorough testing, technical debt obligations need to be incorporated in the contract. Use of tooling such as CAST and SonarQube, or niche tools such as Kiuwan or SQuORE, provides metrics. The pre- and post-measuring indicates the performance of agile teams and of suppliers. Part of the technical debt might be attributable to deliberate decisions of the outsourcing organisation. The remaining technical debt is related to the quality of the supplier's delivery and is indicated as net technical debt. If the net technical debt exceeds the contracted technical debt threshold, the supplier has to improve the quality of the code, called "refactoring," at their own expense. The supplier will allocate (part of) the team in the next sprint(s) in order to reduce the technical debt and will not be compensated for the effort required to reduce the net technical debt. It is a good practice to hold the supplier responsible, for the net technical debt is a fair, effective and efficient mechanism to ensure quality and free up capacity for implementing new functionality in upcoming sprints by minimising future application maintenance effort.

10.3.8 *Do not compensate suppliers for cancelled future sprints and releases, to ensure competitiveness*

Suppliers compensation for cancelled future sprints and releases is a controversial topic in agile software development. It is a good practice to only agree to (up to) four-week notice periods, as the work is performed under a framework agreement. Doing so will give suppliers the opportunity to allocate the involved resources to other projects at the outsourcing organisation or to projects at different clients. By granting a four-week notice period, the commercial risk of underutilisation is sufficiently covered. This assurance avoids the need to add continency to the fees: hourly rates for the initial period as well as fixed prices per story points for the remaining contract term.

Including the above eight guidelines in agile software development contracting transforms the obligations in the contracts from input to output obligations. Output obligations will strengthen the position of the outsourcing company. Also, contracting based on a fixed price per story point enables suppliers to manage their resources better, as the composition of the teams is fully at their discretion.

10.4 Operations in DevOps

DevOps consists of two seamless elements: software development and operations. The DevOps teams engage in continuous integration/continuous delivery (CI/CD) workflows.[19] To manage DevOps, organisations might consider using TOSCA as the standard language to describe a topology of cloud-based services, their components, relationships and the processes that manage them and support DevOps.[20] Software development in DevOps is typically agile software development. Agile software development requires cloud infrastructure to enable fast deployment of new functionality.[21] DevOps requires cloud-native architectures.[22] DevOps is often used in combination with microservices which also require a cloud-native architecture. Each microservice is independently deployable on potentially different infrastructure platforms and technology stacks and communication based on RESTful[23] or RPC-based APIs.[24,25] In adopting microservices, organisations will face challenges in versioning and error-handling issues, as this is more complex in distributed systems[26] and dependencies and tracking dependencies.[27] The next-level development is microservice applications as self-adaptive systems.[28] Due to the increasing threat of cyberattacks in combination with increasing compliance requirements, there is a growing focus on security in DevOps. Also, the acronym DevSecOps has been introduced. Regardless of the acronym, it is important to develop and maintain a specific set of rules to ensure cyber-security. The rule set must be combined with a framework to enable Static Security Testing (SAST) and Dynamic Security Testing (DAST), such as OWASP.[29] To manage all this complexity, cloud orchestration is required.[30] DevOps includes processes and tooling.

The challenges in operations in DevOps are in both selecting and managing, and less so in contracting, as DevOps contracting is straightforward contracting of standard services at fixed rates and difficult when it comes to negotiated terms and conditions, which are not negotiable. The selection of cloud infrastructure services has already been addressed in Chapter 7. Vendor lock-in is the most important consideration in contracting cloud infrastructure services. The supplier lock-in is not only related to the monthly fees but also to costs associated with switching to an alternative cloud platform. Due to dependencies and costs related to the adjustments of the interfaces (APIs), switching is still not very feasible, nor is it straightforward. Therefore, deciding on a large and established supplier is the safest bet. For managing operations in DevOps, organisations have to implement proper governance. The operations teams in DevOps have to include resources with architectural as well as security capabilities. More important is the positioning of the internal IT department, which is responsible for the orchestration and provisioning of cloud infrastructure platforms to the DevOps teams. The internal IT department sets and maintains standards and is a centre of expertise. This centralised approach facilitates the industrialisation required for DevOps.[31] As a good practice, the centre of expertise will have strict service levels for deploying new environments[32] for DevOps teams, as well as service levels for their portfolio; the standard covers +80% of the requirements of the DevOps teams and the remaining request can be implemented by the central team in less than six weeks.

10.5 Conclusions

Due to market dynamics and (as a consequence of these dynamics) the rise of digital transformations, agility has become the norm in implementing new customised functionality. Also, DevOps enables organisations to respond adequately to the dynamics.

Agile software development has caused contracting challenges. Output obligations can only be contracted in due course and require stable development teams to capture the experience and benefits from a played team. Unfortunately, most organisations still contract agile software development based on T&M. This contracting must change soon in order to ensure that agile software development delivers its value. Contracting agile software development based on a fixed price per story point will change the contracts in output-based contracts. The alternative for contracting agile software development based on output obligations, Software as a Service (SaaS) applications, is also tempting for any organisation. However, it is more difficult to achieve competitive advantage with SaaS applications.

Notes

1   https://agilemanifesto.org/
2   Tolfo, C., Wazlawick, R. S., Ferreira, M. G. G., & Forcellini, F. A. (2018). Agile practices and the promotion of entrepreneurial skills in software development. *Journal of Software: Evolution and Process*, *30*(9), e1945.
3   George, J. F., Scheibe, K., Townsend, A. M., & Mennecke, B. (2018). The amorphous nature of agile: No one size fits all. *Journal of Systems and Information Technology*, *20*(2), 241–260.
4   https://www.scaledagileframework.com/
5   https://less.works/less/framework/index – this include a framework for small projects, up to eight teams of eight people, and for agile@scale – LeSS Hugh
6   https://disciplinedagileconsortium.org/
7   Project Management Institute (2018). *Learning to sprint we asked the project management community: What was your greatest challenge when adapting to agile approaches?* (Ser. Voices. project toolkit). Project Management Institute. http://www.pmi.org/.
8   Borrego, G., Morán, A. L., Palacio, R. R., Vizcaíno, A., & García, F. O. (2019). Towards a reduction in architectural knowledge vaporization during agile global software development. *Information and Software Technology*, *112*, 68–82.
9   Tøndel, I. A., Jaatun, M. G., Cruzes, D. S., & Williams, L. (2019). Collaborative security risk estimation in agile software development. *Information & Computer Security*, *27*(4), 508–535.
10 Technical debt was coined by Ward Cunningham in 1992 - Cunningham, W. (1992). The WyCash portfolio management system. *ACM SIGPLAN OOPS Messenger*, *4*(2), 29–30.
11 See Lim, E., Taksande, N., & Seaman, C. (2012). A balancing act: What software practitioners have to say about technical debt. *IEEE Software*, *29*(6), 22–27; Behutiye, W. N., Rodríguez, P., Oivo, M., & Tosun, A. (2017). Analyzing the concept of technical debt in the context of agile software development: A systematic literature review. *Information and Software Technology*, *82*, 139–158.
12 Beulen, E. (2018, February). Implementing and contracting agile and DevOps: A survey in the Netherlands. In Kotlarsky, J., Oshri, I., & Willcocks, L. (Eds.), *International workshop on global sourcing of information technology and business processes* (pp. 124–146). Cham: Springer.
13 The guidelines are developed in close collaboration with C-level representatives, IT executives and subject matter experts of outsourcing organisations, consulting companies and suppliers.
14 In fact, the function point metrics are a benchmark for the story point estimates of the supplier.
15 http://etenders.gov.ie/Media/Default/SiteContent/LegislationGuides/4.%20 Guidance%20on%20Framework%20Agreements.pdf
16 https://less.works/less/framework/index.html
17 http://www.scaledagileframework.com/; empowerment of the product owner is a known omission of this framework.

18 Technical debt reflects the extra development effort required when code that is easy to implement in the short run is used, instead of applying the best overall solution. An example of technical debt is an untouched huge source file that needs to be broken into more manageable pieces.

19 Sachin, L. (2020). Automated performance indicator system for ci/cd & devops developers of software industry using python. *International Journal for Research in Applied Science and Engineering Technology*, *8*(7), 373–379.

20 See Tamburri, D. A., Van den Heuvel, W. J., Lauwers, C., Lipton, P., Palma, D., & Rutkowski, M. (2019). TOSCA-based Intent modelling: Goal-modelling for infrastructure-as-code. *SICS Software-Intensive Cyber-Physical Systems*, *34*(2), 163–172; Wettinger, J., Breitenbücher, U., Kopp, O., & Leymann, F. (2016). Streamlining DevOps automation for cloud applications using TOSCA as standardized metamodel. *Future Generation Computer Systems*, *56*, 317–332.

21 Ebert, C., Gallardo, G., Hernantes, J., & Serrano, N. (2016). Devops. *IEEE Software*, *33*(3), 94–100.

22 See Bass, L. (2017). The software architect and DevOps. *IEEE Software*, *35*(1), 8–10; Waseem, M., Liang, P., & Shahin, M. (2020). A systematic mapping study on microservices architecture in DevOps. *Journal of Systems and Software*, *170*, 110798.

23 Representational State Transfer (REST).

24 Remote Procedure Call (RPC).

25 Balalaie, A., Heydarnoori, A., & Jamshidi, P. (2016). Microservices architecture enables devops: Migration to a cloud-native architecture. *Ieee Software*, *33*(3), 42–52.

26 Jamshidi, P., Pahl, C., Mendonça, N. C., Lewis, J., & Tilkov, S. (2018). Microservices: The journey so far and challenges ahead. *IEEE Software*, *35*(3), 24–35.

27 Ghirotti, S. E., Reilly, T., & Rentz, A. (2018). Tracking and controlling microservice dependencies. *Communications of the ACM*, *61*(11), 98–104.

28 Pahl, C., Garlan, D., Jamshidi, P., & Mendonca, N. C. (2021). Developing self-adaptive microservice systems: Challenges and directions. *Ieee Software*, *38*(2), 70–79.

29 Mansfield-Devine, S. (2018). DevOps: Finding room for security. *Network Security*, *2018*(7), 15–20.

30 See de Carvalho Silva, J., de Oliveira Dantas, A. B., & de Carvalho Junior, F. H. (2019). A scientific workflow management system for orchestration of parallel components in a cloud of large-scale parallel processing services. *Science of Computer Programming*, *173*, 95–127; Qadeer, A., Waqar Malik, A., Ur Rahman, A., Mian Muhammad, H., & Ahmad, A. (2020). Virtual infrastructure orchestration for cloud service deployment. *The Computer Journal*, *63*(2), 295–307.

31 Vithayathil, J. (2018). Will cloud computing make the Information Technology (IT) department obsolete?. *Information Systems Journal*, *28*(4), 634–649.

32 These environments are IaaS (and to a lesser degree PaaS) platforms, such as AWS and Azure. For DevOps, SaaS platforms are not relevant.

11 Compliance

Compliance is also having an impact on IT outsourcing. Any organisation has to structure and continuously change processes and IT services for evolving and increasing global legislation. Also, suppliers have to adapt their services to ensure that their entire portfolio is compliant. This required flexibility is in IT outsourcing contracts facilitated by change control clauses and in the relationship by the concept of trust. Both outsourcing organisations and the suppliers have to deal with this uncertainty. What are the implications of current legislations, such as data protection regulations, and in making legislations, such as digital regulations?[1]

11.1 Introduction

Mostly, the legislation is addressing potential issues related to the increasing opportunities that cloud services are offering. Understanding cloud service offerings and the business models of the suppliers better is a prerequisite to understanding compliance obligations. This is addressed in Section 11.2. For many organisations, data protection legislation is the most important legislation. Cyber-security is becoming an important aspect in compliance. This is explained in Section 11.3. Implications of data protection legislation are explained in Section 11.4. In the future, outsourcing organisations as well as suppliers have to be compliant with the Digital Service Act Package. This will have major implications for IT outsourcing and is detailed in Section 11.5. Also in this chapter, the European Union statement of objective to Amazon.com is explained. The analysis of the anti-trust accusation is detailed in Section 11.6. The conclusions of this chapter are detailed in Section 11.7.

11.2 Cloud services market

In the cloud services market, there are three offerings: Infrastructure as a Service (IaaS), Platform as a Service (PaaS) and Software as a Service (SaaS). In IaaS and PaaS, size matters the most, as this is an oligopoly market with only a few suppliers. In Gartner's 2020 Magic Quadrant Amazon Web Services, Microsoft and Google are identified as leaders and Alibaba Cloud,

DOI: 10.4324/9781003223788-11

Tencent Cloud as well as Oracle and IBM are identified as niche.[2] However, niche still means a major size; also, the functional and technical differences between these seven cloud service providers are decreasing. Especially in IaaS, pricing and pricing structure are becoming the most important differentiators. This differentiator includes service credits in case of an outage. Furthermore, latency requirements are importing in comparing the offerings of the different cloud services suppliers. Finally, the tooling and support for cross cloud management are becoming more important, even more so in the context of the rise of DevOps. This tooling is maturing and expected to be further mature; however in the short- and mid-term, this will not resolve the supplier lock-in concern in cloud computing. In enterprise architecture and IT architecture, outsourcing organisations need to provide clear guidance, and interchangeability between platforms needs to be safeguarded. Despite the interchangeability implication, an increasing number of organisations are building multiple cloud technology stacks, where most outsourcing organisations limited themselves to two main cloud stacks. This strategy is not limited to the large multinational organisations; also, smaller organisations are reducing the supplier lock-in by implementing multiple cloud stacks and accepting the integration challenge as well as the higher cost due to lower volumes.[3]

Furthermore, most outsourcing organisations are contracting predominantly public cloud services; however, industrialised private cloud offerings are available for outsourcing organisations which have highly confidential operations and business processes, such as governments or innovative knowledge-intensive organisations. These private cloud offerings can be deployed in the outsourcing organisation's data centres. Typically, the private cloud costs are significantly higher than the costs for a public cloud.

PaaS offerings are supportive to organisational agility. Levering PaaS building blocks is speeding up the process of releasing functionality. Unfortunately, PaaS cloud offerings of different cloud suppliers are not fully interchangeable, although containerisation is addressing part of the interchangeability challenge. In IT architecture, outsourcing organisations need to make technology stack decisions to ensure that the contracted cloud services and the data exchange between the different technology stack are smooth.

The market of SaaS is very scattered, with large suppliers such as Oracle, Salesforce and SAP, but also many small suppliers. Especially for smaller SaaS suppliers, assessing compliance and security risks is important. This assessment is not limited to an initial pre-contract signing assessment; this is a continuous assessment. Technologies are changing, and larger suppliers are acquiring smaller suppliers at a large scale.

The enterprise architecture and IT architecture challenge for SaaS is much more difficult than for IaaS and PaaS. However, the architectural challenges for SaaS are less fundamental, as IaaS and PaaS are full technology stacks, whereas SaaS is only a silo in the architecture. Therefore, swapping in and out SaaS platforms is less drastic, labour-intensive and costly than migrating IaaS and PaaS platforms.

For all cloud platforms, ensuring proper assurance by audits and certification is important. This includes but is not limited to SOC1–3, SSEA 16, ISO/IEC 27001, ISO/IEC 27017 and ISO/IEC 27018 audits. Most outsourcing organisations rely on third-party statements. Most cloud contracts rightfully include no provisions for outsourcing organisations to audit the services and cloud service delivery organisations. The implication of outsourcing organisation audit will be a potential disturbance of the service provisioning, as most cloud services are highly industrialised. Third-party statements should be sufficient for outsourcing organisations and governing regulatory bodies.

11.3 Security risks and cyber insurance

On the back of the compliance impact, security of cloud services is also an important topic. A decade ago, there were security and confidentiality concerns related to cloud computing in most outsourcing organisations. This has impacted the use of cloud computing. Over time, this has changed; currently, the belief is that the offerings of the large cloud providers provide a higher assurance than outsourcing organisation's internal IT departments can provide. For the smaller SaaS suppliers, this is a bit more challenging. The focus of the chief information security officer has to be on assessing the security provisions in these smaller SaaS solutions.

The increase in cyber-security incidents, not limited to cloud computing, has initiated cyber-security insurance offerings. Cyber-security threat and the need for a cyber-security insurance policy are discussed in board rooms.[4] This topic will be in the agenda of Board of Management as the impact and intensity of cyber-attacks will continue to grow. KPMG reports in their 2020 report: "increased cyber-security threats – more than four in ten (41%) of organisations have experienced increased incidents mainly from spear phishing and malware attacks."[5]

Insurance offerings include compensation for the loss of data, rebuilding IT services and re-installing underlying data, additional external costs associated with rebuilding, such as technical subject matter experts and an external legal-council, and even ransom payment.[6] The paying and insuring ransom is a sensitive topic. The impact from ransomware on the business and the reputation of an organisation can be considerable. Cyber-criminals typically make a good assessment of their ransom requests. However, decisions on paying ransom are rightfully not only based on business cases. Furthermore, organisations need to factor in the risk that paying ransom is not an absolute guarantee that the cyber-criminals will provide the encryption key(s) after receiving the ransom.

The market for cyber-security insurances is maturing. The cyber-security insurers also trigger compliance by addressing the under-preparation and under-compliance gaps. Prior to accepting a policy holder, an assessment has to be performed. The outcome of this assessment set the exemptions, own risk and caps, the general conditions and of course the insurance premium. Another possible outcome can be a mutually agreed improvement programme to decrease cyber-security risks over time, as an example multi-factor authentication in place in all countries in six months. The cyber insurer will closely monitor the progress of this project and will be included in the project governance for this project: participating in project meetings and receiving project updates. Cyber-security insurers also offer risk management services and introductions to solid consulting organisations. Talesh labels this as institutionalised risk management techniques.[7] Cyber-security insurers also support organisations by providing interpretations of the law and when policy holders are the victims of a cyber-attack. Therefore, cyber-security insurers positively contribute to avoiding cyber-crime.

11.4 Data protection legislation[8]

Since 25 May 2018, the new European privacy regulation, the General Data Protection Regulation (GDPR), is in force.[9] This regulation is implemented in all local privacy laws in all EU and EEA countries (countries part of the European Economic Area Agreement). According to the GDPR directive, the definition of personal data is all information related to a person, such as names, photos, e-mail addresses, bank details, posts on social networks, location data, medical information and IP addresses. This does not distinguish between personal data of private individuals, or of individuals at companies or public organisations – the person is the person. Business-to-business communications also involve interaction between individuals, who exchange information with and about each other.

Who does it apply to? The regulation applies to all companies that interact with individuals in the European Union and store personal information about those individuals, including companies in other continents. This gives citizens in EU and EEA countries more control over their personal data and ensures that their information is protected across Europe.

The directive distinguishes between the data controller and the data processor. The controller is the main decision-maker; the data controller determines the purposes for which and the means by which personal data are processed. Thus, if a company or organisation decides "why" and "how" personal data should be processed, it is the data controller. The data processor in relation to personal data indicates any person (other than an employee of the data controller) who processes the data on behalf of the data controller. The role of the data processor is in particular interesting in relation to outsourcing.

The GDPR sets out seven principles for the lawful processing of personal data. Information-processing includes all that can be done with data: the collection, organisation, structuring, storage, alteration, consultation, use, communication, combination, restriction, erasure or destruction of personal data. Broadly, the seven principles are as follows:

- Lawfulness, fairness and transparency
- Purpose limitation
- Data minimisation

- Accuracy
- Storage limitation
- Integrity and confidentiality (security)
- Accountability.

The data controller and the data processor both have responsibilities in this respect. Both should provide sufficient guarantees that the required confidentiality, integrity and availability of personal data can be ensured. A critical point of attention for the data controller is that the data processor appointed by data controller is able to provide this assurance. So, a major concern is to consider the capacity of the processor to perform the contract in accordance with the GDPR. For example, this can be demonstrated by the participation of the processor in a certification programme approved by supervisory authorities or the adoption by the processor of a code of conduct. If this is not the case with existing processors, contracts with these parties should not be renewed.

For its part, the processor must also maintain the necessary independence from the controller, for example, when deciding whether or not it can transfer personal data to a third country. While processors are required to follow the relevant data controller's instructions with regard to the data processing, no matter what those instructions are, they may only transfer personal data to a third country (in the absence of an adequacy decision) if the controller or processor has provided appropriate safeguards and on condition that data subjects have enforceable rights in that country with respect to the data.

11.4.1 The effect of GDPR on IT outsourcing

The GDPR makes the outsourcing of IT more complex, especially if countries outside the European zone (EU and EEA) are involved. The outsourcing organisation and the supplier will have to be critical of their privacy and security measures to be applied.[10] From an economic point of view, this means that compliancy costs will increase. Since the outsourcing company is responsible for the assessment of the supplier in this regard, it can be expected that the so-called agency costs will increase.

Also, the GDPR introduces the accountability principle for the proper application of the GDPR rules. This principle makes clear that controllers and processors bear responsibility for being compliant with the GDPR and they must be able to demonstrate compliance. The latter implies the presence of robust controls, appropriate reporting, and assessment and evaluation procedures.

Such laws have serious consequences for all outsourcing relationships: suppliers will then have to meet the requirements set by these laws and their extra efforts and accountability will have to be paid for. For new contracts, the prices will be higher; for existing contracts, the fees will have to be renegotiated. Nevertheless, considering the growing importance of IT services for any company's business, a move towards such higher prices seems inevitable.

Furthermore, the GDPR has a wider definition of data processing than its predecessor – the Data Protection Directive which was in force from 1995 to 2018. This is increasing the obligations of suppliers. Also, the increasing obligations in case of data breaches will impact the involvement of suppliers. Suppliers have to factor in additional effort to supply their clients in case of a data breach. Similar for the tracking of processing activities as detailed in the GDPR. In supplier tooling, additional activities have to be tracked and reported on to the authorities.[11]

11.4.2 Data Protection Officer

To ensure a proper governance related to the GDPR, the role and responsibilities of the Data Protection Officer (DPO) are detailed in this legislation in clauses 37–39.[12] The DPO reports directly to "the highest management level" in the organisation. Under the GDPR, the DPO is responsible for informing the organisation on the data protection obligations and providing awareness training and preparation for related audits, monitoring the organisations compliance. Furthermore, the DPO is involved in Data Protection Impact Assessments. Under the GDPR, these assessments are mandatory for any change in the IT landscape, such as the implementation of a new software application or adjusting existing software applications. In these assessments, the DPO is working closely with the architects, security specialists and the suppliers to ensure compliance.

The DPO is also the contact point for the European Union Information Commissioner's Office and any other relevant supervisory authority, on all data protection issues, including data breach reporting. The DPO is also responsible for handling or orchestrating the data subject access requests. Obviously, the DPO is also responsible for resolving any underlying issues related to data breaches.

For avoidance of doubt, only in three situations organisations in the European Union are mandatory.[13] Any public authority or body has to appoint a DPO. Also, organisations which have core activities that require regular and systematic monitoring of data subjects on a large scale have to appoint a DPO. Furthermore, also organisations which have core activities involving large-scale processing of special categories of personal data and data relating to criminal convictions have to appoint a DPO.

11.4.3 Data privacy shield

To ensure a GDPR-compliant data exchange with organisations in the US, the privacy data shield was installed. On 16 July 2020, the European court concluded that the privacy shield is invalid per immediate effect.[14] The rational for this ruling was that the privacy shield provided inadequate protections for the privacy and data protection rights of people whose personal information is transferred from Europe to the US. The first argument was that the US national security can overrule the rights and freedom of European Union data subjects. Second, the US judiciary may request access to more data than is strictly necessary. To address this gap, large suppliers such as Microsoft have publicly committed to privacy shield principles and have self-certified its compliance with its requirements. Also, the European Commission has approved Google's model contract clauses as a means of ensuring adequate protection when transferring data outside of the European Economic Area. Organisations can also consider European Union data storage and for organisations outside the European Union can consider an ISO 27701 certification. This certification also qualifies for GDPR compliance.

11.5 Digital Services Act Package[15]

The proposed Digital Service Act Package consists of Digital Service Act (DSA) and the Digital Market Act (DMA). The European Union has proposed these acts to ensure a proper online business engagement and to protect the European Union citizens. The legal basis is Article 114 of the Treaty on the Functioning of the European Union ("TFEU"). Existing laws, such as Regulation (EU) 2019/1150 and Directive (EU) 2019/2161, will be dealt with as lex specialis, and will override the DSA. DSA and DMA are forced by 2023 at the earliest. It is the expectation that both the DSA and the DPA be standard setters at the global level, which is similar to the GDPR.

11.5.1 Digital Services Act

The DSA is adapting commercial law and civil law rules for commercial entities operating online. The DSA addresses intermediate services, hosting services and very large online platforms, which reach +10% of the EU's consumers.

Suppliers have to implement measures to ensure compliance once this legislation becomes effective, such as transparency measures for online platforms, research access to key data, effective user safeguards, notice-and-takedown measures to combat illegal goods, services and content. The user safeguard includes flagging mechanisms. Furthermore, online marketplaces have obligations to allow traceability of business users. The proposal also includes serious fines, up to 6% of platform's global turnover.

It defines clear responsibilities and accountability for suppliers of intermediary services, and in particular online platforms, such as social media and marketplaces. The obligations include due diligence services, such as notice-and-action procedures.

11.5.2 Digital Market Act[16]

The DMA will ensure fair and open digital markets. The basis of the DMA are P2B regulations – Regulation (EU) 2019/1150 of the European Parliament and of the Council of 20 June 2019 on promoting fairness and transparency for business users of online intermediation services. This proposed legislation is envisioned to foster innovation, growth and competitiveness.

In Europe, there are currently a few large gatekeepers as active. These gatekeepers are a threat for business users. Gatekeepers have a significant impact on the internal market, operate one or more important gateway to customers and enjoy or are expected to enjoy an entrenched and durable position in their operation. The scope of this proposed legislation is the digital sector, including core platform services (online intermediation services, social networks, video sharing services, number-independent interpersonal electronic communication services), operating systems, cloud services and advertising services.

In the DMA, the obligations for gatekeepers are detailed. The obligations include allowing third parties to inter-operate with the gatekeepers' services in specific situations, as well as allowing business users to access data generated in their use of the gatekeeper's platform. Also, gatekeepers have provided advertisers on the gatekeeper's platform with the tools and information necessary to carry out independent verification of their advertisements hosted by the gatekeeper. Furthermore, gatekeepers have to allow business users to promote offers and conclude contracts with their customers outside the gatekeeper's platform.

Gatekeepers must not treat services and products offered by the gatekeeper itself more favourably in ranking than similar services or products offered by third parties on the gatekeeper's platform. Also, gatekeepers should not prevent consumers from linking up to businesses outside the gatekeeper's platform and not prevent users from un-installing any pre-installed software or app if they wish so.

The fines in the proposed DMA fines are high: 10% of companies' platform turnover, or periodically 5% of average daily turnover. There is even the possibility that gatekeepers are forced to sell parts of the business.

11.6 Amazon.com[17]

Platforms are growing at an unprecedented speed. This includes marketplaces such as Alibaba and Amazon. In this section, the focus is on Amazon.com. Amazon is the owner of the platform, whereas Amazon Web Services is the provider. Amazon and independent retailers sell their products on the platform to consumers. Amazon.com therefore has a dual role: (1) it provides a marketplace where independent sellers can sell their products directly to consumers, and (2) it sells products as a retailer on the same marketplace, in competition with the independent sellers. Furthermore, Amazon.com is offering fulfilment services to the independent sellers.

On 12 November 2020, the European Union sent Statement of Objections to Amazon for the use of non-public independent seller data and opens second investigation into its e-commerce business practices. The Commission's pre-liminary findings show that very large quantities of non-public seller data are available to employees of Amazon's retail business and flow directly into the automated systems of that business, which aggregate these data and use them to calibrate Amazon's retail offers and strategic business decisions to the detriment of the other marketplace sellers.

Amazon's business practices might artificially favour its own retail offers and offers of marketplace sellers that use Amazon's logistics and delivery services (the so-called "fulfilment by Amazon or FBA sellers"). In particular, the Commission will investigate whether the criteria that Amazon sets to select the winner of the "Buy Box" and to enable sellers to offer products to Prime users, under Amazon's Prime loyalty programme, lead to preferential treatment of Amazon's retail business or of the sellers that use Amazon's logistics and delivery services. Also, there are possibilities for marketplace sellers to effectively reach Prime users.

If confirmed, this would infringe on Article 102 of the Treaty on the Functioning of the European Union (TFEU) that prohibits the abuse of a dominant market position.

11.7 Conclusions

It is safe to assume that in future additional and more restrictive compliance, obligations will be imposed. Also, further consolidation in the SaaS market can be expected. As a consequence of these two developments, IT outsourcing will be pushed into the contracting and managing of standard services. This is potentially reducing the agility of organisations and the opportunities to innovate. Also, these developments will make contracting more formal.

As a consequence of these developments, the entry of new suppliers to the markets will also be reduced; entry barriers will be higher due to higher required initial product and services investments. This will potentially have an impact on not only the competitiveness of the market but again on innovation.

What would be an important step forward is an attempt to avoid as much as possible local differentiation in legislation. This will reduce the complexity for outsourcing organisations and reduce the development cost for new services and the maintenance costs of existing servers.

Furthermore, there is the question of governmental initiatives such as GAIA-X,[18] a European cloud service, as an alternative for cloud suppliers such as Amazon Web Services, Microsoft and Google will make the difference. GAIA-X is a combined German and French initiative. Building a safe environment is the starting point for this EU initiative; however, the current main participants are limited to Germany and France, including leading technology companies in these countries, despite the 10b Euro European development budget. As scale is important, the main question is if there is room for an additional supplier in this growing market. The entrance barriers for this market are very high, as veteran suppliers such as IBM and Oracle are, according to Gartner, not leaders in the market. This will make a European governmental initiative (that most like) become hard to impossible to become successful. Time will tell.

Notes

1 Examples are by the European Union proposed Digital Service Act Package.
2 Gartner (2020). *Magic quadrant for cloud infrastructure & platform services.* Raj Bala, Bob Gill, Dennis Smith, David Wright, Kevin Ji, 1 September – report ID G00441742.
3 Cloud service providers offer most of their services in price bands. Lower volumes result in the increase of unit price, as price bands with lower volumes have higher unit prices.
4 Miller, L. (2019). Cyber insurance. *Journal of Law & Cyber Warfare*, 7(2), 147–182.
5 Harvey Nash and KPMG (2020). CIO report. https://home.kpmg/xx/en/home/insights/2020/09/harvey-nash-kpmg-cio-survey-2020-everything-changed-or-did-it.html - accessed 23 March 2021
6 Cyber-criminals targeting cyber insurance companies to get insights into their cyber-security policy holders and the thresholds for ransom. This is a real concern for Insurance firm CNA Financial, a US-based prominent cyber-security insurer – see https://www.scmagazine.com/home/security-news/ransomware/policy-holders-may-be-the-primary-target-in-hack-of-cyber-insurance-provider-cna/ – accessed 27 March 2021.
7 Talesh, S. A. (2018). Data breach, privacy, and cyber insurance: How insurance companies act as "compliance managers" for businesses. *Law & Social Inquiry*, 43(2), 417–440.
8 See for overviews of the applicable data protection legislation in specific countries across the globe. https://unctad.org/page/data-protection-and-privacy-legislation-worldwide or https://www.dlapiperdataprotection.com/ – accessed 27 March 2021
9 See for more details https://gdpr-info.eu/ – accessed 27 March 2021
10 Gozman, D., & Willcocks, L. (2019). The emerging Cloud Dilemma: Balancing innovation with cross-border privacy and outsourcing regulations. *Journal of Business Research*, 97, 235–256.
11 Lincke, K., & Nourbakhsh, A. (2017). An analysis of the GDPR's effects on the future of cloud outsourcing: Winds of regulatory change threaten the ubiquity of the cloud. *Computer Law Review International*, 18(6), 179–184.
12 Articles 37–39 of the GDPR set out its DPO-related requirements: when one must be appointed (Article 37), the nature of their position in the organisation (Article 38) and the tasks they must carry out (Article 39).
13 In addition, local legislation can enforce organisation to appoint a DPO – for example, Germany has more strict obligations. Also, the European Union encourage appoint a DPO for any organisation – European Article 29 Working Party (WP29).
14 See for the detailed judgement https://curia.europa.eu/juris/document/document.jsf;jsessionid=C3870AA7000B921065B0CAC3F40B07CB?text=&docid=228677&pageIndex=0&doclang=en&mode=req&dir=&occ=first&part=1&cid=9982258 – accessed 27 March 2021.

15 See for additional information https://ec.europa.eu/digital-single-market/en/digital-services-act-package – accessed 27 March 2021.

16 See for more information https://ec.europa.eu/info/strategy/priorities-2019-2024/europe-fit-digital-age/digital-markets-act-ensuring-fair-and-open-digital-markets_en – accessed 27 March 2021.

17 This case study is based on the statement of objective of the European Union – https://ec.europa.eu/commission/presscorner/detail/en/ip_20_2077 – accessed 23 March 2021. At the time of publishing this book, the outcome of this formal anti-trust investigation was not known.

18 For more detailed information, see https://www.data-infrastructure.eu/GAIAX/Navigation/EN/Home/home.html – accessed 23 March 2021.

12 Looking forward

Due to the COVID-19 pandemic, the outsourcing spend declined slightly in 2020. However the outsourcing spend is still significant, Gartner projects the global outsourcing spend at \$3.4 trillion.[1] However, technology innovations organisations have given more value for their money – which one can clearly see in IaaS pricing. However, also in application development, supported by PaaS, such as Microsoft Azure, SAP Cloud or Salesforce's Heroku, the productivity of application development teams has significantly increased over time. Outsourcing is here to stay, but what can be expected in the years to come?

12.1 Introduction

In this chapter, there are three current developments in outsourcing technology: (1) pay-as-you-go and pay-as-you-use contracting, (2) compliance and ethical outsourcing considerations and (3) value chain outsourcing opportunities. This chapter reflects on the implications of these current developments on managing IT outsourcing. This reflection on all three developments includes various aspects of cloud services. In Section 12.3.1, crowdsourcing is explained, including the ethical considerations such as employment rights for gig workers. Also, these platforms are powered by cloud services.

12.2 Pay-as-you-go and pay-as-you-use contracting

The outsourcing journey is still very dynamic. Future demand is harder to predict as the business is more dynamic than ever. Also, the supplier landscape is constantly changing. Start-up companies either become tech giants or are acquired by tech giants. Alternatively, tech giants mimic the start-up's technology and integrate the innovative functionality in the products.

This set challenges for outsourcing organisations as this is impacting the architecture and the technology stacks significantly.

As a consequence of the above setting, a long-term strategy for IT is becoming increasingly difficult from outsourcing organisations. The required flexibility in contracting services is increasing; the flexibility is also reflected in IT outsourcing pricing concepts. Fixed price IT outsourcing contracts

DOI: 10.4324/9781003223788-12

are no longer fit for purpose.[2] The increase in cloud services, such as IaaS, PaaS and SaaS, supports the transformation from predominantly fixed price outsourcing contracting to flexible price outsourcing contracting.[3] Pay-as-you-go contracts, utility-based pricing based on spot prices and reservations that are widely applied in cloud computing are around for over a decade[4] and are now becoming the norm. Also, pay-as-you-use contracts are on the rise. The pay-as-you-use contracts are based on functional pricing. Contracts based on pay-as-you-like/feel and pay-as-you-can are emerging. These contracts are based on an open stack and fully enable flexible contracting.[5]

Pay-as-you-go pricing combined with interchangeable modularised technology stack supports required flexibility. Interchangeable modularisation is predominantly associated with PaaS and SaaS; however, the authors of this book expect in future that IaaS will be cannibalised by PaaS and SaaS, as the competitive advantage of building up one's own functionality stack from scratch will decrease over time. In addition, the concept of containerisation[6] is relevant for Platform as a Service (PaaS) platforms. The applications are managed and orchestrated through containers as the application packaging and deployment mechanism. The container platform tools are a prerequisite for DevOps. Most legacy applications require significant refactoring (rewrite) to enable containerisation. Continuously running these legacy applications on bare metal or virtual machines up and until decommissioning is sometimes a better alternative. Nevertheless, smartly parameterising SaaS products and configuration of the functionality with PaaS building blocks is the way to go.

Obviously, there are also architectural considerations that need to be taken into account. One of the challenges is facilitating a dual-cloud supplier strategy. Most large organisations have embraced a dual-cloud strategy to reduce the supplier lock-in. This strategy reduces achieving economies of scale and makes managing technology stacks more complex. Over time, the interchangeability between different cloud platforms is expected to further increase. Also, provisions for fast processing need to be addressed in the architecture. To ensure speed-edge computing, bringing processing power and data storage closer to the end user has to be considered. Furthermore, technical cloud enhancements and improved pricing structures facilitate artificial intelligence (AI) and machine learning (ML) in the cloud. In the future, cognitive systems will no longer be the default choice for AI and ML.

This required flexibility also sets challenges for contract management of outsourcing organisations. One flexibility is estimating and managing the cloud computing costs. Allocations are more straightforward with pay-as-you-go pricing models but challenging for organisations with strict annual budget rounds, such as most governmental organisations. Also, real-world experience in developing, delivering and pricing of IT services is required to be successful in contract management roles. In the future, one can expect to see only professionals with 10+ years of supplier experience in account and product management roles. Their experience is required to guide outsourcing organisations, ensure service and contract flexibility and being an equal-level counterpart for contract and delivery managers of suppliers.

12.3 Compliance and ethical outsourcing considerations

Compliance obligations for the outsourcing organisation and the suppliers, as detailed in Chapter 11, are expected to grow. For the data volume, an exponential growth is expected. In 2024, the data/information created, captured, copied and consumed worldwide is estimated at 149 zettabytes.[7] This data growth combined with the anticipated growth of processing power, in future supplemented with the large-scale availability of quantum computing,[8] will increase the possibilities of data analytics significantly. This will increase the ethical challenges in outsourcing.

These increased risk exposures will drive up the charges and fees of suppliers, not limited to the increase in the liabilities and the increased likelihood of being liable. Suppliers need to build up knowledge to ensure that their services are compliant and remain compliant in future. Also, suppliers need to offer services to the outsourcing organisations to update their clients on implications of changing laws and regulations. Furthermore, the outsourcing contracts need clear provisions detailing the implications of changes in laws and regulations. Mutual transparency about potential risks related to a breach of compliance and ethical issues is essential for successful IT outsourcing organisations. Outsourcing organisations need to invest significant effort in strengthening their governance to manage these risks.

Furthermore, suppliers have to put additional effort in auditing and certification. Technologies such as blockchain can be used to ensure the reliability of the data,[9] especially when there are multiple actors collaborating in the governance. With regard to certification outsourcing, organisations and suppliers need to be mindful that certification should not hinder innovation.[10]

The ethical considerations are predominantly with the outsourcing organisations as these are organisation-specific and are related to data, analytics and algorithms. Changes in the ethical beliefs are also potentially triggering outsourcing contract changes. These changes are subject to the change control clauses and the cost impact has to be agreed upon upfront. The costs of these changes are typically born by the outsourcing company, as this change is a unilateral change. Suppliers can offer services to advise with regard to ethical considerations and standards. In addition, suppliers can offer services to audit an outsourcing organisation by leveraging the ethical framework of the outsourcing organisation or any other framework. Outsourcing organisations are encouraged to frequently assess their algorithms to ensure that they meet their ethical standards.

12.3.1 Crowdsourcing

Crowdsourcing has been around for over a decade and is still evolving and still very current in gig economy. Introduced by How[11], and defined in detail by Kleeman et al.[12] as… a form of the integration of users or consumers in internal processes of value creation. The essence of crowdsourcing is the intentional mobilisation for commercial exploitation of creative ideas and other forms of work performed by consumer.

Crowdsourcing is enabled by platforms,[13] such as Uber or Just Eat. The most important crowdsourcing challenge for these platforms is if the crowd workers are platform employees. In Supreme Court, ruling in the UK was that Uber drivers must be treated as workers rather than self-employed. This ruling could mean that thousands of Uber drivers in the UK are entitled to minimum wage and holiday pay. The consideration of the Supreme Court included the following elements: the fare is set by the platform, the platform is basically dictating the driver's earnings, the contract terms are unilaterally set by the platform, the platform allocates requests and rejecting rides can be penalised by the platform and the platform monitors the star rating and can terminate the relationship if services are not improving. Also, in the US, there is legislation related to fair wages: Fair Labour Standard Act from 1938. The UK ruling from the Supreme Court might also impact current law suites and the new law suites.[14,15]

For other crowdsourcing platforms, this court ruling is less of a challenge as the platform is not, or to a lesser degree, required or involved in the service provisioning of the gig worker as much as the Uber or other driver and/or delivery platforms. These non-driver and delivery platforms are focusing on connecting gig workers with their (potential) clients.

From the outsourcing organisation perspective, attention is required to loss of knowledge, as maintaining the relationship with a community of crowd workers is challenging. Also, making explicit agreements on intellectual property rights with crowd workers is not straightforward. Furthermore, poor-quality entries drive the costs for the outsourcing company selection process up and potentially impact contracting timelines. Also, the coordination effort required should not be underestimated by outsourcing companies. Finally, the rating systems do not always provide a true insight into the quality of the services delivered by the crowd worker.

All in all, despite the size of crowdsourcing and high-end platforms such as TopCoder to engage with, is crowdsourcing for outsourcing organisations not an obvious choice? Nevertheless, for some individual roles such as data scientist or cloud architect, crowdsourcing might be a feasible option. Also, crowdsourcing has definitely benefited from the COVID-19 pandemic; remote working has really taken off.

12.4 Value chain partnering – creating an ecosystem across the value chain to foster innovation

Participating in global value chains is attractive as this is generating more economic growth than the participation on domain value chains. Transforming from participating from domain value chains into global value chains, economic upgrading, is a trade-off between fragmentation costs and switching costs.[16] If the fragmentation costs are low, making the change will be less attractive.[17] Also, power-dependence and bargaining power in domain value chains can limit the attractiveness to transform from a domain value chain into a global value chain.[16] Nevertheless, many organisations are making this change, which will have implications for the partnering strategy.

As the next partnering level, organisations power their ecosystems with cross value chain IT outsourcing partnerships. This fosters innovations and increases competitive advantage for ecosystem organisations and their suppliers. The outsourcing implications are that the traditional outsourcing and cloud contracts are supplemented with consortia outsourcing contracts. These contracts include exclusivity and typically have a longer duration (three to five years) and are less descriptive. In fact, these contracts are similar to generic innovations contracts with a loosely coupled contract regime.[18] These contracts also require specific clauses related to intellectual property ownership, which is similar to generic innovations contracts; however, they are more complex, as the number of organisations and suppliers involved is higher by nature than in traditional outsourcing contracts. There is a similar challenge related to data ownership and the exchange of data in the value chain. Most organisations already have difficulties with internal data management,[19] let alone data management across a value chain. This issue is not so much a technical issue; the power balance in a value chain is directly related to the agreements on what data are shared in what format and when.

The outsourcing complexity further increases as organisations participate in multiple value chains and their participation in value chains is not stable. In making this work, the relation aspect needs to be implemented. Mechanisms, as researched by Kano,[20] are selectivity, inclusion of non-business intermediaries, joint strategising, relational capital, multilateral feedback and rules for equitable value distribution. These mechanisms have to be also included in the governance related to the IT outsourcing contracts.

12.5 Conclusion

The main question is, where will organisations be five to ten years from now? The answers to this question will come soon enough, but surely the role of technology and IT in profit as well as in not-for-profit organisations will most likely be significantly greater than today. Also, a continuation of the growth of outsourcing can be expected. With regard to innovations, internal IT departments are simply too small and they are not able to attract and retain the required talent. To foster innovation, partnering with a combination of start-ups and tech giants is needed. The supplier's core business is not only delivery services but also to innovate their own services portfolio.

This leaves outsourcing organisations with demand management, the identification and managing of the requirements and safeguarding the architecture and the technology choices, as well as (cyber) security of their organisations[21] and contract management. Contract management is beyond supplier management and focuses on creating value by outsourcing. For any organisation and supplier, lots of success means creating value by outsourcing.

Notes

1 Gartner (2020). https://www.gartner.com/en/newsroom/press-releases/2020-05-13-gartner-says-global-it-spending-to-decline-8-percent-in-2020-due-to-impact-of-covid19 - accessed 21 March 2021

2 Dos, S. J. C., & Da, S. M. M. (2015). Price management in it outsourcing contracts. The path to flexibility. *Journal of Revenue and Pricing Management, 14*(5), 342–364.

3 See Lee, I. (2019). Pricing schemes and profit-maximizing pricing for cloud services. *Journal of Revenue and Pricing Management, 18*(2), 112–122; Nicola, D. (2020). Pricing cloud IaaS computing services. *Journal of Cloud Computing, 9*(1), 14.

4 Corbett, M. (2004). *The outsourcing revolution. Why it makes sense and how to do it right*. Chicago, IL: Dearborn Trade Publishing.

5 Wu, C., Buyya, R., & Ramamohanarao, K. (2019). Cloud pricing models: Taxonomy, survey, and interdisciplinary challenges. *ACM Computing Surveys (CSUR), 52*(6), 1–36.

6 Examples of an orchestration tool are Docker and Kubernetes.

7 https://www.statista.com/statistics/871513/worldwide-data-created/ - accessed 23 March 2021

8 Möller, M., & Vuik, C. (2017). On the impact of quantum computing technology on future developments in high-performance scientific computing. *Ethics and Information Technology, 19*(4), 253–269.

9 Wang, H., Wang, X. A., Xiao, S., & Liu, J. S. (2021). Decentralized data outsourcing auditing protocol based on blockchain. *Journal of Ambient Intelligence and Humanized Computing, 12*(2), 2703–2714.

10 Gopalakrishnan, S., & Zhang, H. (2019). The link between supplier certification and growth in it outsourcing: A tale of two stories. *International Journal of Production Research, 57*(13), 4228–4243.

11 Howe, J., The rise of crowdsourcing. *Wired, 14*(6) (2006) - https://www.wired.com/2006/06/crowds/ - assessed 21 March 2021

12 Kleemann, F., Voß, G. G., & Rieder, K. (2008). Un(der) paid innovators: The commercial utilization of consumer work through crowdsourcing. *Science, Technology & Innovation Studies, 4*(1), 5–26.

13 Kaganer, E., Carmel, E., Hirschheim, R., & Olsen, T. (2013). Managing the human cloud. *MIT Sloan Management Review, 54*(2), 23.

14 BBC 2021, https://www.bbc.com/news/business-56123668 accessed 21 March 2021

15 Supreme Court UK, https://www.supremecourt.uk/press-summary/uksc-2019-0029.html accessed 21 March 2021

16 Dindial, M., Clegg, J., & Voss, H. (2020). Between a rock and a hard place: A critique of economic upgrading in global value chains. *Global Strategy Journal, 10*(3), 473–495.

17 Beverelli, C., Stolzenburg, V., Koopman, R. B., & Neumueller, S. (2019). Domestic value chains as stepping stones to global value chain integration. *The World Economy, 42*(5), 1467–1494.

18 Aubert, B. A., Kishore, R., & Iriyama, A. (2015). Exploring and managing the 'innovation through outsourcing' paradox. *The Journal of Strategic Information Systems, 24*(4), 255–269.

19 Vilminko-Heikkinen, R., & Pekkola, S. (2019). Changes in roles, responsibilities and ownership in organizing master data management. *International Journal of Information Management, 47*, 76–87.

20 Kano, L. (2018). Global value chain governance: A relational perspective. *Journal of International Business Studies, 49*(6), 684–705.

21 Beulen, E. (2018). *Information management leads top line information technology initiatives and contributes to bottom line targets: The chief information officer is a technical innovator and custodian of the IT architecture*. Tilburg: Tilburg University.

Index

Note: **Bold** page numbers refer to tables; *italic* page numbers refer to figures and page numbers followed by "n" denote endnotes.

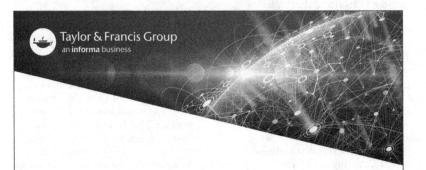

Printed in the United States
by Baker & Taylor Publisher Services